The Aeneid of Vergil

AENEAS

The Aeneid of Vergil

TRANSLATED BY

Kevin Guinagh

REVISED EDITION

Holt, Rinehart and Winston

NEW YORK • CHICAGO • SAN FRANCISCO • ATLANTA • DALLAS
MONTREAL • TORONTO • LONDON • SYDNEY

Library of Congress Catalog Card Number: 72–123478
SBN: 03–083186–5
Printed in the United States of America
01234 68 987654321

· Introduction ·

Shortly after defeating Antony and his Egyptian queen in a naval battle at Actium, off the west coast of Greece, Gaius Julius Caesar Octavianus, whom we call Octavian or Augustus, became the undisputed master of the civilized world. Though he was little beyond the age when he might legitimately have run for the quaestorship, the lowest political office in the Roman course of honors, he had already been in public life for thirteen years—from 44 B.C., when Julius Caesar, his granduncle, had been assassinated.

Octavian's victory brought peace to the Roman world. Two years after Actium, the temple of Janus Quirinus was closed, an indication that the god of war was chained within its walls. Octavian was determined to keep the world at peace.

He well knew the history of the bloody century that had preceded his victory over Antony. It had been an era of internal conflict, which began when the Gracchi, who were brothers, championed the cause of the landless and the disfranchised. Their social reforms were aimed at distributing more widely some of the gains that had been won by Rome in its march to power from a town along the Tiber to the ends of the Mediterranean basin. Their proposals set off violence in which the Capital witnessed the fearful spectacle of Roman senators clubbing citizens who opposed their cherished privileges. Both of these fearless leaders lost their lives because of their sympathy with the popular cause. Shortly thereafter the two opposing factions squared off against each other in two political parties: one, called the Optimates, derived its strength from the aristocrats and their followers; the other, the Populares, sponsored democratic, antisenatorial action and numbered in its ranks many disgruntled aristocrats and that vast mass of the proletariat that opposed special privileges for the senatorial class. During this fateful century the popular cause made considerable progress under the leadership of Marius. A brilliant general, conqueror of Jugurtha and northern tribes that had threatened Italy, he made soldiering a profession, thus opening a career to poor freemen. Thenceforth soldiers became personally attached to their generals, who were forced to seek not only military exploits to keep them employed but bonuses and land grants with which to reward their victorious troops.

The unwillingness of the Romans to share citizenship with their allies brought on the so-called Social War (90–88 B.C.) in which Rome, after suffering severe losses at the hands of her new enemies, was forced to make concessions to save herself. In this struggle both Marius and Sulla distinguished themselves, and when hostilities were over, these generals renewed their personal struggle for power. When the Marians gained the upper hand in Rome, many Optimates lost their lives and their possessions; when the aristocratic Sulla returned to Italy from the East, he inaugurated a reign of terror, wreaking such vengeance on those who opposed him that one might think he was dealing with conquered enemies instead of fellow citizens. After his death a champion of the popular party gained the ascendancy for a short time, only to be put down by generals doing the bidding of the Senate. The struggle was continued in Spain where Sertorius, a follower of Marius, headed a revolt of Lusitanians that was finally crushed by Pompey, an agent of the Senate. While this struggle was being waged in Spain, Roman troops were facing Mithridates in Asia Minor, and revolting gladiators in Italy rallied to their cause 70,000 slaves for desperate battle.

Even though Rome triumphed, these wars decimated the manpower and the economic resources of the country. But other costly campaigns were still to come. Caesar's legions conquered Gaul in the years between 58 and 51 B.C.; Crassus, eager to win military fame, led Roman troops to fight Parthians; Pompey, who had fought pirates and warred in Asia Minor, stayed in Italy where he sought to further his own ambitions. Hostility between Caesar and Pompey brought on a civil war from which Caesar emerged victorious. During this century of revolution, control frequently passed from one party to the other; it suited Caesar's purposes, however, to put an end to this alternate seizure of power and subsequent reprisal. In 45 B.C. he met the last organized opposition at the battle of Munda in Spain. In the following year Caesar was assassinated.

The conspirators naively thought that Roman society would be restored to republican processes if Caesar were disposed of, but after the deed a great battle for power developed between the followers of Caesar and the conspirators, who hoped to witness a rebirth of the ideals of the Republic. Confusion was general. Caesar, like many another dictator, left no plan for succession, but he had made a will, and by its terms the bulk of his estate went to Gaius Octavius, whom he adopted as his son and who immediately took Caesar's name, changing his own to Octavian. Any observer, looking at the possible successors to the power of Julius Caesar, might express the conviction, as Cicero did, that this sickly heir to the fortunes of mighty Caesar would be quickly set aside. However, Octavian was far from being the weakling that he seemed to be. What he lacked in physical stamina was offset by his shrewdness. He seemed to realize that Caesar's error had been his open desire to rule alone. Octavian resolved to make no such mistake but rather to display a willingness to be of service to the Senate and his countrymen. If the patrimony left him and the Roman citizens had been swallowed up by Antony, Octavian, with his eyes on a more distant goal, decided not to make an issue of the theft. He sold his own properties in order to pay off the legacies Caesar had bequeathed the citizens—a move that gained him great popularity. He had a persuasive skill that brought the Caesarean leaders together; he pushed for the punishment of the assassins of Julius Caesar, and two years after the death of his adoptive father, stood with Antony as joint victor over the Republican forces at the battle of Philippi, in Macedonia.

The feeling that existed between these two leaders was never cordial. Though each had taken for his sphere a half of the Roman world—Antony the East and Octavian the West—it was inevitable that they should eventually come into armed conflict. When this did take place at Actium, Octavian's victory was complete. A bleeding world that had lived at war or in the shadow of war for over a hundred years gladly accepted the principate of Octavian with its promise of peace.

After the battle of Philippi, Antony gave his fellow victor the unpleasant task of settling 170,000 veterans on land in the neighborhood of certain cities that had sided with Brutus, among others, Cremona and Mantua, and when the lands that had been provided were not sufficient to take care of the troops, numerous small landholders were evicted. Then Octavian settled down to the work of making his own position solid by carefully choosing the more desirable privileges and avoiding unpopular offices, by expelling Sextus Pompey from Sicily, and by making preparations for the coming struggle with Antony.

After the victory at Actium, then, Octavian could look back on a century of conflict that had drained the lifeblood of the country. He now turned to the problem of reconstructing an Italy that had forgotten its gods, its ancient virtues, the patriotism of early Republican days, and the peace of agriculture. By re-establishing neglected priesthoods, rebuilding temples, purifying public morals, and luring people back to the soil, he aimed to restore to Roman society the old stability that had been shaken by so much internal disorder.

Octavian was well aware of the value of literature in the promotion of these ideals and counted heavily on his friend Maecenas, a writer whose work has not survived, to sponsor men whose literary talent promised to be an ornament to the spirit that he was striving to create. Noble birth was no passport to membership in this group. In politics the "new man" had a difficult time in establishing himself, as Cicero well knew, but in literature lack of aristocratic birth was no deterrent to recognition.

The poet held in highest esteem in this circle of Maecenas was

Vergil. More than any other he devoted his talents to the promotion of Augustan ideals. He was, it seems, richly rewarded for his loyalty to the cause, enjoying a town house in Rome and a villa in Campania, though this latter may have been given him in compensation for his father's estate, from which he was forcibly ejected in the resettlement of the region around Mantua. At any rate, membership in this coterie left him financially free to devote himself exclusively to poetry.

From this it must not be inferred that Vergil was a hireling, that he praised the Julian family simply because he was well paid, a statement that is sometimes made by critics of the poet. Not every poet laureate is insincere. One must not ignore the fact that Vergil was by nature a pacifist. Unlike Octavian, he seems never to have borne arms, but he entertained genuine admiration for the man who had brought Italy back to the ways of peace after a century of revolution. If he placed his entire talent at the disposal of the new regime, even accepting suggestions of themes that were dear to Augustus and Maecenas, we need not conclude that he was a flatterer. It is fairer to suppose that he was an ardent admirer of the First Citizen and his policies and sought to promote the reconstruction that Augustus had in mind. That his language bordered on the extravagant should not be thought unusual in an epic poet. He spoke of Julius Caesar and Octavian as gods, but the word had a different meaning from what it has today.

THE WORKS OF VERGIL

The authorship of a group of minor poems attributed by some to Vergil and referred to as the *Vergilian Appendix* has never been definitely established, though a great deal of scholarly research has been focused on them. No matter who their author is, they will continue to interest few except scholars in the field of Latin literature.

The earliest verses that we have of the poet, the *Eclogues,* or *Bucolics,* were written before 39 B.C. Modeled on the *Idylls* of the Greek poet Theocritus, these pastorals picture a world of poetic peasants who express their thoughts in a very artificial style. In the first and ninth pieces he touches on the evictions in which he eventually lost his farm, but it is difficult to determine from the veiled imagery of his poetry just how much Vergil was permanently affected by these seizures. Certainly he is rather lighthearted about the invasion of his rights. Other eclogues treat of the loves of shepherds, evidently without any hidden reference to real personalities or current events. The most famous of the series is the fourth, really not a pastoral, which is dedicated to Asinius Pollio and looks forward in joyous anticipation to the expected birth of a child whose identity is not certainly known. Through the Middle Ages this poem was held in high regard because it was thought to be a divine revelation, foretelling the coming of the Messiah as recorded in the prophecy of Isaiah.

Italy had given its best to war for many years; as a result the soil had been neglected. Even when soldiers were settled on farms, they were not always disposed to stay there; for years they had been laying fields waste, and now they had to be lured to cultivate them and to interest themselves in the quiet, lonesome tasks of the farmer. At the urging of Maecenas, Vergil undertook the composition of the *Georgics,* a work on agriculture, an important phase of the reconstruction. He took particular pleasure in this theme, for he had been reared on a farm and not only knew the countryside, but loved it. In the first four lines of the first book of the *Georgics* he indicated the material he would treat in the four books:

> What makes the crops rich, under what star it is proper to plow the earth, Maecenas, and to wed the vines to the elms, what care the cattle need, what attention the breeding of the herd, how great the experience required for keeping thrifty bees, straightway I shall begin to sing.

He spent seven years at this poem, the product of his mature genius, presenting it to his patron Maecenas in 29 B.C. after polishing the work until he was completely satisfied with it.

He was evidently not subjected to any pressure to bring the task to a hurried conclusion, since he averaged little more than a line a day. It was this labor of the file that Tennyson had in mind when he wrote of Vergil,

> who would write ten lines, they say,
> At dawn, and lavish all the golden day
> To make them wealthier in his reader's eyes.

Most critics who deal with Latin literature have held this poem in high regard; Addison called it perfect, and Dryden maintained it was the best poem of the best poet. The modern reader, to whom the happy turn of many a beautiful expression is lost in translation, is not likely to share the enthusiasm of the specialist for the *Georgics;* nor will he find the scientific observations on agriculture illuminating, though the lengthy digressions are charming.

Octavian was very much interested in seeing Vergil write a national epic which by its praise of the past glories of the Roman race would promote Roman patriotism and pride. In the *Georgics* Vergil promised to write an epic in praise of the battles of Caesar, as Octavian was known to his contemporaries, but when the poet gave the subject some thought, he must have come to realize that contemporary achievements, no matter how heroic, are not proper material for the epic; that the exaggerated feats of men personally known to the readers might be received with ridicule. It may well be, as some critics have held, that Vergil took Octavian as his model for Aeneas, but there is no solid basis for such an interpretation.

Aeneas was not entirely the invention of Vergil. In the twentieth book of the *Iliad,* Homer tells us that this hero was destined to survive the Trojan War. He had already begun to battle with the Greek champion Achilles when Poseidon took note of this single combat and addressed the gods, telling them that Aeneas would surely go down to Hades, slain by Achilles, if the contest were allowed to continue. The god urged them to guide Aeneas out of death's path, for it was the will of heaven that the race of Dardanus, whom Zeus loved above all the children born to him from the daughters of men, should not perish utterly. The anger of Zeus was not directed against Aeneas but against the race of Priam. (The genealogical table, preceding the glossary, shows that these two Trojans were of different families.) Stesichorus, the Greek poet of Sicily, who lived about 600 B.C., sang of Aeneas' coming to the West. A tradition dating back to the third century mentioned the hero's arrival in Latium. Naevius, who died about 204 B.C., wrote a poem, now lost, on the First Punic War, in which he had served. It was here that Vergil found his material on the flight of Aeneas with his father, his reception at Carthage, and his landing in Latium. The legend was embellished by Ennius, Varro, and others before Vergil gave it final form in the *Aeneid*. Vergil found it suitable for his purpose to link the Ilian hero with the Roman race; thus the family of Caesar could claim descent from the gods, since the Trojans sprang from Jupiter, and Aeneas himself was the son of the goddess Venus.

Roman writers generally imitated the writings of the Greeks, whom they recognized as their literary masters. The conquerors of the world were extremely conservative in their ideas and reproduced for their countrymen the treasures of Greek literature, suiting them to their purposes and gaining for their own works a certain unearned increment because the subject had already been tested by centuries of popularity. It was quite natural for Vergil to pattern his epic on Homer's; not to have done so would have argued a lack of respect for the master. Vergil had imitated Hesiod in his *Georgics* and had stated the fact in his work; in the *Aeneid* his debt of inspiration was clear to all. But there were basic differences. Since Homer had sung of life in primitive times, his story appealed to primitive instincts; Vergil, adapting these ideas, had to satisfy the tastes of a refined audience and produce a more civilized epic. The wanderings of Aeneas were taking place at the time when Odysseus was slowly making his way back to his home in Ithaca, but many centuries intervened between the composition of the two works. As might be supposed, the spirit of Homer's *Odyssey* is quite different from that of Vergil's *Aeneid,* as one might expect the return of a very human hero from a victorious campaign to differ from the anxious search of a godlike hero for the land where heaven had promised him a settlement. In the first six books of the *Aeneid,* Vergil tells of the wanderings of Aeneas through the Mediterranean basin from Troy to the Tiber; in the second six books the *Iliad* is his model. As the modern reader finds the *Odyssey* of Homer more absorbing than the *Iliad,* so he will find the first six of the twelve books of the *Aeneid* more interesting, as their composition must have been to the poet himself.

This preference is reflected in what is read in secondary schools today where a teacher is grateful if a class covers four books, regularly chosen from the first six. Often students are not aware that the *Aeneid* has a second half. Indeed, too frequently little thought is given to the content of the complete epic. During the last two weeks of the year's study of the masterpiece, it would seem advisable to set aside the Latin and ask students to read and discuss the whole tale of Aeneas in English translation.

BACKGROUND OF THE STORY

Some knowledge of the events preceding the opening lines of the *Aeneid* will be helpful to the reader looking into the poem for the first time. At the very beginning one is made aware that Aeneas and his followers are exiles from their ancestral city of Troy. They are seeking another home in the West where they hope to start life anew, safe from the anger of Juno, the wife and sister of Jupiter.

This savage anger of Juno and her relentless pursuit of the friendless and guiltless Aeneas will strike the reader as strange conduct in a goddess who calls herself the queen of heaven. Vergil pictures Aeneas as the innocent victim of a feud between Juno and Venus. This can be traced back to the marriage of Peleus and Thetis, to which all the gods and goddesses were invited except Discord, who, nevertheless, was able to toss into the assembly a golden apple on which were engraved the words:

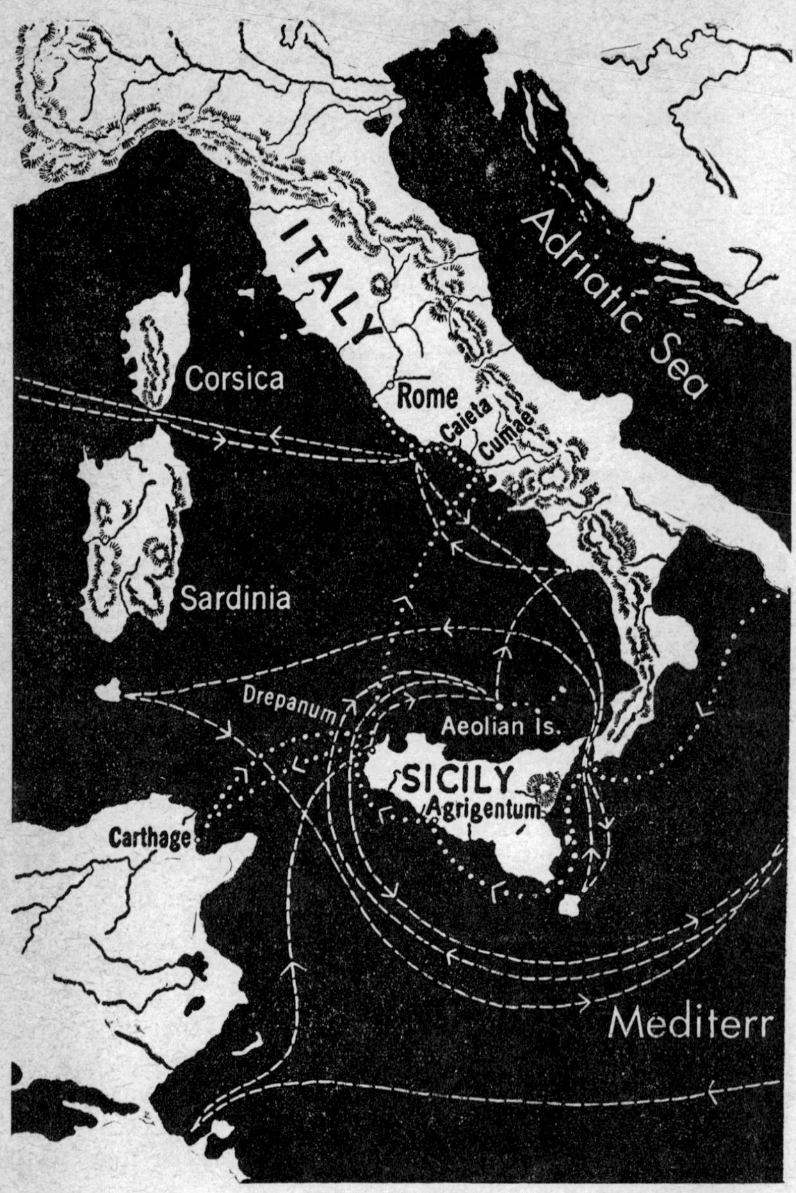
ITALY
Adriatic Sea
Corsica
Rome
Caieta
Cumae
Sardinia
Drepanum
Aeolian Is.
SICILY
Agrigentum
Carthage
Mediterr

THRACE
Aenus
Troy
Antandrus
Buthrotum
GREECE
Lesbos
Actium
Athens
Delos
Sparta
Pergamus
anean Sea
Crete
Route of Æneas
Route of Ulysses

"Let the beauty take it." Three of the goddesses laid claim to being the fairest: Venus, Minerva, and Juno. Jupiter was unwilling to make a decision in such a delicate matter, and so delegated the judging of this beauty contest to Paris, Priam's unrecognized son, who, because of the prophecies and ill omens attending his birth, had been exposed by his father's order on Mount Ida. The child was subsequently reared by a shepherd who found him, miraculously saved from death, several days after he had been abandoned. Mercury was ordered to guide the three goddesses to Paris. Eager to gain the golden apple, each offered the young shepherd a bribe: Juno promised him political power, Minerva wisdom, Venus the most beautiful woman in the world. Being young, he chose Venus—a tragic error.

Paris, now accepted by his father, who seems to have forgotten the dire prophecies attending his son's birth, left Troy to visit Greece where he fell in love with Helen, who eloped with him during the absence of her husband Menelaus in Crete. To redress this wrong done their king, the Greeks went to war with the Trojans, whom they finally defeated after ten years through the stratagem of the wooden horse. Many of the great Trojan heroes perished in the last fateful hours of the city. Aeneas battled valiantly but, being divinely admonished that resistance was futile and that he should rescue his family from the burning city, he gave up the fight.

When the story begins, Aeneas has already been moving about through the Mediterranean for seven years, vainly searching for the place where his new kingdom was destined to rise.

Juno nourished a deep hatred of the Trojans for another reason. Her daughter Hebe, the cupbearer of Jove, because of some awkwardness in pouring wine, was replaced by Ganymede, the grandson of the founder of the Trojan race. Because of the slight her daughter had received, Juno became jealous of Ganymede and entertained a deep hatred for everything Trojan.

In Aeneas Vergil created a hero who embodied all those virtues that a Roman should practice. The usual epithet he applies to him is *pius,* which means dutiful, reverent, respectful. He shows great solicitude for the safety of his aged father and a genuine deference to his opinions, not a mere humoring of his aged parent. Aeneas is proud of his young son Ascanius and greatly concerned about the establishment of the kingdom over which the boy will eventually rule. He loved his wife Creusa, though we would hardly call his attitude toward her romantic. In contrast to the conduct of that other wanderer Odysseus, there is never any suggestion in the life of the Trojan hero that he was especially interested in any of the women who followed him in their flight from Troy. His love for his fatherland and for his fellow citizens was profound. His attitude toward the gods is one of complete devotion. In all matters touching religious observance he is most scrupulous. Indeed, Vergil's epic is a religious poem. Let anyone who is inclined to doubt this open the book at any point; he will not read far until he comes upon a prayer, a sign from heaven, an oracle, a sacrifice, or even the appearance of a divine being. It is the constant concern of Aeneas to ascertain the will of the gods and to follow this out to the letter, no matter how great the personal sacrifice involved. Vergil made his hero a model in whom the Romans could find ample inspiration, for the poet gave him all the ideals they should cherish: patriotism, filial devotion, parental love, conformity to the will of heaven, and a scrupulousness in carrying out the honors due the gods. Vergil made his hero the epitome of all the olden virtues which Octavian was seeking to revive. Aeneas never loses his self-control, never blasphemes, is never unjust, deceitful, or careless in the performance of any of his obligations. There is no flaw in his character; he is never guilty of sin. Aeneas, although a great warrior, prefers peace to war. Indeed, King Latinus and Aeneas were well on the way to a friendly understanding when Juno employed Alecto, one of the Furies, to foment war. Ascanius, aided by the Fury, killed a pet deer of Silvia, daughter of Tyrrhus, who was in charge of the royal stables. War was thus forced upon Aeneas; he had not caused it, he did not desire it, but once battle was joined, there could be no retreating until victory was won, a typically Roman attitude. He fights heroically and slays a host of enemies, yet he is no truculent savage, delighting in slaughter. When he defeats Turnus in single combat, he is disposed to listen to his pleas until he notices that his victim is wearing the belt of which he had despoiled the youthful Pallas, the son of Aeneas' ally, King Evander. It is then that he slays his victim, but he does not tie him to his chariot and drag him about the walls of the city, as Achilles dragged Hector about the walls of Troy.

For many readers the simple truth is that Aeneas is too noble and too virtuous: in a word, he is too good, his virtue too oppressive. His critics cite his relationship with Queen Dido (Book IV) to support their contention that he is ungrateful and cruel. He and his fleet had been overtaken by a storm between Sicily and Carthage. Landing on the shore, they were utterly at the mercy of the Carthaginians. Instead of treating Aeneas and his followers as invaders, she banqueted them. When the remains of the feast were cleared away, she heard from his lips the sad story of the last hours of Troy, their escape, and their troubles by land and sea up to the moment when she befriended them. She welcomed the hero and could not help falling in love with him. After Aeneas had enjoyed the queen's hospitality for an extended period—indeed it was her understanding that they were married—Mercury, the messenger of the gods, was sent from heaven to inform him that this was not the future that destiny had in store for him. He must leave Carthage at once.

Immediately she detected his changed attitude and, frantic with grief, tried to induce him to delay his departure until she could get accustomed to the idea of living without him. When she realized that her pleadings were of no avail, she began to remind him of what she had done for him. The love he had felt toward her must now have changed to pity, which is no substitute. He could explain everything to her, but she was hysterical and would not let him speak. After she recovered from a fainting spell, she sent her sister Anna to him, hoping that she could induce him to reconsider, but he would not soften. It was heaven's will, he said. That night, while Aeneas was asleep on one of the ships, Mercury appeared and urged him to set sail at once, reminding him that woman is a fickle and changeable thing, which was hardly applicable in the case of the queen. In spite of the dangers of setting sail on a wintry sea, he gave the order to leave at once, fearful of the revenge Dido might take on him and his fellow exiles. In her despair she committed suicide before his ship was out of sight.

The ancient Romans did not read this episode as tearfully as we do. First of all, Carthage was Rome's ancient enemy with whom she had fought three exhausting wars, ending in the total destruction of Carthage. But apart from this natural hatred of things Punic, Augustus himself had similarly treated his first wife Scribonia by divorcing her on the very day that she bore him a daughter, Julia, the only child he ever had. Nor did he show any consideration for this same daughter's love life, for, in order to build a family tree, he married her three times, last of all to Tiberius, the future emperor, who was forced to divorce the wife he loved to satisfy the ambitions of Octavian. When his daughter became immoral, he banished her forever from the court to the bleak island of Pandataria; later, for a like reason he sent her daughter of the same name into exile. Doubtless Octavian could justify in his own mind such conduct.

From the Roman point of view, Dido was the aggressor in her marriage with Aeneas, an intolerable assumption of a male prerogative. The Romans knew the story of how Medea had helped Jason bring back the Golden Fleece on condition that he marry her: this he did, only to desert her later. Theseus, too, had received help from Ariadne in his fight with the Minotaur on the island of Crete. Seeming to fulfill his promise to marry her, Theseus took Ariadne with him, only to desert her when he reached the island of Naxos on his return to Athens.

Vergil's heroine, then, was receiving treatment that was not unfamiliar to Romans.

Moreover, Dido was guilty of another fault. After her husband Sychaeus had been murdered by her own brother, she vowed that she would never marry again. This vow she had broken, and Romans regarded such violations with extreme severity. When, for example, vestal virgins, vowed to virginity, were convicted of any laxity with men, they were buried alive. In showing no mercy to those who had failed to keep their promises to the gods, the Romans were not demonstrating any special enthusiasm for virtue; rather they felt that they must punish the delinquents lest the gods hurl their wrath against the whole community.

Those who regard Aeneas as a cad for deserting Dido feel a deep sympathy for Turnus, who is already engaged to Lavinia when Aeneas appears on the scene. Because of an oracle to the effect that his daughter should marry a stranger, her father withdrew his blessing from Turnus in favor of Aeneas. The native Italian prince resented what he considered an injustice, and in his resentment he slew great numbers of Trojans and their allies before he finally met Aeneas in single combat. At the very end of the action Turnus was defeated because Jupiter ordered Juno to cease aiding him. He lost because his sister Juturna was forced to desert him and because one of the Furies in the form of a bird was sent to terrify him. It was Turnus' destiny to fall as it was Aeneas' to conquer. If Turnus were a devout man, he would have complied with the oracle revealed to Latinus that his daughter was to marry a stranger, but one cannot imagine that the haughty, irascible Turnus would meekly retreat at the arrival of the refugee Aeneas.

The modern reader will be perplexed at the savage anger of the goddess Juno. The poet asks at the beginning of the epic if such great wrath can dwell in a divine breast, and leaves us to infer that such conduct is scandalous. Actually there is little virtue in the divinities of the ancient epics. Vergil inherited this machinery from the distant past where the gods had been made by man to man's likeness.

In adopting these supernatural powers, then, he was accepting the polite, the comfortable tradition. As a well-educated and enlightened Roman, Vergil could hardly have believed literally in the individual existence of the gods and goddesses as he depicted them in the *Aeneid.* In his youth he had been a disciple of Siro, the Epicurean teacher, and at that time he must have examined the myths of the gods rather critically. His literary style was influenced by Lucretius' *The Nature of Things,* in which the gods are considered indifferent to mankind, powerless to harm or to help men, in sharp contrast to the powers attributed to the various divinities in the *Aeneid.* Vergil did not follow the school of Epicurus; he was rather eclectic in his philosophy, adopting ideas from Stoicism and Platonism. He knew that he could not change the traditional attitude of the Romans toward the gods, and therefore he worked with the symbols that his readers could understand and accept, just as Lucretius began his poem with an invocation to Venus, who had no personal existence for him. We have a hint of Aeneas' philosophy of the supernatural in VI,724ff (p. 159) where Anchises expresses the doctrine of a world soul, an all-pervading mind infused into all nature. Tennyson in his admirable poem, "To Virgil," stated the poet's conviction graphically when he wrote: "Thou that seest Universal Nature moved by Universal Mind."

We must not look into the conduct of the deities for examples of lofty living and high virtue. Aware that these devices were outmoded, the poet created Aeneas, who is really the god in the story. The world must not look to the gods for ideals but to Aeneas. Because Vergil pictures Aeneas as divine, he carefully avoided putting into the hero's character anything base.

To maintain that Aeneas should have stayed with Dido in Carthage in spite of the order Mercury brought from Jupiter is to misunderstand Aeneas' character and his mission. Much as he was attached to her, he could not linger after the clear command from heaven. More romantic heroes may violate all laws, divine and human, to keep their promises to a heroine, but this is not the type of hero that Vergil created. To make him consistent in his dutifulness he must leave the queen. It is true that he remained quite a long time in Carthage, but this was due to an understanding between Venus, who acquiesced in what she considered an amorous episode, and Juno, who thought of the union as permanent. When it suited Venus she spoke to Jupiter about her son Aeneas' plight, and the father of heaven immediately sent Mercury to tell the hero to be on his way. If he lingered too long before considering the idea of departure, the fault is not in Aeneas but in the gods, who did not reveal their will to him.

If, however, we are to indulge in what is known in Biblical studies as the higher criticism, and to regard Mercury not as a god but merely a conviction that slowly takes hold of Aeneas, who is suffering from boredom, if the machinations of Venus and her son Cupid are merely symbols for the passion that rose in the heart of the lonely queen when she met this handsome, unattached warrior, then all the imprecations that critics have heaped on Aeneas are deserved; he is a hypocrite and his pose of piety is revolting. But such an interpretation, while intriguing in some phases of the epic, will offer difficulties when stretched to cover all the instances of supernatural manifestation in the poem.

VERGIL IN LITERARY TRADITION

The influence of Vergil on European literature has been continuous and extensive. In his own day he became a classic and he was always read, even in the darkest period of the early Middle Ages. It was quite natural that he should be accepted in the ages of faith, even though he was a pagan, for his epic was religious in tone and pure in thought and diction, a rare combination in a Latin poet. That the *Aeneid* was great literature was never called into question until relatively modern times when, perhaps because of the rising emphasis on scientific truth, it has been somewhat neglected. But whether the tale is true or not is a question one does not put to a poet, for he always asks his reader to look beyond the symbols, beyond the apparent story. Certainly it was believed by many readers down through the Middle Ages, and for that reason left a strong impression on the thought of the centuries following its appearance until the eighteenth century. Outside of literature Vergil's influence throughout the Middle Ages entered into such fields as magic and necromancy; these nonliterary influences may be studied by the curious student in the works of Comparetti and Spargo cited in the bibliography.

The great writers inspired by Vergil are numerous and include, among others, Dante, Tasso, Chaucer, Milton, Spenser, Marlowe, Tennyson, and Wordsworth.

In spite of his wide influence, critics have at times tried to prove that literary invention is not one of Vergil's strong points. The ancient author Macrobius looked into his borrowings from Greek and Latin classics, ranging from parts of lines to whole incidents from Homer. However, if one examines these, he will find that they are at times no more than dim echoes of what Vergil, widely read in Latin and Greek, retained in his memory. Then, too, he may have regarded elegant expressions in the work of Ennius as literary flourishes whose source would be generally recognized by intelligent readers, just as writers today use Biblical expressions or familiar phrases from Shakespeare without thinking of giving the author. When one reads Apollonius of Rhodes, for example, to see just how much Vergil borrowed from the story of Medea for his Dido episode, he will discover that the debt is questionable and at best slight. The same indebtedness to other poets may be charged against Homer and Shakespeare, but it is to the credit of both poets that they took what others gave them and recast it so that the identity of the contribution was virtually lost.

Biographical and Textual Note

Publius Vergilius Maro was born October 15, 70 B.C., at Andes, a village near Mantua, just north of the Po River where the family had a small farm. Though in modest circumstances, the father gave his son a good education, first at Cremona and later at Milan and Rome. In the capital he studied under Siro, a notable expounder of the doctrines of Epicurus. In the distribution of land to veterans after the battle of Philippi in 42 B.C., he lost his farm, but through the intercession of the governor of the region, Asinius Pollio, friend of the young poet, it was restored. Later when his patron was absent, his property was again seized; this time it seems that he was fortunate to escape with his life. It is quite probable that Maecenas gave him an estate in Campania as compensation for the loss he sustained. Though rustic in appearance, he was the principal ornament of the literary circle sponsored by Maecenas and was responsible for introducing Horace to Maecenas, a favor that was deeply appreciated by the younger poet, as we can judge by the number of times he refers to Vergil in his poems. He never married. In 19 B.C. he undertook a journey to Greece where he intended to put the finishing touches on the *Aeneid,* the work that occupied the last eleven years of his life. At Athens he met Augustus, who was returning from the East, and fell in line with his suggestion that he return to Italy with the imperial entourage. During the voyage he became ill of a fever and died on September 21, 19 B.C., a few days after landing at Brundisium, the modern Brindisi. His body was brought to Naples, where his tomb became a shrine. It was Vergil's desire that his epic be destroyed, since it had not received the polishing he had hoped to give it; but Augustus forbade the poet's literary executors, Varius Rufus and Plotius Tucca, to carry out his wishes.

The present translation of the *Aeneid* follows in the main the Latin edition of the great Italian scholar, Remigio Sabbadini, revised by Concetto Marchesi. Lines they regarded as spurious are bracketed.

In five issues of "The Classical World" for 1958 (vol. 51) there is a survey entitled "Recent Work on Vergil (1940–56)." In the same journal for 1964 (vol. 57, no. 5) this study was continued in "Recent Work on Vergil (1957–63)." These extensive surveys are the work of George E. Duckworth. Both were reprinted by The Vergilian Society of America (Exeter, N. H., 1964).

The following selected bibliography in English is intended for the general reader. For the most part these items are available from sources cited, though these are often not the original publishers. Material on the poet's life, about which so little is known, has been examined by Tenney Frank (*Vergil: A Biography,* Henry Holt and Company, New York, 1922), Gilbert Highet in a chapter of his *Poets in a Landscape* (Hamish Hamilton, London, 1957) and Bruno Nardi (*The Youth of Virgil,* Harvard University Press, Cambridge, Mass., 1930). General studies of the poet include Robert Seymour Conway's *Harvard Lectures on the Vergilian Age* (Biblo and Tannen, New York, 1967); T. R. Glover's *Virgil* (Methuen and Company, London, 1930); W. Y. Sellar's *The Roman Poets of the Augustan Age: Virgil* (Biblo and Tannen, New York, 1965). Henry Steele Commager has edited a collection of twelve critical essays entitled *Virgil,* for which he has written an introduction. (Prentice-Hall, Englewood Cliffs, N. J., 1966.) A discussion of the artistry and the meaning of the *Aeneid* is often found in the same work. See D. L. Drew, *The Allegory of the Aeneid* (Basil Blackwell & Mott, Oxford, 1927); Brooks Otis, *Virgil: A Study in Civilized Poetry* (Oxford University Press, New York, 1964); Viktor Pöschl, *The Art of Vergil: Image and Symbol in the Aeneid,* translated by Gerda Seligson (University of Michigan, Ann Arbor, 1962); Henry W. Prescott, *The Development of Virgil's Art* (Russell & Russell, New York, 1963); E. K. Rand, *The Magical Art of Virgil* (Harvard University Press, Cambridge, Mass., 1931). The curious turns that Vergil's fame took in the Middle Ages have been studied extensively by D. Comparetti, *Vergil in the Middle Ages* (Archon Books, Hamden, Conn., 1966) and John Webster Spargo, *Virgil the Necromancer,*

Studies in Virgilian Legends (Harvard University Press, Cambridge, Mass., 1934). For the poet's influence on English literature consult, *From Virgil to Milton* by C. M. Bowra (now published by St. Martin's Press, New York); originally published by Macmillan & Company, London, 1945); *The Classical Tradition* by Gilbert Highet (Oxford University Press, New York, 1949); *Vergil and the English Poets* by Elizabeth Nitchie (Columbia University Press, New York, 1919). There is a chapter on the *Aeneid* in *The Iliad, the Odyssey, and the Epic Tradition* by Charles Rowan Beye (Anchor Books, Doubleday & Company, Garden City, New York, 1966) and in *The Descent from Heaven* by Thomas Greene (Yale University Press, New Haven, Conn., 1963). Lengthy sections on the poet and his work may be found in histories of Latin literature, such as *A Literary History of Rome from the Origins to the Close of the Golden Age* by J. Wight and A. M. Duff (Barnes & Noble, New York, 1960; originally published by T. Fisher Unwin, London, 1909) and *A Handbook of Latin Literature* by H. J. Rose (E. P. Dutton & Co., New York, 1936). The third chapter of Mark Van Doren's *The Noble Voice* (Holt, Rinehart and Winston, New York, 1946) is a decidedly negative lecture on the character of Aeneas. Much more hostile is an article by Robert Graves entitled "The Virgil Cult" published in "The Virginia Quarterly Review" (vol. 38, 1962, pp. 13–35); in this he opposes all things Vergilian and tries to prove that few poets have done so great discredit to their sacred calling as Vergil.

KEVIN GUINAGH

Tampa, Florida
January, 1970

Table of Contents

Book One

JUNO

The following opening lines from the *Aeneid* are included at this point to remind the reader that Vergil wrote his epic in verse.

Arma virumque cano, Troiae qui primus ab oris
Italiam fato profugus Laviniaque venit
litora, multum ille et terris iactatus et alto
vi superum, saevae memorem Iunonis ob iram,
multa quoque et bello passus, dum conderet urbem
inferretque deos Latio, genus unde Latinum
Albanique patres atque altae moenia Romae.
Musa, mihi causas memora, quo numine laeso
quidve dolens regina deum tot volvere casus
insignem pietate virum, tot adire labores
impulerit. tantaene animis caelestibus irae?
Urbs antiqua fuit (Tyrii tenuere coloni)
Karthago, Italiam contra Tiberinaque longe
ostia, dives opum studiisque asperrima belli;
quam Iuno fertur terris magis omnibus unam
posthabita coluisse Samo: hic illius arma,
hic currus fuit; hoc regnum dea gentibus esse,
si qua fata sinant, iam tum tenditque fovetque.
progeniem sed enim Troiano a sanguine duci
audierat, Tyrias olim quae verteret arces;
hinc populum late regem belloque superbum
venturum excidio Libyae: sic volvere Parcas.
id metuens veterisque memor Saturnia belli,
prima quod ad Troiam pro caris gesserat Argis:
necdum etiam causae irarum saevique dolores
exciderant animo; manet alta mente repostum
iudicium Paridis spretaeque iniuria formae
et genus invisum et rapti Ganymedis honores:
his accensa super iactatos aequore toto
Troas, reliquias Danaum atque immitis Achilli,
arcebat longe Latio, multosque per annos
errabant acti fatis maria omnia circum.
tantae molis erat Romanam condere gentem.

• Book One •

THE THEME OF THE AENEID

I sing of arms and the man who, fated to be an exile, was the first to come from the coasts of Troy to Italy and its shores near Lavinium, a man who was much harassed on land and sea by divine power on account of the relentless anger of savage Juno. He suffered much in war, too, while founding the city and bringing his gods to Latium. From him came the Latin race and our Alban ancestors and the walls of high Rome.

O Muse, bring to my mind the reasons why the queen of the gods—was her divine power offended or did she nurse some grievance?—compelled a hero outstanding for his devotion to suffer so many hardships. Can such great anger dwell in heavenly breasts?

THE WRATH OF JUNO

Carthage was an ancient city—colonists from Tyre dwelt there —across from Italy and far from the mouth of the Tiber, rich in resources and fierce in its pursuit of war, the one city, they say, that Juno loved above all cities anywhere, not excepting even Samos. Here were her arms, here was her chariot. Even then the goddess had the intention and cherished the hope that this would be a kingdom for all the nations, if the Fates would allow it. But she had heard that a progeny that one day would overthrow the Tyrian towers was springing from Trojan blood, that from this offspring would come a people, wide-ruling and proud in war, to destroy Libya: thus the Fates had decreed.

Juno, the daughter of Saturn, feared this and remembered the old war which she as leader had waged before Troy in defense of her dear Argos, for even yet the cause of her wrath and her wild resentment had not been erased from her mind. But buried deep in her soul lay the judgment of Paris, the insult to her slighted beauty, that hated race of Troy, and the honors shown the stolen Ganymede. Incensed by these wrongs, she kept the Trojans—those spared by the Greeks and the ruthless Achilles—tossing upon the deep, far from Latium. Driven by fate, they wandered for many years over all the seas. So much toil did the founding of the Roman race involve!

THE SHIPWRECK OF THE TROJANS

Hardly out of sight of the land of Sicily, they were happily sailing over the deep and churning the sea into foam, when Juno, nursing that eternal wound in her breast, pondered:

"Am I, having scarcely begun, to desist as though conquered, without being able to turn the prince of the Trojans away from Italy? Suppose I am forbidden to do so by the Fates. Was not Pallas able to burn a fleet of the Greeks and swamp them in the sea because of the mad violence of one man, Ajax the son of Oileus? After hurling the swift fire of Jove from the clouds, she herself overturned the ships and churned the sea with the wind; she caught Ajax up in a whirlwind as he breathed forth flames from his pierced breast, and impaled him on a sharp crag. But I, the queen of the gods, the sister and spouse of Jove, have been waging war so many years with but one race. Will anyone adore the divinity of Juno henceforth, will any suppliant place an offering upon my altars?"

The goddess, turning over such thoughts in her inflamed mind, came to Aeolia, the home of storms, a breeding ground of wild winds. Here King Aeolus keeps under his control the struggling blasts and the loud tempests, and holds them back with prison bonds. They madly rage with a mighty roar around the door of the mountain, while Aeolus, scepter in hand, sits on his lofty throne and calms their spirit and tempers their anger. If he did not do this, the swift winds would surely carry away the sea, the land, and high heaven, and sweep them aloft through the air. But fearing this, the all-powerful father hid them in dark caverns and piled a mass of high mountains upon them. He gave them a king, who, when ordered, knew by a set decree how to curb them or to give them free rein. To him, then, Juno humbly addressed these words:

"Aeolus—for the father of the gods and the king of men has given you the power to calm the waves and to rouse them with the wind—a race that is hostile to me is sailing the Tuscan Sea, carrying Ilium and its conquered household gods to Italy. Whip fury into the winds, overturn and sink their ships or break them up and cast their bodies into the sea. I have twice seven nymphs with beautiful bodies, and one of these is Deiopea, who has the most lovely form of all. I will join her in permanent wedlock with you and consecrate her as your own in consideration of your merit so that she may spend all her years with you and make you the parent of lovely children."

Aeolus spoke in reply: "My queen, it is your task to determine what you wish; it is my duty to undertake what you command. You have gained for me this kingdom and the scepter from Jupiter. You have given me the right to recline at the banquets of the gods, and you have made me ruler over the storm clouds and tempests."

On uttering these words, he aimed his spear and hurled it into the side of the hollow mountain. Straightway, as if in battle formation, winds rushed forth where the opening was made, and swept over the land in a tornado. They fell upon the deep, and together the Southeast, the South, and the Southwest Wind, teeming with storms, churned the sea to its lowest depths and rolled vast waves to the shores. Then rose the clamor of men and the creaking of ropes. Of a sudden the clouds snatched the light of day from the eyes of the Trojans, and dark night spread over the sea. The heavens resounded and the sky was lighted by frequent flashes of fire. Everything threatened instant death for the men.

Suddenly the limbs of Aeneas grew numb and cold. He groaned and, raising his two hands to the stars, he exclaimed:

"Thrice and four times happy are you whose lot it was to die under the high walls of Troy within sight of your fathers! O Diomede son of Tydeus, bravest of the race of the Greeks, to think that I could not have died on the plains of Ilium, that your right hand could not have freed my spirit where valiant Hector lies pierced by the weapon of Achilles the grandson of Aeacus, where huge Sarpedon lies, where the Simois rolls along so many shields and helmets and bodies of brave men swept under the waves."

As he uttered these words, the storm, howling from the north, struck the sail head on and tossed the waves to the stars. The oars were broken. Then the ship turned and offered its side to the waves; a steep mountain of water bore down in a mass. Some men hung on the very tip of the flood; the yawning wave opened to their view the earth between the swells; the sea boiled with sand. The South Wind whirled three ships it had seized onto hidden rocks—these rocks in the midst of the waves the Italians call *The Altars*—a dangerous ridge on the surface of the sea. The Southeast Wind drove three ships from the deep into the shallows and sandbanks—a pitiful sight to behold—dashed them into the shoals and surrounded them with a wall of sand. Before his very eyes a heavy sea crashed from above against one ship, carrying the Lycians and faithful Orontes. The pilot was thrown forward and tossed headlong into the deep. Now the flood whirled the vessel around three times in the same spot, and a rapid whirlpool swallowed it up in the sea. Here and there in the abyss appeared swimmers, the weapons of men, planks, and the treasures of Troy on the waves. Already the storm had overcome the strong ship of Ilioneus, then that of the brave Achates, and those in which Abas and the aged Aletes sailed; the hostile storm entered the loose joints and yawning cracks of the ships' sides.

NEPTUNE CALMS THE SEA

Meantime Neptune perceived that a mighty uproar was spreading over the sea, that a storm had been let loose, and that the quiet waters in the lowest depths were stirred. Much troubled, he looked out upon the deep and raised his placid head from the surface of the waves. He saw the fleet of Aeneas scattered over the face of the deep, and the Trojans overcome by the waves and the downpour from the sky. Juno's cunning and anger did not escape the notice of her brother Neptune. He called the East and the West Winds to himself and straightway spoke to them in this way:

"Has such great pride in your birth taken possession of you? Do you dare mingle the heavens and the earth without my divine order and do you dare raise up such great masses, you Winds, whom I—but first it would be better to quiet the disturbed waves. Hereafter, you will atone for your misdeeds by a much more serious punishment. Hasten your flight and take this message to your king: not to him but to me was the rule of the sea and the savage trident given by lot. He has enormous rocks that belong to you and yours, East Wind; let Aeolus glory in that hall and let him rule in the closed prison of the Winds."

Thus he spoke and swifter than the word he calmed the swelling sea and put to flight the masses of clouds and brought back the sun. Cymothoë and Triton, pushing together, shoved the ships off a sharp rock, while Neptune himself opened up the vast quicksands with his trident and calmed the sea as he glided over the tops of the waves on the light wheels of his chariot. As often when lawlessness has broken out in a great concourse of people, and the ill-bred crowd is savage in spirit, and torches and stones are already flying and madness wields the weapons, then if by chance they behold a man respected for his devoted services, they grow silent and stand ready to listen while his words rule their minds and calm their breasts: so all the clamor of the sea died down, after its lord, looking out upon the face of the deep and riding under the clear heavens, turned his horses and, flying, gave rein to his obedient chariot.

LANDING ON THE COAST OF AFRICA

The weary followers of Aeneas strove to steer a course to the nearest shore and they turned to the coast of Libya. There is a spot in a long recess where an island makes a port by the extension of its arms, on which all the billows from the deep break and spend their force on the distant windings of the bay. On both sides vast rocks and twin crags threaten the sky, and beneath their peaks far and wide the safe sea lies quiet; moreover, a curtain of waving forests, a dark grove with dreadful shadows, overhangs the inlet. Facing seaward there is a cave under projecting crags; within are fresh waters and seats of natural stone, the home of the nymphs. Here no cables hold the weary ships, no anchor catches with its hooked fluke. At this point Aeneas beached seven ships collected from the entire number, and disembarking, the Trojans, with great love for the earth, took possession of the wished-for strand and stretched their limbs, dripping with brine, on the shore. First Achates struck a spark from the flint and nursed the fire with leaves, putting dry fuel round about, and he caught the flame in the tinder. Then, though weary from their toils, they prepared to parch the grain they had saved and to grind it with the millstone.

THE DEER HUNT AND THE FEAST

Meanwhile Aeneas climbed the cliff for a wide view of the deep, hoping to see something of Antheus, tossed about by the wind, and the Phrygian vessels, or Capys, or the arms of Caicus upon the high stern. He saw not a ship in sight but three stags wandering on the shore with all the herd following behind them, the long line feeding in the valleys. Here he stopped and took his bow and his swift arrows, weapons the faithful Achates bore. First, the leaders themselves, bearing high their heads with treelike horns, he laid low, and then the drove. Driving all the herd among the leafy groves, he plied them with weapons; nor did he desist in his victory until seven huge bodies lay upon the ground, equaling the number of the ships. Thereupon he sought the port and distributed them among all his companions. Next, he divided the wine which on the shore of Sicily the good Acestes had put aboard in casks as a gift from the hero on their departure, and he calmed their sad hearts with these words:

"My comrades—for we are not ignorant of evils previously suffered—you who have borne more serious troubles, a god will end these evils, too. You have approached the madness of Scylla and its deep-sounding rocks, you have had the experience of being stoned by the Cyclopes. Renew your spirit, and lay aside gloomy fear; perhaps one day it will be a pleasure to remember these trials. Through diverse mishaps, through many crises we make our way to Latium where the Fates portend a peaceful settlement. There it is right for Troy to rise. Have courage and preserve yourselves for prosperous days."

He uttered these words and, though saddened by great worry, he feigned a look of hope on his face and buried his sorrow down deep in his heart. They girded themselves to prepare a feast on the booty. They ripped the hides from the ribs and laid bare the entrails. Some cut the members into pieces and fastened them, still trembling, on spits; others placed bronze kettles on the shore and kindled a fire. Then they revived their energy with food. Sprawled out on the grass, they filled themselves with old wine and fat venison. After their hunger was satisfied by the food, and the plates were cleared away, they mourned for their lost companions in a long discussion, doubting—now hopeful, now fearful—whether they should believe their comrades were still alive or had met their end and no longer heard when they were called upon. Most of all, dutiful Aeneas mourned the misfortune of spirited Orontes and Amycus, the cruel fate of Lycus, brave Gyas, and brave Cloanthus.

COMPLAINT OF VENUS

And when all this was over, Jupiter, looking down from the summit of the sky upon the sail-winged sea, the broad lands, the shores, and the scattered peoples, stood on the highest pinnacle of heaven and fixed his gaze on the kingdom of Libya. Venus, her bright eyes blurred with tears, mournfully addressed him while such cares troubled his heart:

"O you who rule the affairs of men and gods with your eternal decrees and terrify with your thunderbolt, what crime could my Aeneas, what offense could the Trojans have committed against you? Even after they have suffered many disasters, are they still shut off from the entire world because they wish to go to Italy? You definitely promised that one day with the passing of the years, there would be Romans from the revived line of Teucer, that there would be leaders who would hold the sea and the land under their complete sway. What consideration has changed you, my father? Indeed it was for this reason that I was consoled at the fall and the sorrowful destruction of Troy, balancing adverse fate with the hope of a happier fate, but now the same fortune pursues these men harassed by so many misfortunes. Great king, what end do you propose for their toils? After having slipped through the line of the Achaeans, Antenor was able to penetrate safely to the Illyrian bay and the heart of the kingdom of the Liburnians, and go beyond the source of the Timavus, from which through nine mouths the water breaks forth with deafening mountain roar and deluges the land with its resounding flood. But there that hero founded the city of Padua and established a settlement of the Teucrians, gave his name to the race, and set up the arms of Troy. Now undisturbed he rests in quiet peace, but we, your progeny, to whom you promise the citadel of heaven, are betrayed and our ships lost—unspeakable crime—because of the wrath of one, Juno, and we are kept far from the shores of Italy. Is this the honor shown to piety? Is this the way you restore us to power?"

JUPITER'S PROPHECY ABOUT THE ROMANS

The father of men and gods, smiling upon her with the look that calms the storms in the sky, lightly kissed the lips of his daughter and then spoke these words to her:

"Spare your fear, goddess of Cythera. The fate of your dear ones remains unchanged: you shall see the city and the promised walls of Lavinium, and you shall raise the greathearted Aeneas to the stars of heaven; nor has any new decision changed my mind. He shall wage—for I will speak out, since this worry consumes you, and unrolling the scroll further, I will disclose the secrets of fate—he shall wage a great war in Italy, and he shall crush wild peoples and set up laws for men and build walls, until the third summer sees him ruling over Latium, and the third winter passes after the subjection of the Rutulians. But the boy Ascanius, to whom is now added the surname Julus—he was Ilus while the state of Ilium was in power—shall complete in his rule thirty great circling years of revolving months and transfer his kingdom from the seat of Lavinium and strongly fortify Alba Longa.

"Here the race of Hector shall rule for full three hundred years until a royal priestess, Ilia, with child by Mars, shall bring forth twins. One of these, Romulus, happily wearing the tawny skin of the wolf that nursed him, shall carry on the Roman race and build walls sacred to Mars, and call this people the Romans from his name. Over these I place no bounds, either of empire or time; I have given them rule without end. Nay, even vengeful Juno, who now strikes fear into the sea, the land, and the sky, shall alter her plans for the better, and with me shall cherish the Roman masters of the world and the race that wears the toga.

"This is my pleasure. As the years glide by, an age shall

come when the house of Assaracus shall reduce to slavery Phthia and famed Mycenae, and shall dominate conquered Argos. From this illustrious line Trojan Caesar shall be born, whose rule shall reach ocean's bounds and whose fame shall rise to the stars—Julius, a name handed down from the great Julus. Be assured that one day you shall receive him in heaven, laden with spoils from the East; he, too, shall be invoked in prayer. Then the fierce ages, having laid aside war, shall grow mild; white-clad Faith, Vesta, and Quirinus with his brother Remus shall establish the laws, and the awful gates of war shall be closed with tight joints of iron. Impious Fury, sitting inside on his savage armor and bound with a hundred bronze knots behind his back, shall rage fearfully from his blood-stained mouth."

THE DESCENT OF MERCURY

Thus Jupiter spoke. From on high he sent down Mercury the son of Maia, so that the land and the towers of new Carthage would show hospitality to the Trojans, lest Dido, unaware of the decree of fate, should repel them from her boundaries. He flew through the great expanse of air on an oarage of wings and quickly alighting on the shores of Libya, he fulfilled these commands. Because of the will of the god, the Carthaginians put aside their fierce feelings. The queen especially entertained a friendly spirit and a kindly attitude toward the Trojans.

AENEAS MEETS HIS MOTHER, VENUS

But dutiful Aeneas, after turning over many ideas in his mind during the night, decided, when first the blessed dawn appeared, to go forth and explore the new region and learn for his companions to what shores they had been blown by the wind and whether men or wild beasts lived there, for he saw the place was uncultivated. He hid the fleet in a wooded inlet under a hollowed-out cliff surrounded by trees and dreadful shadows, and with Achates as his sole companion, he strode forth, brandishing in his hand two spears with broad iron heads. Amid the forest he met his mother in the guise of a maiden wearing the dress and bearing weapons, like a Spartan girl, or like Thracian Harpalyce as she urges on her horses or surpasses in speed the swift Hebrus River. For the huntress had a light bow slung from her shoulder, and she let her hair blow in the wind; her knees were bare and her flowing garments were tied in a knot.

She spoke first: "Ho there! youths, tell me if by chance you have seen one of my sisters wearing a quiver and the skin of a spotted lynx wandering here or pursuing with shouts the tracks of a foaming boar."

So Venus spoke, and the son of Venus answered: "None of your sisters have I heard or seen—but how should I address you, maiden? Your face is hardly that of a mortal, and your voice does not sound human. You are a goddess certainly, or are you the sister of Phoebus or one in blood with the nymphs? Be generous and lighten our toil, whoever you are, and tell us under what sky we are and upon what shores we are tossed; for not knowing this place and its people, we wander about, driven here by the wind and the huge waves. Many a victim shall be slain by our right hand before your altars."

"Indeed I hardly deem myself worthy of such an honor," Venus replied. "It is the custom of Tyrian maids to carry a quiver and to bind their legs high with a purple boot. You see the Punic kingdom, the Tyrians, and the city of Agenor, but on the boundaries are the Libyans, a race unconquerable in war. Dido rules the kingdom, having set out from the city of Tyre to escape her brother. The story of her wrongs is a long one, and the details numerous, but I shall touch upon the main points. Her husband was Sychaeus, the richest landowner among the Phoenicians, loved with a great love by the miserable woman. To him her father had given his virgin daughter, binding her in wedlock at the first favorable omens. But the kingdom of Tyre was held by her brother Pygmalion, who was more savage than any man in crime. Between them hatred arose. Blinded by his love of gold and disregarding the love of his sister, in secret before the altar he sacrilegiously slew with a sword the unsuspecting Sychaeus. For a long time he concealed the deed, and wickedly making many pretenses, deceived the love-sick Dido with vain hope. However, the very image of her buried husband, wondrously raising his pale face, came to her in sleep. Revealing the cruel altar and his breast pierced with the sword, he uncovered all the secret crime of their family. Then he persuaded her to hasten her flight and leave her fatherland, and he disclosed a treasure in the earth, an unknown weight of silver and gold, as help for the journey.

"Moved by these events, Dido prepared herself and her companions for flight. Those assembled who felt a cruel hatred or keen fear of the tyrant; they seized ships which, as it happened, were ready, and they loaded them with gold. The wealth of greedy Pygmalion was carried upon the sea, and a woman was leader of the exploit. They came to the place where now you see huge walls and the citadel of new Carthage rising, and they bought as much land as they could encircle with the hide of a bull, calling it Byrsa for that reason. But who are you, may I ask? From what shores have you come, and to what place are you going?"

The hero sighed and his voice came from the depth of his soul as he answered her queries:

"O goddess, if I should start my story from the very beginning, and there were time to listen to the recital of our troubles, before I should finish, Vesper would bring the day to an end and close the gate of Olympus. By pure chance a storm drove us, already borne over many seas from ancient Troy—perhaps the name of Troy has reached your ears—to the Libyan shores. I, the devout Aeneas, famed beyond the sky, carry abroad with me my household gods, rescued from the enemy. I seek Italy, our fatherland, and our race sprung from high Jupiter. In twice ten ships I set sail on the Phrygian Sea, following the revelations of the oracles, while my goddess mother showed me the way. Hardly seven are left, shattered by the waves and winds. I myself, unknown and needy, wander over the deserts of Libya, repulsed from Europe and Asia."

Though he would have complained further, Venus interrupted him in the midst of his sorrowful recital:

"Whoever you are, not disdained, I believe, by the gods, you breathe the breath of life, you who have come to the Tyrian city. Set out now, and go from here to the threshold of the queen, for I bring you word that your comrades have returned and that the fleet has been restored, driven into a safe haven by the changing winds, now from the north—unless my parents foolishly taught me divination to no end. Look at the line of twelve rejoicing swans which the bird of Jupiter, gliding down from the ethereal regions, has just been chasing in the clear sky. Now they seem either to be alighting on the earth in a long line or to be looking down on those that have already alighted. As on their return they sport with noisy wings and circle the heavens in a flock and utter their cries, so your ships and your comrades are either safe in port or are entering its mouth under full sail. Continue now; direct your steps where this path leads you."

She spoke and as she turned aside, she showed her rosy throat, while the hair of her head breathed forth the divine perfume of ambrosia. Her dress fell to her feet, and she appeared a true goddess in her bearing.

When he recognized his mother, he called after her as she fled:

"Why do you, cruel mother, deceive your son so often with false disguises? Why do I never have a chance to join my hand with yours and hear and speak words that are natural?"

AENEAS ENTERS CARTHAGE

With such words he complained to her, and then directed his steps to the walls. But as they went along, the goddess Venus shielded them with an obscuring fog and spread around them a thick veil of mist so that no one could see or touch them, or cause their delay or demand the reason for their coming. Rising aloft, she departed for Paphos and joyously returned to her shrine where the hundred altars of her temple smoke with Arabian incense and are fragrant with fresh wreaths.

Meanwhile they hurried along the way where the path directed. Soon they were ascending the very high hill which rises above the city and looks down upon the towers opposite. Aeneas marveled at the mass of buildings, once huts; he marveled at the gates, the clamor, and the paved roads. The Tyrians attacked the work eagerly, some constructing the walls, building the citadel, and rolling up stones with their hands, others selecting a lot for a home and bounding it with a furrow. They were setting up laws, electing magistrates and an august senate. Here some were excavating the harbor, yonder others were seeking broad foundations for the theater and cutting out rough columns from the rocks, the lofty ornaments for the future stage. They labored as do the bees under the sun of early summer throughout the flowering countryside when they lead out the grown offspring of the race, or when they store up liquid honey, or fill the cells with sweet nectar, or receive the burdens of those that come, or, forming a battle line, keep the lazy brood of drones from the hive; the work proceeds at fever pitch, and the fragrant honey is redolent of thyme.

"O happy you whose walls are already rising!" Aeneas said as he looked up at the battlements of the city. Cloaked in a mist—wondrous to behold—he walked through their midst, mingling with the men though observed by no one.

In the heart of the city there was a grove, a most pleasant spot because of its shade, where on their arrival, the Phoenicians, after being tossed about by the waves and the storm, had dug up the sign that royal Juno had promised, the head of a spirited horse, which indicated that the race would be outstanding in war and easily survive in the ages to come. Here Sidonian Dido had founded for Juno a great temple, rich in gifts and in the ever-present power of the goddess. It had a bronze threshold at the top of the steps, beams bound with bronze, and bronze doors on creaking hinges. At the sight of this spectacle in the grove Aeneas' fears were quieted for the first time; here first he dared hope for safety and feel some confidence after his misfortune. While waiting for the queen, he gazed at each object in the great temple and marveled at the good fortune of the city, the skills of the competing artists, and the toil represented in these works. He saw the Trojan battle lines drawn up and the war already known in story throughout the whole world, the sons of Atreus, and Priam, and Achilles, who was enraged at both sides. He stopped and weeping said:

"Achates, what place, what region on the earth is not already full of our sufferings? Look at Priam! Even here praiseworthy action has its own reward. Human experience is full of sorrow and the lot of man depresses the mind. Put aside your fear; this fame will bring some safety to you."

Thus he spoke and he feasted his soul on the lifeless picture, and as he sighed deeply, many a tear rolled down his cheeks. For he saw at one spot how the warlike Greeks were fleeing and the Trojan youths were pressing on, while at another the Trojans were retreating and crested Achilles was pursuing in a chariot. Weeping, he recognized not far from this the snowy tents of Rhesus. These the savage Diomede the son of Tydeus destroyed amid much slaughter by a surprise attack in their first sleep, and turned the spirited horses of Rhesus back into the camp before they had tasted the pastures of Troy or drunk from the river Xanthus. In another scene, fleeing Troilus was pictured, luckless youth unequal in combat to Achilles! He had lost his weapons and was being dragged along by the horses, and though on his back, he stayed with the empty chariot, still holding to his reins. His head and hair were dragged along the ground, and the dust was marked with his trailing spear. At the same time, the Trojan women with loosened hair were going to the temple of unfair Pallas. They carried her robe, humbly sorrowful as they beat their breasts with their hands. But the unfriendly goddess kept her eyes fixed on the ground. Thrice Achilles had dragged Hector around the walls of Troy and was pictured as selling the lifeless body for gold. Then indeed Aeneas uttered a heavy sigh from the bottom of his heart on seeing the spoils, the chariots, the body of his friend, and Priam stretching forth his unarmed hands. In among the Greek chieftains Aeneas recognized himself also, the Eastern battle lines, and the weapons of dark Memnon. Infuriated Penthesilea led the battle lines of the crescent-shielded Amazons and raged in the midst of thousands; a warrior maid with a golden binding about her bare breasts, she dared contend with men.

While Trojan Aeneas was looking at these marvels, while he stood musing, riveted in one gaze, Queen Dido, a woman of surpassing loveliness, entered the temple in the company of a great crowd of youths. As on the banks of the Eurotas or over the ridges of Cynthus, Diana leads her dances, attended on all sides by a thousand oreads (she bears her quiver on her shoulder and towers over all the goddesses as she walks along, while joy fills the silent heart of her mother Latona), thus happy Dido moved amid the men, directing their work and the future kingdom. Then at the door of the cell of the goddess, in the middle of the vaulted temple, Dido, surrounded by armed men, seated herself upon her high throne. She administered justice and made laws for the men. By fair assignments she was making equal the toil involved in the work or was drawing lots. Suddenly Aeneas saw approaching in a great crowd Antheus, Sergestus, brave Cloanthus, and others of the Trojans whom the dark storm had scattered upon the sea and carried away to other shores. At the same time Aeneas and Achates in their astonishment were struck dumb with joy and fear. They eagerly desired to shake hands with their comrades, but the uncertainty of their own position disturbed their minds. They remained hidden and cloaked with the hollow cloud, waiting to see what fortune the men would have, on what shore they had left their fleet, and why they were coming here;

for men chosen from all the ships were walking along, begging for mercy, and were entering the temple amid shouts.

THE SPEECH OF ILIONEUS

After they had entered and were given an opportunity to speak, Ilioneus, the senior among them, began quietly:

"O queen, to whom Jupiter has given the right to found a new city and to curb proud tribes with laws, we miserable Trojans, borne by the winds over all the seas, beseech you: ward off unspeakable fires from our ships, spare a devout race, and look at our condition a little more closely. We have not come to lay waste with the sword the homes of Libya or drive captured booty to the shore. We have no such violence in mind; there is no such insolence in conquered men.

"There is a place that the Greeks call Hesperia, an ancient land, powerful in arms and rich in its soil. Oenotrian men once inhabited it. The story goes that now their descendants have called it Italy, from the name of their leader, Italus. This was our course when stormy Orion, suddenly rising from the waves, drove us into hidden shallows and scattered us far apart before the raging winds over the waves of the turbulent sea and into the impassable rocks. A few of us sailed to your shores. What race of men is this, what country so barbarous as to permit such treatment? We are refused the hospitality of the coast. They start a war, and forbid us to stay on the edge of the shore. If you scorn the human race and the weapons of men, yet remember that the gods are mindful of right and wrong.

"Aeneas was our ruler. No man was more virtuous than he nor more renowned for piety or warlike deeds at arms. If the Fates still preserve him, if he still breathes the air of heaven and does not already rest in the cruel shadow of death, we have no fear; nor would you repent striving to anticipate him in kindness. In the region of Sicily are the cities and the armed might of famed Acestes sprung from Trojan blood. Permit us to beach our fleet shattered by the winds, to hew beams from the forests, and to trim oars so that, if we are allowed to sail for Italy after recovering our companions and our leader, we may joyfully seek Latium. But if hope of recovery has been lost and, best of Trojan fathers, the sea of Libya holds you and no hope remains for Julus, then at least let us sail to Sicilian waters and the prepared settlements of King Acestes, whence we have been driven here."

Thus spoke Ilioneus and all the Dardanians shouted their approval.

DIDO WELCOMES ILIONEUS

Then Dido answered briefly, lowering her eyes: "Free your hearts of fear, Teucrians, put aside your cares. The difficulty of our situation and the newness of the kingdom compel me to take such precautions and to protect the borders far and wide with patrols. Who could be ignorant of the race of the followers of Aeneas, of the city of Troy, the courage of its men, and the conflagration of so great a war? We Carthaginians do not bear such unfeeling hearts, nor does the Sun harness his horses so far from the city of Tyre. Whether you desire great Hesperia and the Saturnian fields of Italy or Eryx as your country and Acestes as your king, I will send you away safe with my help and I will aid you with my resources. Do you even wish to settle in this kingdom on an equal footing with me? The city I am setting up is yours; beach your craft. Trojan and Tyrian will be treated by me with no discrimination. Would that King Aeneas himself, buffeted by the same storm, were present! Indeed I will send reliable men along the shores and I will order them to search the uttermost bounds of Libya to see if, tossed ashore, he wanders in some forest or city."

APPEARANCE OF AENEAS AND RECEPTION BY DIDO

Aroused by these words, brave Achates and father Aeneas were now eager to break forth from the cloud. First, Achates addressed Aeneas:

"Goddess-born, what feeling now rises in your mind? You see that everything is safe, that the fleet and our companions have been recovered. One is absent, one whom in the midst of the flood we ourselves saw drown. Everything else agrees with the words of your mother."

Hardly had he spoken these words when the surrounding cloud parted and disappeared into the clear air. Aeneas stood revealed. His face and shoulders shone in the bright light like those of a god, for his goddess mother herself had bestowed beautiful locks on her son, a glowing light to his youth, and happy charm to his eyes, as workmanship adds beauty to ivory or as silver or Parian marble is bound by yellow gold.

Then he addressed the queen and to the surprise of all, he suddenly spoke: "I whom you seek am here before you, Aeneas of Troy, snatched from the waves of Libya. You alone pity the unspeakable sufferings of Troy and share your city and home with us, the remnants left by the Greeks. Already exhausted by all the disasters of land and sea, and needing everything, neither we nor whatever remains anywhere of the Trojan race scattered through the whole world have the power to show you, Dido, the gratitude that is your due. May the gods give you a just reward, if any power cares for the pious, if there is any justice anywhere and a mind conscious of right. What happy age produced you? What great parents gave birth to you? As long as the rivers flow to the sea, as long as shadows pass over the slopes of the mountains, and the heavens feed the stars, always your honor and your name and your praise shall live, no matter what lands call me."

After speaking thus, he grasped his friend Ilioneus with his right hand and Serestus with his left and then the others and brave Gyas and brave Cloanthus.

Sidonian Dido was astonished first at the appearance and then at the great misfortune of the man, and thus she spoke:

"What fate pursues you, goddess-born, through so many dangers? What power drives you to these barbarous shores? Are you that famed Aeneas whom lovely Venus bore to Trojan Anchises on the bank of the Phrygian river Simois? And indeed I remember Teucer's coming to Sidon after being exiled from his father's land, when he sought a new kingdom with the help of Belus, my father, who was laying Cyprus waste and was holding it under his victorious sway. Already at that time the fall of the Trojan city was known to me, and your name, too, and the Greek kings. Though my father was their enemy, he praised the Teucrians exceedingly and wished that he were descended from the ancient lineage of the Teucrians. Come now, young men, enter our palace. A similar fate willed that I, too, after being buffeted by many trials, should in the end come to rest on this land. Not unacquainted with evil, I know how to help the unfortunate."

Thus she spoke. At the same time she led Aeneas into the royal palace and ordered a sacrifice in the temples of the gods. In the meantime, for his companions she sent to the shore twenty bulls, a hundred bristling backs of great hogs, and a hundred fat lambs with their mothers, gifts for the joyous day. The interior of the house was decked out resplendent in royal luxury, and they prepared a banquet in the middle of the palace. Here were embroidered coverlets of royal purple and on the tables heavy silver upon which the brave deeds of their fathers were engraved in gold, a long series of events descending through so many men from the ancient origin of the race.

Aeneas—for a father's love did not suffer his mind to rest quietly—sent swift Achates ahead to the ships to carry this news to Ascanius and to lead him to the walls. All the anxiety of a loving parent was centered on Ascanius. Moreover, Aeneas ordered him to bring gifts saved from the ruins of Troy, a robe stiff with ornaments of gold, a veil edged with yellow acanthus, ornaments of the Grecian Helen, marvelous gifts from her mother, Leda, which Helen had brought from Mycenae when she went to Troy and her unlawful marriage; a scepter, too, which Ilione, the eldest of Priam's daughters, had once carried, a necklace of pearls, and a crown doubly decorated with gems and gold. Hastening to carry out these commands, Achates made his way to the ships.

THE WILES OF VENUS

But the goddess of Cythera turned over in her mind new artifices and new plans so that Cupid, his features and appearance changed, would come in place of sweet Ascanius and by gifts enkindle the queen to the madness of love and infuse fire into her very marrow, for Venus feared the double-dealing house of the deceitful Tyrians. The savage spirit of Juno roused her, and her anxiety returned at night. Therefore she addressed winged Love with these words:

"Son, my strength, my only great power, you who despise mighty Jupiter's bolts that killed Typhon, to you I fly as a suppliant, begging your intercession. You know how your brother Aeneas has been tossed about on all the shores of the sea because of the hatred of bitter Juno, and you have often grieved at my sorrow. Now Phoenician Dido holds him and delays him with flattering words. I fear the course this hospitality of Juno may take; she will hardly yield at this decisive moment. Wherefore, I plan to trick Dido beforehand and surround her with the flames of love so that she will not change her mind through the assistance of some power, but will be held fast to me because of her great love for Aeneas. Heed now my instructions as to how you can do this. The royal child Ascanius, at the behest of his dear father, is preparing, my dearest love, to go to the Sidonian city, bearing gifts saved from the sea and the flames of Troy. When he is buried in sleep I will hide him upon high Cythera or at the sacred shrine in Idalium so that he cannot discover the ruse or make his presence known. Counterfeit his appearance for not more than one night, and as a lad put on the known features of the boy so that, when happy Dido holds you in her lap amid the royal banqueting and the wine drinking, when she embraces you and gives you sweet kisses, you may breathe into her the hidden fire and poison her secretly."

Cupid obeyed the words of his dear mother, and removing his wings, happily walked along with the stride of Julus. But Venus sprinkled quiet sleep over the limbs of Ascanius, and the goddess, pressing him to her breast, carried him aloft into the high groves of Idalia where soft marjoram, breathing forth fragrance amid flowers and pleasant shade, surrounded him.

THE BANQUET

And now, happy in his guide Achates, Cupid, obeying Venus' command, walked along, carrying royal gifts for the Tyrians. When he arrived, the queen had already composed herself upon a golden couch in the center of the hall amid stately hangings. Now father Aeneas and the Trojan youth assembled and reclined upon purple-draped couches. The servants gave them water for their hands and served bread from baskets and brought them napkins of fine texture. In a nearby hall there were fifty maidservants whose duty it was to arrange in order the long line of food and to honor the household gods by tending the fires. There were a hundred maidservants and just as many menservants of the same age whose task it was to load the tables with the feast and put the cups in place. When invited to recline on the embroidered couches, the Tyrians gathered in great numbers throughout the happy halls. They marveled at the gifts of Aeneas, they marveled at Julus and the beaming countenance of the god and his simulated speech; they marveled at the mantle and the veil embroidered with yellow acanthus. Most of all, unhappy Dido, destined to future ruin, could not satisfy her mind but was on fire as she gazed, and was moved equally by the boy and the gifts. When he had embraced Aeneas and clung to his neck, satisfying the great love of his supposed parent, Cupid approached the queen. With her eyes, with her whole heart she clung to him, at times fondling him on her lap, unconscious of what a powerful god possessed her in her misery. But he, mindful of his mother of Acidalia, little by little began to wipe away the memory of Sychaeus and tried with a living love to change her mind long at peace and her heart unaccustomed to love.

When the first lull at the banquet came and the tables were removed, they set up great bowls and wreathed the wine cups. There followed a din in the palace as their voices rolled through the spacious halls. Burning lamps hung from the gold-covered ceiling and torches conquered the night with their fires. At this point the queen called for the libation bowl, heavy with gold and gems, which Belus and all descended from Belus were wont to use, and she filled it with wine. Then there was silence in the palace.

"Jupiter, for they say that you set up the laws of hospitality, grant that this day may be a happy one for the Tyrians and for those who set out from Troy, and that our descendants may remember this day. May Bacchus, the giver of joy, be present, and good Juno; and you, Tyrians, celebrate this meeting in a friendly spirit."

She spoke and poured into the goblet on the table an offering of wine, and after the libation, she touched the edge lightly with her lips, and then tauntingly gave it to Bitias. He eagerly drained the foaming bowl and drank from the full goblet of gold; afterward the other chieftains drank. The long-haired Iopas, whom the great Atlas taught, played upon his golden lyre. He sang of the wandering moon and the eclipses of the sun; whence came mankind and cattle; whence the storms and lightning. He sang of Arcturus, the rainy Hyades, and the twin bears; why the winter sun hastens so fast to dip in the ocean, and what delay holds back the long nights.

The Tyrians redoubled their applause and so did the Trojans. Unhappy Dido prolonged the night with varied talk and drank deep draughts of love, asking many questions about

Priam and many about Hector—now under whose banner the son of Aurora had come, now what kind of steeds Diomede had, now how powerful Achilles was.

"Come, good guest," she said, "tell us from the very beginning the deception of the Greeks, the disasters of your followers, and your wanderings, for already the seventh summer finds you still wandering over all the land and sea."

Book Two

MINERVA

Book Two

AENEAS BEGINS HIS STORY

All grew silent and waited, their eager faces turned to him. Thereupon father Aeneas began speaking from his high couch:

"O queen, you order me to renew an unspeakable sorrow, how the Greeks destroyed the wealth of Troy and its lamented kingdom. These miserable sights I myself witnessed; I was a great part of them. What soldier of the Myrmidons, the Dolopes, or harsh Ulysses could keep back his tears when telling such a story? Already the dewy night is descending from the sky and the setting stars counsel sleep. Yet if you have such a great desire to know of our misfortune and to hear in brief the last agony of Troy, although my mind shudders at the remembrance and shrinks back in horror, I will begin."

THE TROJAN HORSE

"Weary of war and repulsed by the Fates, the leaders of the Greeks, seeing that the years were slipping by, built a horse of mountain size inspired by the divine art of Pallas, constructing the ribs from strips of fir. They feigned, so the story went, that it was a votive offering for their return home. There in the dark side they secretly enclosed chosen men, filling the great hollow recesses of the belly with armed soldiers.

"In plain view is Tenedos, an island whose fame is well known. It was rich in resources when the kingdom of Priam stood, but now it is only a bay and a treacherous anchorage for ships. Sailing to this point, they concealed themselves along the deserted shore. We thought that they had gone away and sailed for Mycenae. Thereupon Troy freed itself from its long gloom; the gates were thrown open. It was a pleasure to visit the Doric camp, the deserted spots, and the shore they had left behind. 'Here the band of the Dolopes camped, there was the tent of the savage Achilles; here their fleet anchored, there they used to fight in battle array.' Some were amazed at the fateful gift to the virgin Minerva and marveled at the size of the horse. Either on account of his treachery or because this was the will of the Fates for Troy, Thymoetes was the first to urge that it be drawn within the walls and placed on the citadel. But Capys and those who had better judgment ordered that the Trojans throw this deception of the Greeks, their suspected gift, into the sea and put fire to it, or that they bore through the hollow belly and explore its cavity. The uncertain crowd was split by contrary desires.

"First of all Laocoön, in company with a great crowd, angrily rushed down from the top of the citadel and cried afar off:

" 'O miserable citizens, what great insanity is this? Do you believe that the enemy has sailed away, or do you think that any gifts of the Greeks are free from deceit? Is this Ulysses' reputation? Either the Greeks are hidden in this wooden structure or this machine has been built against our walls to look into our homes and attack the city, or some trick is hidden in it. Do not trust the horse, Trojans. Whatever it is, I fear the Greeks, even though they bring gifts.'

"After he spoke these words, with mighty force he hurled a huge spear into the side, into the rounded framework of the beast's belly. The spear stuck trembling, and when the sides resounded, the hollow cavern re-echoed and gave forth a groan. And if the Fates had not been unkind, if our minds had not been blinded, Laocoön would have forced us to destroy the hidden band of Greeks with the sword. Troy would now be standing, and, lofty tower of Priam, you would still survive."

"Meanwhile, with a great shout, Trojan shepherds came dragging into the king's presence a youth whose hands were bound behind his back. He had freely offered himself, unknown to those who came along, in order to effect this very purpose and open Troy to the Greeks, confident in mind and prepared for either eventuality—to accomplish his deceit or meet certain death. In their desire to see him, Trojan youths rushed in crowds from all directions and strove to make sport of the captive. Listen now to the deceit of the Greeks and from the crime of one man learn to know all the Greeks. For as he stood, perplexed and unarmed, and gazed around at the Phrygian battle lines, he groaned:

" 'Alas, what land, what seas can now receive me? What final doom awaits me in my misery? I have no place anywhere among the Greeks, and, moreover, the angry Trojans demand my blood in punishment.' Because of his complaints our minds were changed, and all hostility was put aside. We urged him to tell to what race he belonged, what news he brought, and wherein his confidence as a captive rested. [At length, putting aside his fear, he spoke]:

" 'Indeed I shall confess the entire truth to you, O king, come what may, nor will I deny that I am of the Greek race. This is my first admission; if Fortune has made me miserable, she will not, though she is malicious, make Sinon deceitful and lying. Perchance, by hearsay, some word has reached your ears about Palamedes the son of Belus and his glory renowned in fame. The Greeks by wicked testimony, under a false charge of treason, condemned this innocent man to death because he opposed the war, and they now mourn him in death. In my early years my poor father sent me here to war as the companion of this kinsman of mine. While Palamedes was safe in power and mighty in the councils of the princes, I, too, bore a certain reputation and dignity. After he left the upper world through the hatred of wily Ulysses—a well-known story—in my affliction I dragged out my sorrowful life amid darkness, and I secretly resented the death of my innocent friend. Nor did I in my madness keep silent, but if the chance would ever be offered, if I should ever return as victor to my ancestral Argos, I promised that I would be his avenger, and I spoke bitter words of hate. The beginning of my misfortune dated from that time. From then on, Ulysses always terrified me with new charges; from that time on, he threw out double-meaning words to the crowd, and conscious of his guilt, he sought means of attacking me. Nor did he rest until, using Calchas as his tool —but why do I recall these unpleasant things? Why do I delay, if you consider all Greeks in one class? It is enough merely to state the fact that I am a Greek. Wreak your vengeance right now. Ulysses the Ithacan would wish it so, and the sons of Atreus would pay you a big price.'

"Then in truth we were afire to know and to ask about his misfortune, ignorant as we were of such great crimes and of Greek cunning. Trembling he went on and said with deceitful heart:

" 'Often the Greeks, worn out from the long war, desired to begin a retreat from Troy and to depart. Would that they had done so! Often a fierce storm at sea prevented them, and the wind terrified them as they were on the point of departing. Then especially did the thunder roll through all the heavens after this horse with its framework of maple beams was built. In doubt we sent Eurypylus to inquire of the oracle of Phoebus, and he brought back these sorrowful words from the shrine: "With the blood of a sacrificed maiden you placated the winds when first, Greeks, you came to the shores of Ilium; with blood your return must be bought and expiation made with a Greek life."

" 'As this message reached the ears of the common soldiers, they were amazed and through the very marrow of their bones there ran a cold shudder. For whom were the Fates preparing this destiny? Whom did Apollo demand? Hereupon, amid great tumult, Ulysses the Ithacan dragged Calchas the prophet into the middle of the crowd and demanded what these orders of the gods meant. And many were already predicting that the cruel crime of the scheming Ulysses was directed against me, and they secretly realized what was to come.

" 'For ten days Calchas was silent and, remaining in seclusion, refused to betray anyone or expose him to death. Finally, driven by the loud shouts of the Ithacan, the prophet spoke out, as agreed, and destined me for the altar. Everybody assented, and what all feared for themselves they allowed when it was turned to the destruction of one wretched man.

" 'Soon the unspeakable day was at hand; the sacred objects were prepared for me, the salted meal and the fillets around my temples. I escaped from death, I confess it, and I broke my bonds, and through the night I lay hidden in the dark amid the sedge along the slimy lake until they should set sail, if perchance they would. Now I have no hope of seeing my ancient fatherland or my dear children and my longed-for father. These they will perhaps demand in punishment on account of my flight, and they will avenge this fault of mine by killing my unhappy family. Wherefore I beseech you by the gods above and the powers conscious of truth, by unsullied honor, if any such thing still remains anywhere among mortals, take pity on such great misfortune, take pity on a soul suffering undeservedly!'

"Because of his tears we spared his life and, more than that, we took pity on him. Priam himself was the first to order that the man's tight-fitting manacles be loosened, and the king spoke to him with such friendly words as these:

" 'Whoever you are, forget about your lost Greeks from now on. You shall be one of us. Speak out the truth to me when I ask you these questions. For what purpose did they build this frame of a massive horse? Who was its author? What is their object? What religious offering is it or what engine of war?' He finished speaking. Sinon, skilled in the Greek art of deceiving, raised his hands freed of their bonds to the stars:

" 'You, O eternal fires and your inviolable power, I call to witness; you, O altars and wicked swords that I escaped, and fillets of the gods which as a victim I bore, it is right for me to break my sacred Greek oath, it is right to hate those men and to bring out into the open all their secrets. I am not held by any laws of the fatherland. Only stand by your promises, and when you are preserved, O Troy, keep faith, if I reveal the truth, if I repay you generously.

"'All the hope of the Greeks and their confidence in the war that had started rested entirely on the help of Pallas. But from the time when Diomede the son of Tydeus and Ulysses the inventor of crimes dared, after killing the guards of the lofty citadel and seizing the sacred image, to carry from the holy temple the fateful Palladium and to touch with bloody hands the fillets of the virgin goddess, Greek hopes began to ebb away and slipping backward, receded. Thenceforth their power was broken, and the mind of the goddess was hostile. Nor did Minerva give signs of this by doubtful warnings. Hardly was the image placed in the camp when blinding flames shot from its angry eyes, and salty sweat flowed down its limbs. Three times the goddess herself—marvelous to relate—sprang up from the ground, bearing her shield and trembling spear. Suddenly Calchas declared that they must attempt to retreat over the seas, that the citadel of Troy could not be destroyed by Greek weapons unless they repeated the omens in Greece and brought back the divine power which had come over the sea with them in their curved ships. And now, as to the reason why they have sailed to their ancestral Mycenae: they are preparing arms and gods as their companions, and they will unexpectedly arrive after recrossing the sea. Thus Calchas explained the omens. After being warned to atone for the offense to the divinity, they set up in place of the Palladium this figure which was to expiate the sorrowful desecration. Nevertheless, Calchas ordered them to raise this huge structure of interjoined timbers to the heavens so that it could not be received through the gates or dragged within the walls or honored by the people according to their ancient religious rites. For if your hand had violated the gift of Minerva, then a great disaster—may the gods rather turn this omen against Calchas himself—

would come to the kingdom of Priam and the Trojans. But if by your hands it had ascended into the city, Asia would come even to the walls of Pelops in a great war: such a fate would be in store for our descendants.'

"By reason of such lying cunning on the part of the perjured Sinon the story was believed. Those men, whom neither Diomede nor Achilles of Larissa, nor ten years of warring, nor a thousand ships could overcome, were tricked by his craftiness and forced tears."

THE DEATH OF LAOCOÖN

"Here another and a much more fearful evil confronted the unfortunate Trojans and disturbed their unforeseeing minds. Laocoön, chosen by lot a priest of Neptune, was solemnly sacrificing a huge bull at the altars, when lo, twin serpents coming from Tenedos through the tranquil deep—I shudder as I tell it—lay upon the sea with immense coils and headed for the shore side by side. Their breasts rode high in the water and their blood-colored crests rose above the waves, while the rest of them trailed behind in the sea, twisting their immense backs in coils. Their sound was heard from the foaming deep. Then they reached the shore. Their eyes were fiery and bloodshot and they licked their hissing mouths with vibrating tongues. We fled, pale at the sight. They approached Laocoön in a direct attack. And first, both serpents twined themselves around the little bodies of his two sons and biting, fed on their miserable members. Afterwards they seized Laocoön as he came with weapons to aid his sons, and they bound him with their great coils. Encircling him twice around the waist and putting their scaly backs twice around his neck, they raised their heads and necks high above him. At the same time, his fillets covered with slime and black poison, he strove to loosen the knots with his hands, all the while raising horrifying shouts to the stars, much like the bellowing heard when a wounded bull has escaped after shaking a poorly aimed ax from its neck. But with a gliding motion the twin dragons escaped to the lofty shrine and sought the citadel of savage Minerva where they found shelter at the feet of the goddess under the circle of her shield."

THE HORSE IS BROUGHT INTO THE CITY

"Then indeed a new terror seized the trembling hearts of all, and the word was passed around that Laocoön had deservedly paid for his crime of striking the sacred wood with his spear and hurling the sacrilegious javelin into the back of the horse. They cried out that the image should be brought to the shrine and the divinity of the goddess petitioned.

"We made a breach in the walls and laid open the defenses of the city. All prepared themselves for the work. They threw rollers under the horse's feet and stretched hempen bonds from its neck. The fateful engine, bristling with arms, entered the walls. Crowding around, boys and unmarried girls sang sacred hymns and rejoiced to touch the rope with their hands. The horse entered and threateningly glided into the middle of the city. Ah fatherland, Ilium, home of the gods, ah Trojan defenses, renowned in war! Four times on the very threshold of the gate the horse halted and four times the sound of arms echoed in its hollow. Nevertheless, heedless and blinded with madness, we pressed on and placed the ill-omened monster in the sacred citadel. Then indeed the fate of the future was uttered by Cassandra, who was never believed by the Trojans because of the command from the god Apollo. Though that day was our last, with festive foliage we unfortunate men decorated the temples of the gods throughout the city.

"Meanwhile the heavens revolved and Night rushed from the ocean, cloaking the earth and the sky and the deceit of the Greeks in deep shadow. The Teucrians, scattered through the city, became silent; deep sleep overcame their weary limbs. Now the Greek fleet with its ships in order was sailing from Tenedos, seeking the known shores through the friendly silence of the quiet moon, when the leading ship gave the flaming signal. Aided by the unjust decrees of the gods, Sinon freed the Greeks enclosed in the horse and stealthily loosened the pine bars. The horse, now open, restored them to the air, and from the hollow structure the joyful leaders, Thessandrus, Sthenelus, and cursed Ulysses, came sliding down the rope which they had dropped, and Acamas and Thoas, Neoptolemus the son of Peleus, noble Machaon, Menelaus, and the very author of the deception, Epeus. They invaded the city, which was buried in sleep and wine. Cutting down the guards, they welcomed all their companions through the open gates and reunited their confederate battle lines."

THE GHOST OF HECTOR APPEARS

"It was the hour when first rest begins for weary mortals and by heaven's favor creeps in most pleasingly. In sleep it seemed to me that sad Hector appeared before my eyes, pouring forth a flood of tears; he was foul with blood and dust and his swollen feet were pierced with thongs, as once when he was dragged along by the chariot. Ah, what a picture! How changed from that Hector who returned wearing the spoils of Achilles, or after throwing Trojan fire on the ships of the Greeks! Now his beard was neglected, his hair matted with blood, and he bore those many wounds received around his ancestral walls. Freely weeping, I seemed to address the hero, uttering these sorrowful words:

" 'Ah, light of Troy, most trusted hope of the Trojans, what has caused your long delay? From what shores do you, long expected, come? With what joy we behold you in our weariness after the many funerals of your kinsmen, after the manifold sufferings of men and the city! What has so cruelly marred your serene face? Why do I see these wounds?'

"He made no reply, nor did he heed my vain inquiries, but with a heavy sigh from the bottom of his heart, he said, 'Ah, flee, goddess-born, and escape from these flames. The enemy holds the walls. Troy is falling from its lofty height. Enough help has been given the fatherland and Priam. If Troy could have been saved by any right hand, already it would have been saved by this one. Troy commends its sacred objects and its household gods to you. Take these as companions of your fate, seek a walled city for them, a great one that you will set up finally after wandering over the seas.' Thus he spoke and in his hands he bore the fillets of powerful Vesta and her eternal fire from the interior sanctuary."

THE SACKING OF THE CITY

"Meanwhile the city was filled with varied expressions of grief. Although the home of my father Anchises was remote and protected by trees, the sounds grew clearer and clearer, and the dreadful clash of arms reached my ears. I was aroused from sleep and I ascended to the highest pinnacle on the roof. I stood listening attentively, like a shepherd on the highest point of a rock hearing a sound and not knowing its cause when flames fanned by the winds fall upon the grain, or the rapid torrent of a mountain stream lays waste the fields, the happy crops, and the labors of the oxen, and sweeps the forests headlong. Then indeed the false faith of the Greeks was manifest and their treachery revealed. Already the spacious house of Deiphobus was ruined by the mounting fire, already the neighboring home of Ucalegon was burning. The broad straits of Sigeum were alight with fire. The shouts of men and the blasts of trumpets were heard. In my madness I took up arms, though I had no clear plan in seizing arms, but my spirit burned to gather a band for battle and to rush into the citadel with my comrades. Furious anger urged on my mind and I remembered that it is a noble thing to die in armor.

"But now, Panthus, after escaping from the weapons of the Greeks, Panthus the son of Othrys, the priest of the citadel of Phoebus, madly rushed to our threshold, carrying in his arms the sacred objects, the conquered gods, and his little grandson.

" 'Where is the main struggle, Panthus? What citadel are we to occupy?' Hardly had I spoken these words when he answered with a groan:

" 'The last day, the inevitable hour has come for Troy. We were Trojans, there was a Troy, and a glory of the Teucrians that was great. Cruel Jupiter has transferred everything to Argos; the Greeks are masters in the burned city. The lofty horse standing in the middle of the fortifications is pouring forth armed men, and victorious Sinon is mockingly setting fires. Some are at the wide-open gates, as many thousands as ever came from great Mycenae. Others have blocked the narrow streets with opposing weapons. Their battle line, prepared for slaughter, stands drawn up with gleaming spears of iron. Resisting in a blind struggle, the first guards of the gates scarcely attempted battle.' "

THE TROJANS COUNTERATTACK

"At such words from the son of Othrys by the will of the gods, I rushed into the flames and to arms, where the dread Fury, where the din and the clamor raised to the heavens called me. Ripheus and Epytus, an expert with arms, added themselves as allies, appearing in the moonlight, and Hypanis and Dymas also came to my side, and the youth Coroebus the son of Mygdon. By chance he had come to Troy in those days, burning in his insane love for Cassandra; as son-in-law he brought help to Priam and the Trojans, unhappy man, who did not heed the commands of his prophetic wife! When I saw them boldly massing for battle, I began with these words:

" 'Youths, hearts brave to no purpose, if you have a fixed desire to follow me in my daring to the very end, let us die and let us rush into the midst of conflict. You see how fortune stands: all the gods by whom this kingdom has stood have deserted us, leaving their temples and their altars. You are coming to the aid of a burned city. The only safety for the conquered lies in hoping for no safety.'

"So fury was added to the spirit of the youths. Thereupon, like raiding wolves in a dark fog, when maddening hunger has driven them out blindly, while their cubs that are left in the lair wait with dry jaws, we went amid the weapons of the enemies into certain death, and we made our way through the midst of the city. Dark night surrounded us with a hovering cloud. Who could describe in speech the defeat and the carnage of that night, or who equal its sorrow with his tears? An ancient city fell, after ruling many years. Very many lifeless bodies lay here and there throughout the streets, in the homes, and on the sacred thresholds of the gods. Nor did the Trojans alone suffer punishment in blood. At times courage returned to the hearts of the conquered and the victorious Greeks fell. Everywhere there was bitter mourning, everywhere consternation, and many a scene of death.

"Androgeos, with a great company at his heels, was the first of the Greeks to encounter us, unwittingly believing that we were his comrades. He first addressed us with friendly words: 'Hurry men! What tardy sloth delays you so long? The others are already sacking burning Troy and bearing it away, and you only now are coming from the high ships?'

"He spoke and suddenly—for trustworthy replies were not forthcoming—he realized that he had fallen into the midst of the enemy. He was startled, and he checked his step as he stopped speaking. As a person who has stepped with heavy tread on a snake unseen among the rough brambles on the ground, trembling draws back as its anger rises and its blue neck swells, in the same way Androgeos, visibly frightened, sprang back.

"We rushed in and in close array surrounded them with arms. Here and there we laid low those who were ignorant of the place and who were overcome by panic. Fortune favored our first adventure.

"Then Coroebus, exulting in the courage born of success, shouted: 'Comrades, let us follow where good Fortune first points out the safe course and where she shows herself favorable. Let us change shields and put on the armor of the

Greeks. Who asks whether an enemy won by guile or courage? They themselves will furnish the arms.'

"After he said this, he donned Androgeos' helmet and his shield with its artistic markings, and he fitted the Greek sword to his side. This Ripheus did and Dymas, too, and all the youths in joyful spirit; everyone armed himself with recent spoils. During the dark night, mingling among the Greeks under a divinity that was unfavorable to us, we fought many battles in hand-to-hand conflict. We sent many of the Greeks down to the lower world. Others fled to the ships hastily seeking the safe shores. Some in base fear climbed again into the huge horse and hid themselves in the hollow they knew.

"Unfortunately it is not right for any man to trust in unwilling gods! Look how Cassandra, the virgin daughter of Priam, her hair streaming, was dragged from the temple, from the very sanctuary of Minerva, vainly raising her gleaming eyes to heaven—her eyes, I say, for shackles bound her tender hands. Coroebus, his mind in a frenzy, could not bear this sight and so threw himself into the midst of the battle, though certain to perish. We all followed and rushed into the thick of the fight. From the high roof of the temple of Minerva we were first assailed by the weapons of our own men and because of the appearance of our arms and their mistaking our Greek crests, a most unfortunate slaughter began.

"In sorrow and anger at having the maiden snatched away, the Greeks gathered from all sides and attacked fierce Ajax, the two sons of Atreus, and all the army of the Dolopes—just as at times when a hurricane has broken out, opposing winds clash, the West Wind and the South and the Southeast proudly riding its horses from the dawn, while forests wail and foam-covered Nereus rages with his trident and stirs the sea to its lowest depth. Those of the foe whom in the shadows of the dark night we had routed by our stratagem and hunted through the whole city, rallied again. They first recognized our shields and deceptive weapons and noted the differing sound of our speech. Immediately we were overwhelmed by numbers. First of all, Coroebus fell by the right hand of Peneleus at the altar of the warlike goddess Minerva; Ripheus, too, fell, a Trojan of outstanding virtue, a righteous man, though to the gods it seemed otherwise. Hypanis and Dymas perished, slain by their comrades; nor did your great piety protect you in your misfortune, Panthus, nor your fillet of Apollo. O ashes of Ilium, the last funeral pyre of my kinsmen, I call you to witness that in your fall I avoided neither their weapons nor any encounters with the Greeks. If it had been the will of the Fates that I should perish, I merited it by the deeds of my arm. Then we were separated, Iphitus and Pelias going with me. Iphitus was already enfeebled by age and Pelias limping from a wound Ulysses gave him. Straightway the din drew us to the palace of Priam."

THE ATTACK ON PRIAM'S PALACE

"Here we saw a really great battle in progress as if there were no other fighting anywhere and no one dying in the whole city. We beheld fierce conflict: the Greeks mounting to the rooftops, moving up under the protection of joined shields, and occupying the threshold. The ladders clung to the walls, and the Greeks climbed step by step at the very posts of the gate. Protecting themselves, they raised their shields toward the weapons with their left hands, and grasped the battlements with their right. In opposition the Trojans pulled apart the towers and the covering of the roofs of the palace. With these as weapons, when they realized that the end had come, they prepared to defend themselves in the extremity of death, and they threw down gilded beams, the lofty ornaments of their ancient ancestors. Other Trojans with drawn swords protected the gates below and held them with a dense line. Our courage was renewed to bring help to the king's palace, to reinforce the men with aid, and to add strength to the conquered.

"There was a threshold with secret doors and a communicating passageway between the sections of Priam's palace, an abandoned postern gate where the pitiful Andromache, while yet the kingdom stood, used time and again to go unaccompanied to her parents-in-law when she took the boy Astyanax to his grandfather. I ascended to the very top of the roof from which the unfortunate Trojans were hurling ineffective weapons with their hands. There was a tower flush with the edge of the wall and rising from the top of the roof to the stars. From there all Troy, the ships of the Greeks, and the Achaean camp used to be visible. After prying round about with iron bars where the top floor showed loose joints, we loosened the tower from its lofty base and pushed it over. Its sudden fall brought a ruinous crash and it fell far out upon the battle lines of the Greeks. Meanwhile the shower of stones and every sort of missile did not cease, but still others kept climbing up.

"Before the entrance, even on the very threshold, Pyrrhus strode about, gleaming in the sheen of his bronze weapons, as a snake fed on poisonous herbs, whose swollen body the cold winter kept protected under the earth, renewed and gleaming with new life after casting aside its skin, coils up its sleek back and reaches high toward the sun with its neck upraised, while it darts its triple-forked tongue from its mouth. Together huge Periphas and the driver of the horses of Achilles, the arm-bearer Automedon, as well as all the youthful band of Scyrians advanced to the palace and hurled flames to the rooftops. Among the first, Pyrrhus, seizing an ax, broke through the tough door and wrenched the bronze posts from their pivots. Then after cutting through the jamb, he hollowed out the strong oak panels and made a great, wide hole. The interior of the house was revealed and the long halls came into view; the private quarters of Priam and the ancient kings lay open and the invaders saw armed guards on the very threshold.

"But within the house, lamentations mingled with wretched confusion, and the vaulted halls far within resounded with the wailing of women; the tumult reached the golden stars. Then trembling mothers wandered through the vast buildings, embracing and kissing the pillars. Pyrrhus attacked with the vigor of his father Achilles; neither bars nor the guards themselves could hold him back. The door, weakened by repeated blows from the battering ram, and the jambs, wrenched from their sockets, collapsed. They made their way by force: they broke through the entrance. Greeks, rushing in, killed the first men and filled the place far and wide with soldiers: not so furiously does a foamy river, bursting its banks, breaking out, and conquering opposing dikes with its flood, pour itself out upon the farms and carry along cattle with their stables over all the fields. I myself saw Neoptolemus in a slaughtering rage and the two sons of Atreus on the threshold. I saw Hecuba and her hundred daughters and Priam, desecrating with his blood amid the altars the fires which he himself had consecrated. Those fifty bridal chambers, such ample promise of offspring, those doorposts, proud with the spoils of barbaric gold, sank in ruins. The Greeks took over where the fire failed."

THE DEATH OF PRIAM

"Perhaps you will inquire what was the fate of Priam. When he beheld the fall of his captured city, the doors of the palace battered in, and the enemy in the very heart of the house, the old man vainly put about his shoulders, trembling from age, his long-unused armor, and he girded himself with his powerless sword and hastened to die in the thick of the enemy.

"In the middle of the palace and under the open sky there was a great altar and nearby a very old laurel drooping over the altar and embracing the household gods in its shade. Here, like doves driven headlong in a dark storm, Hecuba and her daughters sat, vainly clustering around the altars, and embracing the images of the gods. When she saw Priam putting on the armor of his youth, she said:

" 'What madness, my poor husband, has impelled you to gird yourself with these weapons? Where are you rushing? The hour does not need such help or defenders as you, not even if my Hector himself were now present. Come here, I pray. This altar will protect all or you will die at the same time with us.'

"After speaking these words, she drew the aged man to her side and seated him in the sacred place.

"But now, Polites, one of the sons of Priam, after escaping death at the hands of Pyrrhus, fled through the weapons of the enemy down the long porticoes and, though wounded, ran through the empty halls. Raging Pyrrhus pursued him with deadly thrust. Again and again he almost seized him and closed in with his spear. When finally the son came into the very presence of his parents, he collapsed and poured forth his life with much blood.

"Then Priam, although he was already surrounded by death, did not restrain himself nor spare his angry voice: 'For this crime, for this awful deed, may the gods, if there is in heaven any justice that looks to such crimes, pay you your proper deserts and give you your just reward, you who made me see the murder of my son before my very eyes and who defiled the face of a father with the death of a son. Indeed, the great Achilles, of whom you falsely say you are the son, did not so treat Priam, his enemy; he respected the rights and the word of a suppliant and returned the lifeless body of Hector for burial and sent me back into my kingdom.'

"With these words the aged man hurled without force his powerless weapon, which, at once glancing from the resounding bronze, vainly hung from the leather above the ornament of the shield. To him Pyrrhus replied: 'Carry these words, then, and go as messenger to my father Achilles; remember to tell him of my woeful conduct and the degeneracy of Neoptolemus. Now die!'

"While saying this, he dragged to the very altars the trembling old man, slipping in blood gushing from his son, and wound his left hand in Priam's hair. With his right he drew his gleaming sword and buried it up to the hilt in the king's side. This was the destined end of Priam, this the fateful death that carried him off. He beheld Troy in flames and the citadel fallen, the once proud ruler over so many peoples and lands of Asia. His huge trunk lies on the shore, his head torn from his shoulders, a body without a name.

"But then for the first time dreadful horror took possession of me. I was stupefied. The image of my dear parent came to my mind as I saw the king, the same age as he, breathing out his life from a cruel wound. Deserted Creusa came to my mind, and my pillaged house, and the fate of little Julus. I looked around to see what aid was at hand. All in their weariness had deserted and leaped to the ground or exhausted, had thrown themselves into the fire."

THE APPEARANCE OF VENUS

"And now I alone was left when I saw Helen the daughter of Tyndareus keeping close to the temple of Vesta and quietly hiding in a remote corner. The clear fires gave me light as I wandered about, casting my eyes in all directions as I passed. Fearing punishment from the Greeks, the wrath of her deserted husband, and the hostility of the Trojans on account of the overthrow of Troy, Helen, the common fury of Troy and her fatherland, had hidden herself and was seated unseen near the altar. Fires of rage leaped up in my soul; a feeling of anger came into my mind to avenge my falling country and to exact punishment for her crime. 'Will this woman unharmed see Sparta and the Greece of her fathers? Will she ride as queen in a triumph she has won? Will she, escorted by a crowd of Ilian women and Trojan slaves, see her husband, her home, her parents, and her children? Is Priam not slain by the sword? Is Troy not consumed by fire? Has the Trojan shore not often reeked with blood? It shall not be so! For although there is no fame worthy of recording in the punishment of a woman, and the victory does not merit praise, nevertheless I shall be lauded for having destroyed a wicked thing and for having dealt out a just punishment. It will be pleasant to have glutted my spirit with burning vengeance and to have appeased the ashes of my kinsmen.'

"I was muttering such thoughts, swept along by my anger, when my dear mother appeared more clearly to my eyes than ever before, shining through the night with a pure light and revealing herself a goddess in form and stature, as she is usually seen by the heaven dwellers. Seizing my right hand, she restrained me and spoke these words from her rosy lips:

" 'Son, what great sorrow excites your uncontrolled anger? Why do you rage? What has become of your interest in us? Will you not first consider where you have left Anchises, wearied by age, and whether Creusa, your wife, and the boy Ascanius survive? Around them the Greek battle lines are wandering on all sides, and did not my care offer resistance, already flames would have destroyed them, and the enemy's sword would have drunk their blood. You should not hate the sight of Helen of Lacedaemon or blame Paris. The hostility of the gods—of the gods, I say—is destroying this realm and bringing Troy down from her high place.

" 'Look now—for I will completely scatter the cloud that, cast over your eyes, obscures your mortal vision and gathers dark and misty around you. Do not fear any orders from your mother nor refuse to obey her commands. Here where you see shattered defenses and stones torn from stones and smoke billowing with dust, Neptune is demolishing the walls and the foundations which were pried up by his huge trident, and he is destroying the whole city from its very base. Here savage Juno is the first to hold the Scaean gate, and girt with her sword, in a rage she summons her confederate battle line from the ships. Look, Tritonian Pallas has already occupied the top of the citadel, gleaming with her storm cloud and savage Gorgon. Even the father of the gods lends spirit and favoring power to the Greeks. Hasten your flight, my son, and end your vain struggle. I will never desert you; I will place you safe on your father's threshold.'

"She finished speaking and vanished into the thick shades

of the night. Grim specters appeared, great images of powers above hostile to Troy.

"Then finally it seemed to me all Ilium sank in flames and Neptune's Troy was overturned from its very foundations, just as when farmers on the mountaintops strive with might and main to fell an old ash with repeated strokes from a two-edged ax of iron; it constantly threatens to fall, and its foliage trembling, its top sways when the tree is struck, until little by little, overcome by blows, it groans its last and, torn from the ridge, falls with a crash.

"I descended and with divine guidance picked my way between the flames and the enemy; missiles ceased flying and the flames receded."

UNWILLINGNESS OF ANCHISES TO LEAVE TROY

"Now when I came to the threshold of my father's dwelling and our ancestral home, first of all I wished to carry my father into the high mountain and I sought him out first, but he refused to prolong his life beyond the destruction of Troy and to suffer exile.

" 'You, who have young blood, and whose power rests solidly on your own strength,' he said, 'hasten your flight. If the gods had wished me to live on, they would have preserved this abode for me. It is enough and more that I have seen one disaster and have survived the taking of the city once before. After bidding farewell to my body, thus laid out, just as I am, depart. I shall meet death by the deeds of my own hand; the enemy will pity me and will want my armor. To be deprived of burial is a slight loss. Already long-hated by the gods, I have uselessly dragged out my years from the time when the father of the gods and the king of men hurled at me the blasts of his thunder and touched me with his fire.'

"He persisted in saying such things and remained fixed in his purpose. But I and my wife, Creusa, Ascanius, and the whole household broke out in tears, fearing lest my father might wish to drag down everything with himself and yield to the pressure of fate. He refused to stir, holding to his original design, and he remained in the same spot. Again I took up arms and in my great misery I wished for death, for what plan or what chance for deliverance was at hand?

" 'Did you imagine that I could depart, my father, leaving you behind? Have such impious words fallen from my father's lips? If it pleases the gods that from such a great city nothing should be left and this purpose remains fixed in your mind; if it is your pleasure to add yourself and your family to perishing Troy, the gate is open wide for such a death. Soon Pyrrhus will be here, covered with the blood of Priam, Pyrrhus who slaughters a son before the face of his father, a father at the altars. Was it for this reason, dear mother, that you rescued me from weapons and fire; that in the very heart of my home I should see Ascanius and my father and Creusa nearby, lying slaughtered in one another's blood? Arms, men bring on the arms! The last day summons the vanquished. Let me return to the Greeks; let me see the battlefield again! Today not all will die unavenged!'

"Then I again fastened on my sword. I was adjusting my left hand in my shield and proceeding outside the house when suddenly my wife, falling at my feet, blocked the threshold and held out little Julus to his father, saying:

" 'If you are going to your death, take us, too, into it all with you. But if, trusting in experience, you place any reliance on weapons, first protect this house. To whom is little Julus, to whom is your father to be left; to whom am I, whom you once called wife, to be left?' "

ANCHISES DECIDES TO LEAVE

"Crying out such words as these, she was filling the whole house with her weeping when, marvelous to tell, a sudden sign appeared. For between the hands and the faces of the sad parents, from the very top of the head of Julus a slender tip of fire seemed to shine, and a flame, harmless to touch, seemed to lick his soft locks and feed around his temples. We, trembling with fear, hastened to beat out the flaming hair and to extinguish the holy fire with water. But Anchises joyously turned his eyes to the stars and raised his hands to the heavens as he spoke.

" 'O all-powerful Jupiter, if you are swayed by any prayers, look down upon us this one time and, if we merit anything by reason of our piety, then come to our aid, O father, and confirm these omens.'

"Hardly had my aged father finished speaking when it suddenly thundered on the left, and a star falling from the heavens shot through the darkness, leaving a trail of bright light. We saw it glide above the top of the roof of the building and, clearly marking its path, disappear in the forest of Ida. Then the far-reaching track spread a light and the place smoked far and wide with sulfur. Now my father, quite vanquished, stood erect, addressed the gods, and adored the sacred star:

" 'Now indeed there must be no delay. I follow and where you lead, there am I. Gods of my fathers, preserve my home, preserve my grandson. This augury is yours; Troy is in your protection. Indeed, I yield, and do not refuse to go, my son, as your companion.'

"He finished speaking, and already a fire was clearly heard through the buildings and the conflagration rolled the heat closer.

" 'Then come now, dear father, place yourself on my shoulders; your weight will not be a burden to me. Whatever happens, there will be one common danger and one safety for us both. Let little Julus be my companion and let my wife follow our footsteps at some distance. You, servants, pay close attention to what I say. As you leave the city, there is a hill and a lonely old temple of Ceres and nearby an ancient cypress, spared these many years by the reverence of our fathers. From different directions we will come to this same place. You, my father, take the sacred objects in your hands and the household gods of our fathers, for it would be wrong for me to touch them until I cleanse myself in running water, since I have just come from such a great battle and recent slaughter.

"So saying, I spread over my broad shoulders and my lowered neck a garment made of the skin of a tawny lion, and I took up my burden. Little Julus wound his hand in mine and followed his father with unequal steps; my wife trailed in the distance. We made our way through pitch-dark places. Now I, whom neither flying weapons nor Greeks massed in opposing battle lines used to frighten, was terrified by every breeze. Every sound excited me, nervous as I was, fearing equally for my companion and my burden."

THE LOSS OF CREUSA

"I was now approaching the gates, and I felt I had covered all the distance when the sound of many feet seemed to strike my ears, and my father, looking ahead through the darkness, exclaimed:

" 'Son, my son, flee! They are approaching! I see the gleaming shields and the shining bronze!'

"Then some unfriendly power took away my presence of mind in my panic. For while in my course I took the bypaths and left the known routes of the region, alas, I know not whether my wife Creusa was snatched from me by a miserable death, or whether she tarried, or wandering from the road, stopped in her weariness to rest. I never saw her afterward. I did not look back or consider her lost until I came to the mound of ancient Ceres and her sacred abode. Finally, when all had assembled there, she alone was missing, having escaped the notice of her companions, her son, and her husband. What man or god did I not accuse in my madness? What crueler thing did I see in the overturned city? To my comrades I commended Ascanius, my father Anchises, and the Trojan household gods, and I disappeared in the winding valley. I returned to the city and put on my gleaming arms. I resolved to take all those chances once more, to retrace my steps through all of Troy, and to risk my life again in those dangers.

"First I went back to the walls and the dark threshold of the gate through which I had come out, and I tracked the footprints I saw in the night and examined them carefully. The horror on all sides, even the very silence terrified my soul. From there I went home to see if by chance, by mere chance she might have returned there. The Greeks had rushed in and were occupying the whole house. It was too late. The wind was whirling a consuming fire to the top of the roof; the flames were mounting; the waves of fire were raging heavenward. I moved on, returning to the palace of Priam and the citadel. And now in the empty porticoes of Juno's refuge, picked guards, Phoenix and dreadful Ulysses, were standing watch over the booty. Here the wealth of Troy, snatched from burning sanctuaries—tables of the gods, bowls of solid gold, and captured garments—was being piled up on all sides. Boys and trembling mothers stood around in a long line. Even daring to cry out through the darkness, I filled the streets with shouting; sadly I called Creusa again and again, vainly repeating her name.

"As I hunted and raged wildly through the buildings of the city, the phantom shade of unfortunate Creusa herself, her image, larger than I had known, appeared to me. I was startled, my hair stood on end, and my voice stuck in my throat.

"Then she began to speak and to relieve my anxiety with these words: 'What is the use of giving way to a grief so insane, sweet husband? These things do not happen without the approval of the gods. It is not heaven's will that you should take Creusa from here as your helpmate; the great ruler of lofty Olympus does not allow it. You must suffer a long exile, and plow the vast surface of the sea. You will come to the land of Hesperia where Lydian Tiber with gentle current flows amid rich, inhabited fields. There happy events and a kingdom and a royal consort have been provided for you. Brush aside your tears for your beloved Creusa. I shall not see the proud homes of the Myrmidons and the Dolopes. I, a Trojan woman, a daughter-in-law of the goddess Venus, shall not go to be a slave to Greek mothers, but Cybele, the great mother of the gods, is keeping me on these shores. And now, farewell, and cherish the love of our son.'

"When she had uttered these words, she left me weeping and wishing to say much, and vanished into the thin air. Then I tried three times to put my arms about her neck; three times the shade, vainly embraced, escaped my hands much as a gentle breeze or a fleeting dream."

FLIGHT TO THE MOUNTAINS

"After spending the night in this way, I went back to my companions. And here I marveled at finding that a great number of new comrades had assembled there, mothers and husbands and youths gathered for exile, a miserable throng. They came from all sides, willing in mind and prepared with supplies to put out to sea for whatever lands I might wish. And now the morning star was rising over the ridges of lofty Mount Ida and was ushering in the day. The Greeks occupied the guarded thresholds of the gates, and there was no hope of help in sight. I yielded to fate and lifting up my father, I sought the mountains."

Book Three

APOLLO

Book Three

AENEAS SAILS TO THRACE

"After it pleased the gods to destroy Asia's fortunes and the guiltless race of Priam, after proud Ilium fell and all Neptune's Troy was smoking from the very ground, we were driven by divine auguries to seek distant exile in desolate lands. We built a fleet at Antandros, at the foot of Mount Ida in Phrygia, uncertain where the Fates might bring us and where we would be permitted to settle. Then we recruited men. Hardly had the early summer begun when father Anchises, relying on fate, ordered us to set sail. In tears I left the shores of my fatherland, its ports, and the fields where Troy had stood. An exile, I was borne to sea with my comrades, my son, and my great household gods.

"Afar off lay a land of vast fields dear to Mars, tilled by Thracians and once ruled by fierce Lycurgus. From ancient times it was a place of hospitality for Troy, with confederate household gods, while good fortune was ours. I sailed to this place, and on the winding shore I built our first walls, beginning the work in spite of opposing fate, and I gave it the name Aeneadae from my own name."

THE FATE OF POLYDORUS

"I performed the sacred rites to my mother, the daughter of Dione, and to the gods who were kindly disposed toward the work we had begun, and on the shore I sacrificed a sleek bull to the supreme king of the dwellers of heaven. By chance there was nearby a mound on the top of which there were cornel shrubs and a myrtle bristling with many a spear shaft. I approached and, trying to pull from the earth a green growth so that I might cover the altars with leafy boughs, I beheld a horrifying omen, marvelous to tell; for from the first shoot that was pulled up with its broken roots from the soil, drops of dark blood fell, staining the earth with gore. A chill of horror penetrated my body and my blood ran cold with fear. Again I proceeded to pull up a tough sprout of a second tree and to search thoroughly for the hidden reasons: black blood flowed from the bark of the second. Much disturbed, I venerated the woodland nymphs and father Mars, who presides over the Thracian fields, that they might duly bless these signs and lessen the omen. But the third time, after I pulled at the spearlike sapling with greater effort and struggled on my knees against the resisting sand—should I speak or be silent?—a sorrowful moan was heard from the bottom of the mound and a voice, brought back from the dead, was borne to my ears:

" 'Aeneas, why do you mutilate a miserable man? Spare one who is already buried; refrain from desecrating pious hands. I, Trojan-born, am not a stranger to you, nor does this blood flow from a tree trunk. Ah, flee this cruel land, flee this greedy shore; for I am Polydorus. Here an iron crop of spears has covered me, already pierced through, and they have grown into sharp javelins.'

"Then really weighed down in my mind with a double fear, I was amazed, my hair stood on end, and my voice stuck in my throat.

"Once unhappy Priam, when he was beginning to distrust the arms of Dardania and saw that the city was besieged, had secretly sent this Polydorus with a great amount of gold to be reared by the king of Thrace. When the might of the Trojans was broken and fortune had deserted them, the king, a partisan of Agamemnon's victorious arms, broke every sacred obligation: he slew Polydorus and took possession of the gold by force. To what do you not drive the hearts of men, O cursed thirst for gold!

"After terror had left me, I reported these signs of the gods to the chosen chieftains of the people, to my father first, and I asked them for their opinion. All had the same desire, to leave the cursed land, to leave the place of polluted hospitality, and to spread our sails to the winds. Thereupon we began the funeral for Polydorus. A great mass of earth was heaped up in a pile; altars, gloomy with dark fillets and sad cypress, were set up to the spirits of the underworld, and round about stood Trojan women with flowing hair, as was the custom. We offered foaming cups of warm milk and bowls of sacred blood; we laid his spirit to rest in the tomb, and with a loud voice we called upon him for the last time."

THE ORACLE AT DELOS

"Then when first we could place our trust in the open sea, and the winds allowed smooth sailing and the gentle, whispering breeze invited us to the deep, my comrades launched the ships and crowded along the shores. We were wafted from the port, and the land and cities receded.

"In the middle of the sea lies a sacred island, most pleasing to Doris, the mother of the Nereids, and to Aegaean Neptune. Because it was floating about the seas and shores, the dutiful archer Apollo bound it to lofty Myconos and Gyaros, causing it to be motionless and to defy the winds. To this point I sailed. This most pleasant island received us, now weary, in its safe port. Disembarking we venerated the city of Apollo. King Anius, at once king of men and priest of Phoebus, ran out to meet us, his temples bound with fillets of sacred laurel, and recognized his ancient friend Anchises. We joined our right hands in hospitality and entered the buildings.

"I venerated the temple of the god, which was built of ancient stone.

" 'Give us our own home, Thymbraean Apollo; give walls to the weary and a lasting city for our race; preserve the second citadel of Troy, the remains left by the Greeks and savage

Achilles. Whom are we to follow? Where do you order us to go, where to found our settlement? Father, give us a sign and inspire our minds.'

"Hardly had I spoken when everything seemed suddenly to tremble. The temple, the laurel tree of the god, and the entire mountain around seemed to move and the cauldron of the priestess to rumble as the shrine opened. Bowing low, we fell to the earth and a voice was borne to our ears: 'O hardy Trojans, the same earth which bore you first from your ancestral stock shall receive you in its fruitful lap when you return. Seek out your ancient mother. There the house of Aeneas, his children's children, and those who are born from them shall rule over all shores.

"Thus spoke Phoebus Apollo. Great joy with mingled tumult arose, and everyone asked what walls these were to be, to what place Phoebus called the wanderers, and to what region he wished them to return.

"Then my father, turning over in his mind the traditions of ancient men, said: 'Hear, chieftains, and learn your hopes. Crete, the island of great Jupiter, where there is a Mount Ida and the cradle of our race, lies in the middle of the sea. The inhabitants live in a hundred great cities, a very rich realm. From there our earliest ancestor, Teucer, if I rightly recall what I heard, first sailed to the shores of Rhoeteum, and chose the place for a kingdom. Ilium and the citadel of Troy were not yet built; they lived on in the deep valleys. From this place came the Great Mother, the patroness of Mount Cybele, and the bronze cymbals of the Corybants, and the grove of Mount Ida; from there came the inviolable mysteries of her worship and yoked lions pulling the chariot of their mistress. Come then, let us follow where the command of the gods leads, let us propitiate the winds and seek the kingdom of Gnossus. It is not a long voyage; if Jupiter aids us, on the third day the fleet will be beached on the shores of Crete.'

"After speaking these words, he sacrificed due honors upon the altars, a bull to Neptune, a bull to you, handsome Apollo, a black sheep to the storm-god, and a white one to the gentle zephyrs."

THE SETTLEMENT AT CRETE

"A rumor went around that the leader Idomeneus had departed, an exile from his ancestral kingdom, that the shores of Crete were deserted and the homes free of enemies, and that the abandoned settlement still stood. We left the port of Ortygia and, skimming over the sea, skirted about Naxos, on whose heights Bacchic revels were held, green Donusa, Olearos, snowy Paros, the Cyclades, scattered through the sea, and the straits, choppy on account of the many islands. A shout from the sailors rose in mingled rivalry; my comrades urged that we seek the Crete of our forefathers. A rising wind from the stern accompanied us as we went along, and at length we touched on the ancient shores of the Curetes. Then I eagerly built the walls of the desired city, calling it Pergamus, and I urged my followers, proud of that name, to love their homes and to raise a citadel for their dwellings.

"And now the ships were beached on the dry shore. The young people were interested in marriage and the new fields, and I was administering the laws and assigning dwellings, when suddenly there fell upon us from an infected area of the heavens a miserable, wasting plague, and a death-dealing year came upon the trees and the crops. The people gave up their sweet lives or dragged along their sick bodies; then the Dog Star burned the fields crisp. The green dried up and the poor harvest refused sustenance. Again my father urged that, recrossing the sea, we go to the oracle of Phoebus at Ortygia, and after begging pardon, ask how we might end our wearied fortunes, in what quarter the god would order us to seek help, and where to turn our course.

"It was night, and all living things on the earth were deep in sleep. The sacred images of the Phrygian household gods, which I had brought with me out of the fires of the city of Troy, seemed to appear clearly in a flood of light before my eyes as I lay in sleep, where the full moon streamed through the windows set in the wall. Then they spoke and lightened my cares with these words:

" 'What Apollo would say to you if you were to sail for Delos, he here prophesies, and unasked, sends us to your threshold. After the destruction of Troy we followed you and your arms, sailing over the swelling sea in the fleet under your command; we will also raise your future offspring to the stars and give the powers of empire to their city. Prepare great walls for great men, and do not shrink from the long toil of flight. Your settlement must be changed. Delian Apollo did not persuade you to come to these shores, nor did he order you to settle on Crete. There is a place, the Greeks call it by the name Hesperia, an ancient land, powerful in arms and rich in soil; Oenotrians inhabited it. Now the story goes that their descendants call the country Italy from the name of the leader. This is our permanent settlement; thence sprang father Iasius and Dardanus from whom our race first came. Come, rise now and joyfully take this message, not to be doubted, to your aged father: let him seek Corythus in the land of Ausonia. Jupiter denies you the fields of Dicte.'

"Astonished by this vision and the voice of the gods, I leaped from bed. It was not a dream, for I plainly recognized, it seemed, their features, their hair crowned with fillets, and their faces as if present; moreover, a cold sweat flowed from my whole body. I raised my pleading hands and my voice to heaven, and I poured out pure wine upon the hearth. Having made this offering, I joyfully informed Anchises and narrated the vision as it happened. He recognized the double lineage from the two parents, having been deceived by the strange confusion about the ancient locations. Then he said:

" 'Son, harassed by the fate of Troy, Cassandra was the only one to foretell such disasters to me. Now I recall that these things were fated to happen to our race; that she often spoke of Hesperia, often of the Italian kingdom. But who could ever believe that the Trojans would come to the shores of Hesperia? Whom could the prophetess Cassandra ever move in those days? Let us yield to Phoebus and being warned, follow a better course.'

"Thus he spoke and we joyously obeyed his command. We deserted this settlement, too, and, leaving a few behind us, we set sail and crossed the vast sea in the hollow ships."

THE ENCOUNTER WITH THE HARPIES

"After the ships were out in the deep and the land could no longer be seen but only the heavens and the sea on all sides, then over my head burst the murky rain cloud, bringing night and a storm, and the waves grew rough in the darkness. Straightway the winds churned the sea and great billows rose. We were tossed in different directions over the vast flood; the clouds obscured the day and the stormy night took away sight of the heavens; the lightning flashed continuously amid the riven clouds. We were thrown from our course, and we drifted blindly over the sea. Palinurus himself could not distinguish day and night in the heavens, nor could he remember the course in the midst of the waves. For three full uncertain days we floated over the sea in total darkness and for just as many nights without the stars. Finally on the fourth day, for the first time, land seemed to rise out of the deep, revealing mountains afar off whirling up smoke. Down came the sails. We leaped to the oars; without delay the sailors churned the waters with might and main and swept over the dark blue sea.

"The shores of the Strophades first received me when I was rescued from the waves. The Strophades, known by a Greek name, are situated in the great Ionian Sea, islands which grim Celaeno and the other Harpies inhabited ever since the home of Phineus was closed against them, and they left their former tables in fear. There is no portent more dreadful than these Harpies, nor has a more savage plague and scourge of the gods risen even from the Stygian waves. The features of these birds are like those of maidens, their excrement most fetid, their hands hooked, and their faces ever pale from hunger.

"When, on sailing thither, we entered the port, we saw here and there in the fields splendid droves of cattle and a flock of goats, grazing without a goatherd. We rushed upon them with weapons, and we called upon the gods and Jupiter himself to take a part of the booty; then on the winding shore we built up couches and banqueted on a rich feast. But suddenly in a dreadful descent from the mountains, the Harpies swooped down and, beating their wings with a great flapping, snatched away the banquet and befouled everything with their unclean contact; then their fearful cry rose amid the fetid odor. In a long recess under a hollowed cliff [enclosed about with trees and lowering shadows] we set up our tables again and replaced the fire on the altars; coming again out of another quarter of the heavens from secret lairs, the screeching flock hovered over the booty with their hooked claws and polluted the banquet with their mouths.

"Then I ordered my companions to take up arms, proclaiming that war must be fought with a savage race. They did as they were ordered, concealing their swords and hiding their shields here and there in the grass. So, when the Harpies swooped down, screeching along the winding shore, Misenus from his high lookout gave the signal on his hollow trumpet. My companions attacked and attempted a strange kind of warfare to destroy these loathsome birds with swords. But the weapons made no impression on their feathers, nor could they wound their backs. The birds, soaring to the heavens in swift flight, left befouled the half-eaten remains of the booty.

"One of them, Celaeno, an ominous prophetess, perched herself on a high cliff and screeched these words:

" 'And so, sons of Laomedon, you are preparing to declare war, war in return for the slaughter of the cattle and the bullocks, and to expel the innocent Harpies from their ancestral kingdom? Listen, then, and fix deep in your mind these words of mine which the all-powerful father prophesied to Phoebus, and Phoebus Apollo to me, and which I, the greatest of the Furies, now reveal to you. You are seeking Italy in your voyaging, and after calling up the aid of the winds, you shall go to Italy and be allowed to enter the ports, but you shall not surround the city given you with walls until dire hunger, in punishment for the slaughter of our cattle, shall force you to devour with your teeth your very tables.'

"Thus she spoke, and rising on her wings, took refuge in the forest. Then the blood of my companions froze in sudden fear; their spirits fell and they no longer sought peace by arms but through vows and prayers, no matter whether these were gods or fierce and ominous birds. On the shore with outstretched hands, father Anchises invoked the great gods and ordained the honors due them: 'O gods, ward off these threats; gods, avert such a disaster and mercifully save the devout!' Then he ordered the cable to be loosened from the shore and the sheets to be uncoiled and eased off. The winds filled the sails; we skimmed over the foaming waves where the wind and the pilot directed the course. And now in the midst of the sea appeared wooded Zacynthos, Dulichium, Same, and Neritos, steep with rocks. We kept far from the cliffs of Ithaca, the kingdom of Laertes, and we cursed the land that nurtured the savage Ulysses. Soon the clouded peaks of Mount Leucata appeared, and Actium, the promontory feared by the sailors, where Apollo's temple was. In weariness we turned our course toward this place and sailed to the little town; the anchor was thrown from the prow, and the sterns were beached on the shore."

LANDING AT ACTIUM

"Then, finally gaining possession of the unexpected earth, we purified ourselves in Jupiter's sight; we burned our offerings upon the altars and celebrated Trojan games on the shores of Actium. My naked companions, anointed with oil, practiced our country's sports. Escaping so many Greek cities and sailing in flight through the midst of our enemies was cause for rejoicing. Meanwhile the sun made its yearly round and icy winter ruffled the waves with winds from the north. To the front doorposts I attached an arched shield of bronze, carried by great Abas, and I marked the offering with a verse:

These arms Aeneas set up, taken from conquering Greeks.

"Then I ordered that we leave the port and that the men take their places at the rowers' benches. Eagerly my companions rowed over the waves and swept along the surface of the sea. Soon we lost sight of the airy heights of the Phaeacians. Skirting the shores of Epirus, we entered the port of Chaonia and approached the lofty city of Buthrotum."

AENEAS MEETS ANDROMACHE

"Here an unbelievable story greeted our ears, that Helenus the son of Priam was king over Greek cities, having come into possession of the wife and scepter of Pyrrhus the son of Achilles, and that Andromache had again become subject to a husband of her own country. I was amazed and my heart burned with a great desire to address the hero and to know about such a marvelous turn of events. Leaving the fleet on the shore, I set out from the port just when, as it happened, near the city in a grove by the waters of an imitation of the Simois, Andromache was offering to the ashes of Hector a solemn sacrifice and gifts of mourning and was calling upon the spirits of the dead at an empty mound of green sod, which she had consecrated with two altars as a pretext for her weeping. When she saw me coming and hysterically beheld the Trojan weapons about her, frightened by these great portents, she stood paralyzed as she gazed, and warmth left her body.

"She fainted and after a long time finally spoke: 'Is this your real appearance? Are you a true messenger to me, goddess-born? Are you alive? But, if the light of life has left you, where then is Hector?'

"So she spoke, and as she wept, she filled the place with her lamentations. I could scarcely wedge in a few words as she frantically talked, and in my excitement I blurted out now and then:

" 'Indeed I am alive, and I pass my life amid many dangers. Do not doubt; what you see is real. Alas! what misfortune has befallen you, deprived of your great husband, or what good fortune, worthy of your merit, revisits you again? Are you, Andromache, the wife of Hector, still joined in marriage to Pyrrhus?'

"Her countenance fell, and she spoke in a low voice; 'O, Polyxena, sole fortunate daughter of Priam, ordered to die near an enemy's tomb under the very walls of Troy, who did not suffer any drawing of lots nor as a captive touch the bed of a victorious lord! After the burning of the city, borne over various seas, I bore the arrogance of the son of Achilles and the pride of that youth, becoming a mother in slavery. Then he, interested in a Spartan marriage with Hermione, the granddaughter of Leda, handed me as a slave over to the slave Helenus. But inflamed with great love for the wife stolen from him by Pyrrhus and goaded on by the madness caused by his own crimes, Orestes attacked Pyrrhus off guard and killed him at the altar of his father. On the death of Neoptolemus a part of the kingdom was handed over to Helenus, who named the Chaonian fields and all Chaonia after Trojan Chaon, and added Pergamus, this Trojan citadel on the ridge. But what winds, what fates set you on this course? Or what god drove you, unwitting, to our shores? What about the boy Ascanius? Does he survive and does he breathe the air of heaven, [the boy] whom [Creusa bore] to you [during the siege of] Troy? [1] Does the boy still yearn for his lost mother? His father Aeneas and his uncle Hector, do they rouse in him the ancient courage and the manly spirit?' "

---

[1] In this sentence the words in brackets are a conjecture. The original line is incomplete.

MEETING WITH HELENUS; HIS PROPHECY AND COUNSEL

"She was pouring forth these words amid her tears and vainly uttering long lamentations when the hero Helenus the son of Priam advanced from the city with many companions. Recognizing his own kinsmen, he joyfully led them to the gates, and after every word wept without restraint. I walked along and recognized this little Troy and Pergamus, made like the great original, and the empty stream named Xanthus, and I embraced the threshold of the Scaean gate. At the same time the Trojans enjoyed the city of their kinsmen. The king held a reception for them in the wide porticoes; in the middle of the hall they kept pouring out libations of wine, and they held their goblets while the feast was served on gold.

"Now day after day passed. The breezes called to the sails, and the canvas was filled with the swelling south wind.

"I approached the seer, and I questioned him with these words: 'O Trojan-born, interpreter of the gods, you who understand the will of Phoebus, the tripods of Delphi, the laurels of Claros, the stars, the language of birds and their swift-winged omens, come tell me what dangers I should first avoid or what course follow in order to overcome such great misfortunes. Indeed it was revealed that all my course would be fortunate, and all the gods persuaded me to try to reach the remote land of Italy. Only the Harpy Celaeno prophesies a strange warning, horrible to tell, and proclaims that we will suffer the gods' grim wrath and a revolting hunger.'

"Then Helenus, after first killing the bullocks, as was the custom, asked peace of the gods and loosened the fillets of his sacred head, and with his hand he himself led me, awed by the dreadful presence of the god, to your threshold, O Phoebus. The priest then prophesied the following from his inspired lips:

" 'O goddess-born, proof is clear that you are sailing over

the deep under powerful protection. Thus the king of the gods determines fate and arranges one happening after another; this is the order of events. I will make known to you a few of many things so that you may travel more safely over strange seas and be able to settle in the Ausonian port; for the Fates forbid that Helenus know the rest, and Saturnian Juno prevents his speaking further. In the first place, a long, trackless route, along great, far-off stretches of land, separates you from Italy, which, foolish man! you now think close at hand, whose ports you are preparing to enter, as if they were nearby. You must ply the oar on the Sicilian wave and cross the surface of the Ausonian Sea in your ships and visit Lake Avernus and the island of Aeaean Circe before you can establish your city in safe territory. I will tell you the signs; remember to keep them deep in your memory. When in troubled state of mind you shall find at the water's edge of a remote river, under oaks along the bank, a great white sow with a litter of thirty young lying spread out on the ground and her white sucklings about her teats, that shall be the place for the city, the certain rest from your toils. And do not shrink from the future eating of these tables; fate will find a way, and Apollo, if invoked, will be present.

" 'But avoid these lands and this near coast of the Italian shore which is washed by the waves of our sea; all these cities are inhabited by evil Greeks. Here the Narycian Locrians have set up their city, and Idomeneus of Lycte has occupied the Sallentine fields; here is famed though small Petelia, defended by a wall built by the Thessalian leader Philoctetes. Indeed, when the fleet shall be moored across the seas and when, after erecting your altars, you shall pay your vows, cover your head with a purple mantle lest at the sacred sacrifices in honor of the gods any hostile face appear and disturb the omens. Let your comrades keep this custom of the sacred sacrifices, and you yourself keep it: let your descendants devoutly cling to this sacred observance.

" 'But when the wind shall waft you on your departure toward the Sicilian shore and the headlands of narrow Pelorus begin to open up, follow the land and the sea on your left in a great circle; flee the shore and the waters on the right. Once, the story goes, these places, rent by the force of a vast earthquake, split apart, though formerly they were a continuous whole. Such changes a long period of time can bring about. The sea forced its way between and cut off the Italian side from the Sicilian, flowing amid fields and cities, each coast separated by a narrow tide. Scylla holds the right side and savage Charybdis the left. Thrice a day from the very bottom of the abyss the latter swallows straight down vast waves, and again spouts other waves on high and strikes the stars with the water. But a cave holds Scylla in its dark recesses where it sticks out its mouths and drags ships on to the rocks. Above, its features are human and down to the waist it is a maiden with a beautiful breast, while below, it is a sea monster of huge body, its dolphin tails joined to the belly of wolves. It is better that you, delaying, skirt the promontory of Sicilian Pachynus and take the long course around rather than once see the hideous Scylla in its vast cave and the rocks, resounding with sea-hued dogs.

" 'Moreover, if there is any wisdom in Helenus, if any reliance is to be placed in a prophet and Apollo fills his mind with truth, O goddess-born, I will foretell one thing instead of many and repeat again and again this advice: first of all, adore the divinity of great Juno with prayer; chant your vows freely to Juno and win over the powerful queen with suppliant gifts. Thus, finally victorious, you shall reach the borders of Italy after leaving Sicily.

" 'When, after being guided here, you approach the city of Cumae, the sacred lakes, and Avernus with its rustling forests, you shall see the inspired prophetess who tells fortunes at the foot of the cliff and commits her signs and words to leaves. Whatever prophecies the virgin writes down on the leaves she arranges properly and lays aside in the cave. They remain unmoved in their places and do not lose their order; but when at the turn of the hinge a gentle breeze blows them, and the opened door disturbs the light leaves, then she never is interested in seizing them as they fly about in the empty cave, or in putting them back in their place, or in joining the verses together. Uncounseled, people depart, hating the seat of the sibyl. Here, although your companions may grumble and the course may vigorously call the ships to the deep and a favorable wind fill the canvas, let no loss of time on account of the delay be so important in your eyes that you fail to visit the prophetess and with prayer petition the oracle that she may prophesy and freely open her lips in speech. She will explain to you the peoples of Italy and the wars to come and how you may escape or bear each trouble, and after she has been properly honored, she will grant a favorable sailing. These are warnings which I am permitted to give you. Go now and raise Troy, great in deeds, to the heavens.' "

HELENUS AND ANDROMACHE GIVE PARTING GIFTS

"After the prophet had uttered these words in friendly speech, straightway he ordered that gifts heavy with gold and ivory be brought to the ships, and he loaded the keels with a great deal of silver, kettles from Dodona, a cuirass woven of a triple mesh of gold, and a beautiful helmet with crest and waving plumes, the armor of Neoptolemus. These were Helenus' gifts to my father. He added horses and leaders, filled out the crew, and at the same time equipped my comrades with arms.

"Meanwhile Anchises ordered us to prepare the sails for the fleet so that there would be no delay should a favorable wind arise. The interpreter of Phoebus addressed him with great respect: 'O Anchises, considered worthy of a noble marriage with Venus, care of the gods, twice snatched from the ruins of Pergamus, behold your land, Ausonia; hasten to sail there. But you must pass by this side of Italy; that part of Ausonia which is afar off is what Apollo reveals. Go, O father, happy in the devotion of a son. Why do I proceed further, and by my talking delay the rising winds?'

"Not to be outdone by her husband in generosity, Andromache, saddened at our last parting, brought forth garments embroidered with golden threads and a Phrygian cloak for Ascanius, and loaded him down with woven gifts as she spoke these words:

" 'Receive these things, too, and let them be remembrances to you from my hands, child, and let them bear witness to the long love of Andromache the wife of Hector. Take these last gifts from your kinfolk, O sole surviving image for me of my Astyanax. He had such eyes, such hands, such features as you; and now, just your age, he would be growing into manhood with you.'

"Departing I addressed them as my tears began to fall: 'Live in happiness, you who have already realized your destiny; we are called from one fate to another. You have won repose; you do not have to plow the surface of the sea, nor must you seek the ever-receding fields of Ausonia. You see a replica of the Xanthus and the Troy which your hands have built under what I hope are more favorable auspices, a Troy less exposed to the Greeks. If ever I enter the Tiber and the lands near the Tiber and see walls surrounding my people, we will make our two related cities one in spirit—kindred peoples in Epirus and Hesperia, who had the same founder, Dardanus, and suffered the same misfortunes. May that duty remain for our descendants.' "

THE TRIP TO ITALY

"We were borne over the sea near the neighboring promontory of Ceraunia, from which point lies the route to Italy and the shortest course over the waves. Meanwhile the sun went down and the dark mountains were in shadow. After casting lots for the oars, we stretched out near the water on the bosom of the longed-for earth, and lying about on the dry shore, we rested. A deep sleep crept over us in our weariness. Night, driven in her chariot by the Hours, was not yet entering mid-heaven when the alert Palinurus rose from his couch and noted all the winds and tried to catch the sound of the breeze. He marked all the stars gliding in their silent courses, Arcturus and the rainy Hyades and the twin Bears, and he observed Orion, armed with golden weapons. After he saw that everything was calm in the serene heavens, he blew a clear signal from the ship. We moved our camp and undertook the journey, spreading our winged sails.

"After the stars were put to flight, the dawn was beginning to redden when afar off we saw the dark hills of low-lying Italy. First Achates shouted 'Italy!' and his companions greeted Italy with a happy shout.

"Then father Anchises crowned a great bowl, filled it with wine, and standing on the high deck, he called upon the gods: 'Powerful gods of the sea and the land and the storms, give us an easy journey and blow favorable winds.'

"The wished-for breezes rose and soon the port began to widen as we sailed nearer, and the temple of Minerva came into view on the height. My companions furled the sails and turned the prows to the shores. The port was curved in the shape of a bow by the eastern flood; jutting rocks foamed with salty spray, and the harbor itself lay hid. The towering cliffs extended their arms from twin walls and the temple lay distant from the shore. Here I saw the first omen, four horses of snowy brightness grazing far and wide over a grassy field.

"Father Anchises exclaimed: 'O strange land, you bring war; men arm horses for war; these animals portend war. But nevertheless these same horses often become accustomed to pulling the chariot and to bearing peaceful bits under the yoke: there is hope for peace, too.'

"Then we prayed to the sacred power of arms-clashing Pallas, who was the first to receive us in our joy, and before the altars we covered our heads with Trojan veils, and in accord with the most important commands that Helenus had given, we duly offered to Greek Juno the sacrifices he had ordered.

"Without delay, immediately after performing the rites properly, we turned the ends of the sailyards seaward and left the homes of the Greeks and their distrusted fields. From this point the bay of Tarentum, a city founded by Hercules, if the story is true, came into view; further ahead, the temple of Juno at Lacinium appeared on the horizon, and the citadel of Caulon and shipwrecking Scylaceum.

"Then rising afar from the water, Sicilian Aetna was sighted, and we heard a great groaning of the sea and the beating on the distant rocks and the roar of the breakers on the shore; and the shallows boiled up and sand mingled with the surge.

"Then father Anchises cried out: 'Surely this is that famed Charybdis; Helenus foretold these cliffs and these terrifying rocks. Save yourself, my comrades, and all together pull on the oars.'

"They did as they were ordered. First Palinurus turned the straining prow toward the waters on the left: all the crew with the wind strained on the oars toward the left. We were tossed heavenward on a swell of the sea and then when the waves pulled away, we sank down in the very depths where the dead dwell. Three times the cliffs gave out a roar among the hollows of the rocks; three times we saw the spray splashing high and the stars dripping. Meantime the wind and the sun deserted the weary wanderers, and not knowing the route, we edged toward the shores of the Cyclopes."

THE LANDING IN SICILY

"The port was sheltered from the approach of the winds and wide in itself, but nearby Aetna thundered its fearful destruction. Sometimes it belched forth a dark cloud into the air with black swirls of smoke and white-hot ashes, and it tossed up balls of fire that grazed the stars. Meanwhile it vomited forth rocks and the shattered viscera of the mountain; with a groan it whirled molten stone into the air and boiled up from its lowest depth. The story goes that the body of Enceladus, half burned by a bolt of lightning, was pressed down by this mass, and that huge Aetna, placed upon him, breathed out flames from holes in the side of the mountain. As often as he changed from his one tired side to the other, all Sicily quaked with the rumble, and smoke spread over the heavens. That night, protected by the forest, we suffered hideous terror, nor did we see what could cause the sound. For there was no light from the stars nor clear air in the starry heavens, but clouds in a black sky while dark night held the moon under a cloud."

THE RESCUE OF THE DESERTED GREEK

"The following day was dawning with the first rays of light, and Aurora had already scattered the dewy shades from the heavens, when suddenly from the forests, in the last stage of emaciation, the strange form of an unknown man in a pitiable condition came forward and suppliantly extended his hands toward the shore. We looked at him again and again. There was an unspeakable filthiness about him; his beard was matted, and his clothes were held together with thorns; but in all else he was a Greek and once was sent to Troy with his country's arms. When he saw afar off the Dardanian dress and the Trojan arms, frightened for a little at the sight, he froze to the spot and checked his step. Soon with tearful prayers, he ran headlong to the shore:

" 'By the stars, I implore you, by the gods and by heaven's air that we breathe, take me on board, Trojans; carry me to any lands you wish: that will be enough. I admit that I was one of the Greek army. I confess that I warred against the gods of Ilium. For that, if the punishment of my crime is so great, scatter me into the waves and drown me in the vast sea. If I perish, it will be a pleasure to have perished by the hands of men.'

"He finished speaking, and with his arms around our legs, groveling on his knees, he clung to us. We urged him to say who he was and of what blood he came, and then confess what ill fortune pursued him. Father Anchises himself, after a slight delay, extended his hand to the youth and strengthened his courage with this prompt pledge. Finally, after putting aside his fear, he spoke as follows:

" 'I, Achaemenides by name, companion of the unfortunate Ulysses, set out from Ithaca, my homeland, to Troy. Adamastus, my father, was a poor man. Would that his fortune had remained mine! Here my thoughtless companions deserted me in the vast cave of the Cyclops while they left the cruel threshold in panic. His home of blood and gory feasts is dark and spacious. When standing straight, he touches the lofty stars—O gods, turn aside such a scourge as this from the earth!—and it is not easy for anyone to bear the sight of him, nor can one communicate with him in language. He feeds on the vitals and dark blood of wretched men. I myself have looked on when he, lying on his back in the middle of the cave, dashed against a rock two of our number that he had seized with his great hand, causing the threshold to run with blood. I have seen him devour limbs dripping with dark gore while, still warm, they trembled between his teeth. But he did not go unpunished. Ulysses did not allow such crimes, nor was the Ithacan forgetful of himself in this great emergency. For as soon as the Cyclops, filled with feasting and intoxicated with wine, laid his head back and sprawled his great bulk through the cave, belching in his sleep gory matter and pieces mixed with bloody wine, we, after praying to the great gods and assigning ourselves places, together on all sides swarmed about him and bored with a sharp weapon into his eye, a great eye, his only one, which lay concealed under his shaggy forehead like a Greek shield or the lamp of Phoebus, and at length we joyfully avenged the shades of our comrades.'

" 'But flee, ill-fated men, flee, and cut the rope from the shore. Of the same appearance and size as Polyphemus, who encloses his wool-bearing flocks in the hollow cave and milks them, a hundred other terrible Cyclopes live near these curved shores and wander here and there over the high mountains. Three times the horns of the moon have already filled themselves with light. During this time I have dragged out my life in the forests among the deserted haunts and homes of wild animals, watching the huge Cyclopes from the cliff and trembling at the sound of their feet and their voices. The branches give poor food—berries and cornel cherries with large stones—and I have lived on the roots of herbs that I pulled up. On the watch for everything, I sighted this fleet, the first to come to these shores. I resolved to hand myself over to it, no matter what it might prove to be. It is enough to have escaped this cursed race. Rather take this life of mine by whatever death you will.' "

THE CYCLOPES

"Hardly had he spoken these words when on the top of the mountain we saw the shepherd Polyphemus moving his enormous bulk among the flocks and seeking the known shores, a frightful monster, shapeless and huge, whose sight had been destroyed. The trunk of a pine tree in his hand guided and steadied his steps. The wool-bearing sheep, the sole pleasure and consolation of the evil man, accompanied him. After he touched the deep waves and came to the sea, in its water he washed out the blood flowing from the socket of his eye, grinding his teeth and groaning, and though he was walking in the middle of the sea, the water did not yet touch his high sides. We afar off hastened our flight from there in fear, after receiving so deserving a suppliant, and we quietly cut the cable, and bending low, we swept the sea with struggling oars. He heard and turned his steps toward the sound of the noise. In fact, when no opportunity was given him to seize anything with his right hand, and he was not able to breast the Ionian waves in his pursuit, he raised a great outcry, at which the sea and all the waves trembled and the land of Italy far within its borders was startled and Aetna rumbled in its hollow caverns.

"Then the race of the Cyclopes rushed excitedly from the forests and the high mountains down to the port, and they lined the shore. We saw the brothers of Aetna vainly standing with glowering eyes, their high heads reaching to heaven, a terrifying council, as when airy oaks or cone-bearing cypresses stand together on a high mountain amid a lofty forest of Jupiter or a grove of Diana. Sudden fear drove us headlong wherever the ropes lay ready and the sails billowed with favorable winds. On the other hand, the instructions of Helenus warned us to hold to our course, for either side, Scylla or Charybdis, was little removed from death. The sure thing was to sail back over our route. Suddenly, however, the North Wind blew from its narrow home at Pelorus. I sailed past the river Pantagias' mouth of natural rock, the gulf of Megara, and low-lying Thapsus. Achaemenides, the companion of the unlucky Ulysses, pointed out such places as these while we sailed along the shores over which he had wandered.

"Jutting into the Sicanian Gulf lay the stormy promontory of Plemyrium; former peoples gave it the name Ortygia. The story goes that the Alpheus River of Elis made its hidden way under the sea to this place; now, Arethusa, it flows from your mouth with Sicilian waters. On order from Anchises, we venerated the great divinities of the place. I sailed by the very rich soil of the stagnant Helorus. Then we skirted along the lofty cliffs and the projecting crags of Pachynus and afar off in the distance Camarina came into view—its lake, the Fates had promised, would never be moved—and the fields around Gela, and Gela itself, so called from the name of the impetuous river. Then steep Acragas showed in the distance its very great defenses, once the breeding place of high-spirited horses; and after the winds arose, I left you, Selinus, famous for palm trees, and I skirted the shoals of Lilybaeum, dangerous because of hidden stones."

DEATH OF ANCHISES

"Then the port and the joyless shore of Drepanum received me. Here after being driven by so many storms on the sea, what grief! I lost my father, Anchises, the solace of all my care and woe. Here, alas, O best of fathers, rescued in vain from so many dangers, you deserted me. The prophet Helenus, when he warned of many horrors, did not foretell this sorrow to me, nor did the accursed Celaeno. Here at Drepanum was my last trial, here the end of my long journeying. When I left there, some god forced me to your shores."

Thus father Aeneas alone recounted to all his listeners the fates of the gods and explained his course. Finally he grew silent and, coming to an end, he rested.

Book Four

CUPID

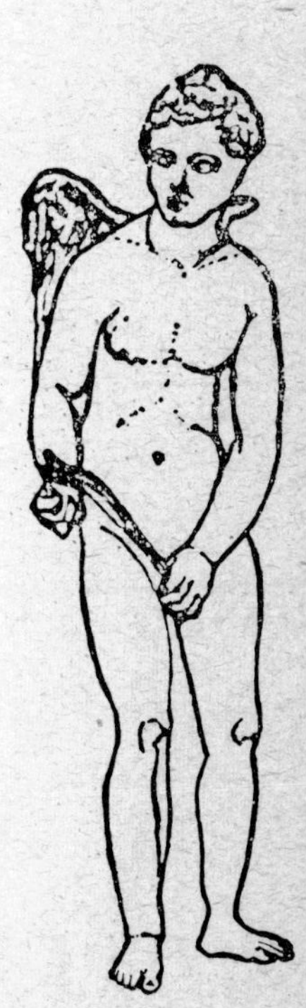

Book Four

DIDO'S PASSION FOR AENEAS

Now the queen, already suffering from the sharp pangs of love, nursed a wound in her veins and was consumed by a hidden flame. Often the courage of the man, often the honor of his race came back to her mind. His features and his words were buried deep in her heart, nor did her grief allow her body quiet rest.

The following dawn was lighting the earth with the rays of the sun and had already scattered the dewy shades from the heavens, when she hysterically spoke to her loving sister in this way:

"Anna, my sister, what dreams terrify me in my indecision! Who is this foreign guest that has come to our settlement? What a noble countenance, what a stout heart, what weapons! Indeed I believe, nor is my confidence vain, that he belongs to the race of the gods. Fear reveals a low-born spirit. Alas! by what ill fortune he was tossed about! What prolonged wars he related! If my purpose were not fixed and steadfast to be united with no one in the bonds of marriage after my first love deserted and deceived me by his death; had I not been so disgusted with marriage, perhaps I might have yielded to this one temptation. Anna—I confess it—since the death of my unfortunate husband Sychaeus, and the scattering of the household gods by a brother's crime, only this man has touched my heart and shaken my resolution. I recognize the traces of the old flame. But I should wish either that the depths of the earth swallow me or that the all-powerful father drive me with his thunderbolt to the shades, the pale shades and the dead of night in Erebus, before I would violate you, O

Honor, or break my oath to you. He who first married me carried away my love with him. May he hold it and keep it with him in the tomb."

After she spoke these words, tears began to well from her heart.

"Sister mine," Anna replied, "more beloved than the light of life, will you in loneliness and sorrow waste all your youth and know neither darling children nor the blessings of love? Do you believe that ashes or buried spirits care about your vow? Granted that no suitors either of Libya or, before, from Tyre ever turned you from your sad resolution; granted that you have despised Iarbas and the other leaders, whom Africa, a land rich in triumphs, has nourished, will you struggle against a pleasing love? And do you not realize in whose fields you have settled? On this side, the Gaetulian cities, a race insuperable in war, and the uncurbed Numidians, and the unfriendly Syrtes surround you; on the other side, a region deserted because of drought, and the Barcaeans raging far and wide. Why should I speak of an impending war from Tyre and the threats of your brother? Indeed, I think that the Trojan ships have followed this course with the wind under the auspices of the gods and the favor of Juno. With such a marriage what a city you will see arise, what a kingdom! Punic glory with the aid of the Trojans will rise to what great heights! Only ask the favor of the gods, and after you have offered your sacrifices, show the Trojans hospitality and invent reasons for their delay, while the winter rages on the sea and Orion is stormy, while the ships are wrecked and the weather is unfavorable."

With these words Anna inflamed Dido's heart with passionate love, instilled hope into her doubting mind, and overcame her scruples. First, they approached the shrines and prayed for peace at all the altars; following the custom, they sacrificed choice sheep to the lawgiver Ceres, to Phoebus, to father Lyaeus, and above all to Juno, who has special concern for the bonds of marriage. Most beauteous Dido, holding a bowl in her right hand, poured wine between the horns of a white cow, or facing the statues of the gods, approached the altars on which were rich offerings, and she daily renewed her gifts and anxiously examined the quivering entrails when the breasts of the victims were slit open.

Ah, ignorant minds of the seers! How can offerings, how can temples help one who is madly in love? Meanwhile the flame consumed the tender heart of her being and quietly smoldered in her breast. Unhappy Dido was afire with love and madly wandered throughout the city like an arrow-pierced hind caught unaware, which a shepherd, plying his weapons, has wounded afar off among the Cretan groves; without knowing it, he has left his flying shaft in the animal, which wanders in its flight through the forests and the glades of Dicte with the deadly reed clinging to its side.

Now she took Aeneas with her through the midst of the fortifications and she showed the rich Sidonian resources and the city already prepared. She began to talk and stammered in the midst of her speaking. Then as the day came to a close, she sought a repetition of the banquet and in her madness asked to hear once more the sufferings of Troy, and again hung on his words as he told the story. Afterward, when all had departed and the darkened moon in its turn withdrew its light and the setting stars suggested sleep, alone she grieved in the empty house and lay on the couch he had left. Though they were apart, she saw and heard him, or captivated by the resemblance to his father, she held Ascanius on her lap, to see if she could disguise a love that must not even be uttered. The towers, already started, ceased to rise, and the young men did not engage in military exercises, nor were the port and the defenses ready for war. The buildings and the high, threatening walls were interrupted, and the crane reaching to the sky was idle.

JUNO AND VENUS CONFER

As soon as the dear wife of Jupiter perceived that Dido was held fast by this passion and that gossip did not check her madness, the daughter of Saturn approached Venus with these words:

"You and your boy are truly winning noteworthy praise and splendid spoils, a great and memorable name if one woman has been overcome by the craftiness of two gods. Nor does it escape me that you, fearful of our fortifications, have regarded the homes of high Carthage with suspicion. But what is to be the limit of this or to what purpose do we now prolong this great struggle? Why do we not rather arrange an everlasting peace and a marriage pact? You have what you sought with your whole soul: Dido is aflame with love; the fire has spread throughout her body. Let us, therefore, rule this people in common under equal auspices; allow her to obey a Trojan husband and to hand over the Tyrians to you as dowry."

Feeling that Juno had spoken deceitfully so as to divert the kingdom of Italy to the shores of Libya, Venus began to reply to her in this way:

"Who would be so insane as to refuse such offers, or who prefer to contend in a war with you, if it were only certain that Fortune would follow the arrangement which you suggest. But because of the Fates I am in doubt whether Jupiter would wish that there be one city for the Tyrians and the Trojans, or whether he would approve the mingling of these peoples or their being allied by treaties. You are his wife; for you it is right to test his mind by pleading. Proceed; I will follow."

Then royal Juno replied in this way: "That task shall be my concern. Attend now, and I will explain in a few words how this affair can be carried out. Aeneas and unhappy Dido are making plans to go hunting together in the forest when tomorrow's sun begins to rise and its rays reveal the world. While the hunters hurry about and encircle the glades with nets, I will pour down on them a dark rain cloud mixed with hail, and I will shake all the heavens with thunder. Their comrades shall flee and be concealed by the dark night; Dido and the Trojan leader shall come to the same cave. I will be there and if I can be certain of your compliance, I will join them in permanent marriage and pronounce her his very own. This shall be their marriage rite."

Not opposing her request, the maid of Cythera agreed and laughed on detecting the ruse.

THE ROYAL HUNT

Meanwhile the rising Dawn had come out of the ocean. When the sun was up, chosen youths went through the gates; Massylian horsemen with large-meshed nets, snares, wide-bladed hunting spears, and keen-scented dogs rushed out. At the threshold the princes of the Carthaginians awaited the queen, tarrying in her bedchamber. Her horse, resplendent in purple and gold, stood stamping as he fiercely champed his foaming bit. At length, in the company of a great troop, she came forth, clothed in a Sidonian cloak with an embroidered edge. She carried a golden quiver, her hair was held in place with a golden band, and a golden clasp bound up her purple garment. Happy Julus and his Phrygian companions also joined the train. Aeneas himself, more handsome than all the others, came forward as her companion and united his group with hers. As when Apollo leaves his winter home in Lycia and the river Xanthus to visit his mother's Delos, and revives the choruses, while mingling Cretans, Dryopes, and painted Agathyrsi chant wildly around the altars—the god himself, his weapons sounding on his shoulders, walks along the ridges of Cynthus and after smoothing his flowing hair, lays a soft wreath upon it and fastens it with a golden band: with no less vigor Aeneas strode along and an equal glory shone on his noble countenance.

After they came into the high mountains and the trackless fens, suddenly wild goats, driven from a rocky height, ran down from the ridges; from another direction deer ran across the open fields and after leaving the mountains, gathered for flight in dusty droves. Now the boy Ascanius rode gleefully through the midst of the valleys upon a spirited horse and passed one after another, as he raced along and wished that in answer to his prayers a foaming boar would appear among the tame flocks and a tawny lion come down from the mountain.

Meanwhile the heavens were filled with loud thunder, and rain mixed with hail followed. Scattered Tyrian comrades, Trojan youths, and the Dardanian grandson of Venus in fear sought diverse shelter in the fields as torrents rushed from the mountains. Dido and the Trojan leader came to the same cave. Earth first and then Juno as bridal matron gave the sign to begin the rite; the lightning flashed and the heavens were witness to the marriage, while the nymphs wailed from the highest peak. That day was the prime cause of her death and of her troubles; for she was not disturbed by appearances or gossip, nor did she any longer merely plan a furtive love. She called it marriage; with this name she covered over her fault.

GOSSIP

Suddenly Rumor went through the great cities of Libya, Rumor than which there is no swifter evil. She thrives on movement and increases her power by her traveling; at first she is small through fear; soon she raises herself into the air, walks upon the ground, and hides her head among the clouds. The parent Earth, irritated by the wrath of the gods, produced her, they say, last of all, the sister of Coeus and Enceladus. She is swift of foot and fleet of wing, a dreadful, huge monster, which for every feather on her body has just as many watchful eyes beneath—marvelous to tell—and just as many tongues and mouths sound, and she pricks up just as many ears. At night she flies screeching through the midst of the sky, nor does she close her eyes in sweet sleep. During the day, like a guard she sits either on the ridge of the highest roof or on lofty towers and terrifies great cities, as persistent a spreader of the false and depraved as of the true. Then gladly she kept filling the people with many different kinds of gossip and gave out fact and fiction in equal measure: that Aeneas, born of Trojan blood, had come, and the beautiful Dido had deemed herself worthy to be joined in marriage to him; that now they were enjoying themselves in luxury the whole winter long, the prisoners of wicked lust, unmindful of their kingdoms. Here and there the foul goddess put these words into the mouths of men. Straightway she turned her course to King Iarbas and enkindled his mind with these stories and magnified his wrath.

THE JEALOUSY OF IARBAS

Iarbas, the son of Hammon by a ravished Libyan nymph, had built a hundred great temples to Jove throughout his broad kingdom, erected a hundred altars, and consecrated perpetual fire—the everlasting sentinel of the gods. The ground in these temples was rich with the blood of flocks, and their thresholds bloomed with various wreaths. Out of his mind and enraged by bitter gossip, he is said to have prayed to Jupiter earnestly as a suppliant with hands upraised before the altars, in the midst of the sacred images of the gods:

"All-powerful Jupiter, to whom the Moorish race is now making an offering of wine after having feasted on embroidered couches, do you see these things? Do we cringe in vain, father, when you hurl your thunderbolt, and does unaimed lightning in the clouds terrify our minds and mingle meaningless thunder? A woman, wandering within our borders, built a small city after paying a price. We gave her the shore to be plowed and laws governing the place, and she has refused marriage with us and received Aeneas as her lord into the kingdom. Now this Paris with his effeminate train, a Maeonian cap tied under his chin, his hair dripping with perfume, seizes his prey, while, of course, we bring gifts to your temples and reverence an empty myth."

MERCURY DESCENDS TO AENEAS

The all-powerful Jupiter listened to him as he uttered this prayer with his hands touching the altar, and he turned his gaze toward the walls of the kingdom and the lovers, unmindful of their better reputation. Then he addressed Mercury in these words and gave him these commands:

"Come now, son, call the zephyrs and glide down on wings to the Trojan leader, who now is lingering in Tyrian Carthage, ignoring the cities given him by the Fates. Speak to him and carry these words of mine on the swift breezes. His most beautiful mother did not promise that he would be such a man, and she did not twice save him from Greek weapons for this purpose. But she did promise that he would be the one to rule an Italy destined for empire and raging with war; that he would bring forth a race from the noble blood of Teucer and put the whole world under its laws. If no desire for the glory of such great exploits enkindles him, and he does not endure labor for his own praise, does the father begrudge Ascanius the citadels of Rome? What is he accomplishing or with what hope does he tarry among an unfriendly people without thought of his Italian offspring and the Lavinian fields? Let him sail away. This is my final word; let this be our command."

He finished speaking. Mercury prepared to obey the order of his great father. First, he fastened on his feet golden sandals, which carry him aloft on wings with a speed equal to that of the rapid winds over the sea or the earth. Then he seized his rod. With this he calls forth the pale shades from Orcus or at another time sends them down to the gloomy nether regions; with this he induces sleep and takes it away and closes men's eyes in death. Relying on this wand, he drives away winds and flies through turbid clouds. Now flying, he sighted the peak and the steep sides of long-suffering Atlas, who supports the heavens on his head, Atlas, whose pine-forested head, encircled with black clouds, is beaten by wind and rain; deep snow covers his shoulders, while rivers fall from the chin of the aged man, and his bristling beard is stiff with ice.

Mercury, poised on even wings, first stopped there; from that point he dove headlong with all his weight down to the waves. Like a bird that flies low along the shores, the fish-teeming reefs, and the sea, Mercury, the grandson of Atlas, flew between heaven and earth near the sandy shore of Libya and cut through the winds.

As soon as he touched the dwellings with his winged feet, he saw Aeneas laying the foundations for towers and new homes. He wore a sword, glittering with yellow jasper; hanging from his shoulders gleamed a cloak of Tyrian purple, which Dido had made as a gift for him, having woven thin gold into the web. Straightway the god accosted him:

"Are you now laying the foundations of lofty Carthage and, a slave to your wife, building a beautiful city, forgetful, alas, of your kingdom and your own affairs? The ruler of the gods himself, who turns the heavens and the earth with his power, sends me down from bright Olympus to you; he orders me to bring these commands on the high winds. What are you planning? What prospect is there in wasting your time in the land of Libya? If no glory in great enterprises moves you [and you undertake no exploit leading to your own fame], consider growing Ascanius and the future of your heir Julus, to whom the kingdom of Italy and the Roman territory belong."

After Mercury delivered his message, he suddenly left mortal view and vanished far from sight into thin air.

But Aeneas, crazed at the vision, was speechless. His hair stood on end from fright, and his voice stuck in his throat. Shocked at this awful warning and command of the gods, he was eager to flee and to leave this sweet land. But what could he do? With what excuse could he dare approach the love-mad queen? How could he broach the matter? He turned his swift mind now to this and now to that solution; torn in different directions, he considered all the possibilities. As he wavered, it seemed that this was the better opinion: he summoned

Mnestheus, Sergestus, and brave Serestus and ordered them to fit out the fleet quietly, gather their companions at the shore, prepare arms, and conceal the reason for the change in his plans. Meanwhile, he himself, when good Dido did not realize or suspect that their great love was being broken up, would test the approaches and discover what would be the most favorable time to speak and what the propitious course in this crisis. All joyfully obeyed the command with speed and carried out what was ordered.

DIDO'S ANGER AND AENEAS' DEFENSE

But the queen perceived the scheme in advance—who can deceive a lover?—and at once surmised their future movements, fearful even when all was well. That same impious Rumor brought word to the furious woman that the fleet was being made ready and the sailing planned. Out of her mind, she raged and, inflamed with anger, madly rushed through the whole city, like a worshiper of Bacchus at the movement of the sacred emblems, when the biennial revels rouse her with the Bacchic cry, and Mount Cithaeron calls her with a shout. Finally, she lashed out at Aeneas with these words:

"Did you even expect, you traitor, that you could conceal such a great crime and depart secretly from my land? Does not our love hold you, does not the pledge you once gave, does not Dido on the threshold of death with its cruel funeral rites deter you? Why are you rather building a fleet in the winter and hastening, cruel man, to go over the deep in the midst of winds from the north? Why is this? If you were not seeking foreign land and unknown homes, if ancient Troy still remained, would the fleet sail to Troy over the stormy sea? Are you fleeing from me? By these tears and the pledge you gave—since I have nothing else left me in my misery—by our marriage, by the celebration already begun, if I have deserved anything at all from you or if anything about me was ever endearing to you, I beg of you, have mercy on my falling house and give up this idea, if there is still any use in my pleading. Because of you the Libyan races and the rulers of the Nomads hate me and the Tyrians are hostile; because of you, too, my self-respect is gone and also my former reputation, by which alone I was on the road to becoming immortal. To whom are you leaving me at the threshold of death, stranger, since this is the only name that remains in place of husband? But why do I delay until perhaps my brother Pygmalion will destroy my walls, or Iarbas the Gaetulian will lead me away a captive? If before your flight, at least a child had been born to me, if in the hall some little Aeneas were playing whose features would, in spite of everything, recall you to me, indeed I should not seem entirely deceived and deserted."

She finished speaking. Because of Jupiter's warning he kept his eyes fixed and with a struggle put down the pain in his heart. At length he spoke a few words:

"I will never deny, queen, that you have deserved praise for the long list of favors you can enumerate, nor will I be reluctant to remember Elissa as long as I have a memory, as long as my spirit rules this body. In defense of my actions I shall say a few words. I did not hope—do not imagine that—to conceal this flight by stealth. I never proposed marriage or entered into such a pact. If the Fates would suffer me to live my life according to my own designs, to settle my difficulties as I wished, I should first of all cherish the city of Troy and those that remain of my kinsmen; the high roofs of Priam would be standing and with my hand I would have erected a Troy restored for the vanquished. But now Grynean Apollo has ordered me to hasten to great Italy, and so has the Lycian oracle of Apollo. That is my love, that my fatherland. If the citadels of Carthage and the sight of your Libyan city hold you, a Phoenician woman, tell me why should you be envious if Trojans settle in the land of Ausonia? It is right for us, too, to seek a foreign kingdom. As often as night shrouds the earth with its dewy shades, as often as the fiery stars rise, the troubled ghost of my father Anchises warns me and terrifies me in my sleep. I am rebuked for the wrong done to the dear life of the boy Ascanius, whom I am defrauding of the kingdom of Hesperia and his destined fields. Even now, the messenger of the gods, sent by Jupiter himself—I swear by your head and mine—delivered these orders through the swift air; I myself saw the god entering the walls of the city, and I drank in his voice with these ears. Cease to torment me and yourself with your complaints. I do not seek Italy of my own accord."

As he uttered these words, she looked at him askance, rolling her eyes from this side to that. Scanning him with sullen gaze from head to foot, on fire with anger she addressed him:

"No goddess was your parent, nor was Dardanus the founder of your race, perfidious man, but the fierce Caucasus bore you amid rough crags, and Hyrcanian tigresses nursed you. For why do I disguise my feelings, why am I saving myself for greater wrongs? Was he distressed at my weeping? Did he lower his gaze? Did he, overcome, shed tears or did he have pity on a lover? What petitions shall I present? And to whom? Now neither great Juno nor Jupiter looks upon these crimes with just eyes. Nowhere is faithfulness certain. I received him when he was tossed on the shore and needy, and in by madness I settled him in a part of the kingdom. I rescued his fleet that was lost, and I brought back his companions from death.

"Ah, I have been made mad by the Furies! First the augur Apollo, then the Lycian oracle, now the messenger of the gods, sent by Jove himself, bears dreadful commands through the air. I suppose this is the labor of the gods; problems like this disturb them in their leisure. I do not detain you, nor do I refute your words. Go sail with the winds to Italy, seek your kingdom through the waves. Indeed I hope that, if divine favor can effect anything, you will suffer punishment in the midst of the reefs and that you will often call out the name of Dido. Though absent, I will follow with dark torches, and when cold death separates my body from my soul, as a ghost I will haunt you everywhere. You shall pay the punishment, evil man. I shall hear and this story will come to me in the realm of the dead."

With these words she broke off in the middle of her talk and, sore at heart, fled the light of day. Turning from his gaze, she departed, leaving him reluctant through fear to speak much, though preparing to say a great deal. Her servants took her up and bore her in a dead faint to her marble bedchamber and placed her upon her couch.

THE TROJANS PREPARE TO DEPART

But although dutiful Aeneas desired to assuage her grief and to drive away her cares with consoling words, though his grief was great and his mind wavering because of his great love, nevertheless he heeded the commands of the gods and went back to the fleet. Then, indeed, the Trojans set to work, dragging down the high ships along the entire shore. Keels covered with pitch floated in the water. In their zeal to flee, they brought green oars of unwrought oak from the forest. One could see them hastening their departure from the whole city, much as when ants, mindful of the winter, carry off a great pile of grain and put it under cover. The dark line goes through the fields, and they drag their booty along a narrow track through the grass; some, leaning against large grains, push with their shoulders, while others urge on the lines and rebuke the sluggards, and all the route is a fever of activity.

ANNA APPEALS TO AENEAS

What feelings were yours, Dido, when you beheld such scenes! What sighs you breathed when from the top of the citadel you viewed the shores alive with activity far and wide, when you saw all the sea before your eyes a scene of such great confusion! O wicked love, to what do you not impel the human heart? She was driven to weep and then again to try to win her pleas, humbly submitting her proud spirit to love, lest she should leave some remedy untried and die in vain.

"Anna, you see the hustling about the entire coast. They have assembled from all sides; already the canvas invites the breezes, and the happy sailors have placed garlands on the ships. If I could expect such a great sorrow as this, sister, I shall be able to bear it. But, Anna, do this one thing for me—for that traitor was accustomed to cherish you alone and even to entrust his secret feelings to you; you alone knew how to approach the man gently, you knew his humors. Go, sister, and humbly address my proud enemy. I did not swear with the Greeks at Aulis to destroy the Trojan race, nor did I send a fleet to Pergamus, nor did I violate the ashes of the spirit of father Anchises. Why does he refuse to admit my words into his cruel ears? Where is he rushing? Let him give this final gift to his wretched lover; let him wait for an easy flight and favorable winds. I do not beg now for the former marriage which he has betrayed, nor that he give up his beautiful Latium and relinquish his kingdom. I ask for a breathing time, a period to calm my frenzy, until fortune teaches me to bear up under my trials. I beg this last favor—have mercy on your sister—and when he grants it to me, I shall repay you many times over at my death."

With such words as these she pleaded, and her miserable sister delivered again and again such complaints. But no pleading moved him, nor did he listen to any words in a yielding mood. The Fates stood in the way, and some god stopped up the kindly ears of the man. And as when northern blasts from the Alps strive among themselves, now from this direction and again from that, to uproot a strong oak of age-old timber, creaking follows and piles of leaves cover the earth when the branches are shaken; yet it clings to the cliffs, and as far as its top extends into the heavens, so far do its roots go deep into the earth. In just the same way the hero was buffeted from this side and that by constant pleas and he felt a deep sense of anguish in his heart. But his mind remained unmoved, and Anna's tears fell to no purpose.

DIDO'S FRENZY; PREPARATION FOR SUICIDE

Then indeed unfortunate Dido, frightened by the Fates, prayed for death and loathed to look upon the vault of the heavens. What impelled her the more certainly to finish what she had begun and to leave the light of day was this, that when she was placing gifts upon the incense-burning altars—horrible to relate!—she saw the sacred waters become black and the wine that was poured out turn into foul blood. This was seen by no one, nor did she tell it even to her sister. Moreover, there was among the buildings a marble temple to her former husband. This she cherished with great reverence and wreathed with snowy fleece and festive branches. From there her husband's voice seemed to be heard calling to her when dark night covered the earth and the lonely owl upon the roof tops often complained with its funereal cry and gave out long, mournful sounds. Moreover, many predictions of devout prophets horrified her with their terrible warnings. In dreams fierce Aeneas himself pursued her in her frenzy. She always seemed to be left alone, always to be traveling on a long journey, unaccompanied, and seeking the Tyrians in a deserted land: just as crazed Pentheus saw the on-rushing Furies, twin suns, and a double Thebes; or as when Orestes the son of Agamemnon, pursued on the stage, fled from his mother, who was armed with torches and dark serpents, while the avenging Furies settled on his threshold.

Therefore, overcome by her grief, she became mad and decided to die. She considered secretly the time and the manner, and concealing her plan with a deceptive countenance and wearing an expression of serene hope on her face, she approached her sad sister with these words:

"Sister, I have found a way—congratulate your sister—to

return him to me or free me from loving him. Near the ocean's end and the setting sun, there is the farthest outpost of the Ethiopians, where great Atlas turns upon his shoulder the world, studded with flaming stars. A priestess of the Libyan race from this region has been suggested to me; she was the guardian of the temple of the Hesperides and used to give food to the dragon and preserve the sacred boughs on the tree, scattering liquid honey and sleep-bearing poppy. This woman promises by her incantations to free minds at will but to weigh others down with heavy care; to stop the water in the rivers and to turn the stars backward. She causes the ghosts of the night to stir about; you shall hear the earth rumbling under your feet and the ash trees descend from the mountains. I call the gods and you and your sweet life, dear sister, to witness that I have unwillingly availed myself of the arts of magic. Secretly within the house erect a pyre heavenward and place upon it the arms that the detestable man left hanging in the bedchamber, and all his clothing, and the marriage bed on which I perished. It is a delight to destroy all the memories of this wicked man, and the priestess shows how to do it."

After she uttered these words, she grew silent and at the same time a pallor came over her face. However, Anna did not believe that her sister was concealing her death in these strange rites, nor did she imagine that there was such great fury in her mind, nor did she fear a disaster greater than the death of Sychaeus. She therefore obeyed her commands.

But the queen, after constructing a great pine and oak pyre in the shrine under the open heaven and decorating the place with wreaths and garlands of funereal foliage, placed upon the couch his garments, the sword he had left, and his effigy, well aware of what was to come. There stood the altars round about. The priestess with flowing hair chanted the names of three hundred gods, and Erebus, Chaos, and triple Hecate, the three forms of the virgin Diana. Moreover, the priestess had sprinkled round about the feigned waters of the fountain of Avernus, and Dido had scattered the salted meal. Growing herbs with the juice of black poison, cut with a bronze sickle in the light of the moon, had been hunted and, before it could be devoured by the mother, the love-charm taken from the forehead of a young horse. Near the altar, with pure hands, one foot free of its sandal and her garment loosened, Dido, on the brink of death, called upon the gods and the stars, conscious of her fate. Then she prayed to any god at all who, just and sympathetic, might have an interest in those whose love is unrequited.

It was night, and over the earth wearied creatures were enjoying peaceful sleep, and the forests and the savage seas had become calm. It was the time when the stars revolve in the middle of their course, when all the land is quiet, when the cattle and the bright-colored birds, those that fly over the lakes far and wide and those that live in the thickets in the rough countryside, take their rest in the silent night. But Dido, unhappy in mind, did not forget her troubles, nor did she ever relax in sleep or welcome the peace of the night to her eyes or heart. Her cares redoubled and her love, returning, raged again, and she was tossed on a great tide of anger. So then, she strengthened her resolution and turned over these words in her heart:

"Well, what am I to do? Shall I, the object of derision, resort to my former suitors? Shall I, a suppliant, seek marriage with the Nomads whom I have already scorned so frequently as husbands? Shall I follow the Trojan fleet and these last commands given to the Trojans? Shall I do it because it pleases those who were formerly aided by my help and because gratitude for an ancient favor remains deep in their minds? But suppose I am willing. Who will allow me or receive me, an object of hatred, upon their proud ships? Alas, abandoned woman, are you still ignorant and do you not yet realize the perjury of the race of Laomedon? What, then, shall I do? Shall I accompany those rejoicing sailors alone? Shall I sail crowded together with all the band of my Tyrian followers? Shall I take those men to sea again whom I could hardly uproot from the city of Sidon, and order them to unfurl their sails to the winds? Nay, rather die, as you have deserved, and avert grief with the sword. Won over by my tears, you, sister, first loaded me down with these evils when I was madly in love, and you exposed me to the enemy. Why was I not allowed to pass my life without sin, free from a second marriage, and to escape such worries, like some animal of the field? I did not keep the word I gave to the ashes of Sychaeus!"

And she kept pouring forth such complaints as these from her heart.

MERCURY AGAIN URGES DEPARTURE

Aeneas on his high ship was buried in sleep, certain of departure, now that everything was properly prepared. The form of the god, returning with the same features, appeared to him in sleep, like Mercury in every respect, in voice and complexion, with blond hair and limbs of youthful beauty, and again seemed to warn him in this way:

"Goddess-born, can you in your folly sleep in such danger as this and not perceive the perils immediately surrounding you? Do you not hear the favorable zephyrs blowing? She, now certain of death, plots treachery and dreadful wickedness in her heart, and tosses on a changing tide of anger. Will you not flee from here in all haste while you have the power to flee? Soon you will see the water tossing with ships and alight with savage torches; you will see the shore ablaze with fire if the dawn finds you lingering in this land. Come now, away! Do not tarry! Woman is ever a fickle and changeable thing."

With these words he disappeared into the dark night. Then, indeed, Aeneas, startled by the sudden appearance of the god, leaped up from sleep and ordered his companions about:

"Awake quickly, my men! Take your place at the oars! Quickly free the sails! Lo, a god sent from high heaven again goads me to hasten the flight and to cut the twisted ropes. We follow you, O holy one of the gods, whoever you are, and once more we obey your command with joy. Be present and propitiously aid us. Make the stars in the sky favorable."

So speaking, he seized his gleaming sword from its sheath and struck the cables with the drawn weapon. At the same time, a like zeal filled all of them, and there was a great hustle and bustle. They left the shores, and the fleet covered the sea; with might and main they churned the foam and swept over the blue waters.

THE QUEEN'S FURY

And now Dawn, leaving the saffron couch of Tithonus, was scattering the first rays of a new day over the earth. As soon as the queen saw from her watchtower that the light was growing bright and the fleet was proceeding under full sail, as soon as she realized that the shore and the port were cleared of rowers, striking her beautiful breast three or four times and tearing her golden hair, she said:

"Ah, Jupiter! will this man go away after he has made a mockery of our kingdom? Will some men not bring weapons and pursue them from the whole city? Will others not launch the ships at the docks? Go, bring fire quickly! Use your weapons! Pull on the oars! What am I saying? Where am I? Unhappy Dido, what madness confuses your mind? Are you now repenting of your wicked deeds? Then that was proper when you gave him the scepter. Look at the pledged fidelity of this man, who, they say, is carrying his ancestral household gods with him, who bore upon his shoulders his father advanced in years! Could I not have seized him and torn his body to pieces and scattered it over the waves? Could I not have butchered his companions and Ascanius himself with the sword and placed him as food on his father's table? Suppose the outcome of the battle would have been doubtful. It might have been, but whom should I have feared when I was about to die? I ought to have thrown torches into their camp, filled the holds with flames, destroyed father and son together with their race, and thrown myself on top of it all."

DIDO'S CURSE

"O Sun, illuminating all the works of the earth with your flame, O Juno, conscious witness of these troubles, Hecate, whose name is called out at night at city crossroads, and you, avenging Furies and gods of dying Elissa, receive these offerings, turn your power against these evil men who deserve punishment, and hear our prayers. If it must be that this cursed person touch port and come to land, if this is what the will of Jove demands and this end is settled, then, vexed by the warring arms of a bold people, exiled from his borders, and torn from the embrace of Julus, may he beg for help, and may he see the shameful death of his kin. When he has surrendered himself to the stipulations of an unfair treaty of peace, may he not enjoy his kingdom or the light of life, but die before his day and lie unburied in the midst of the sand. I beg these favors and I pour out this last word with my blood. Then, Tyrians, hate his offspring and all the race that is to be, and send these gifts to my ashes. Let there be no love for this people nor any treaties with them. May some avenger of our blood rise up to pursue the Trojan colonists with fire and sword whenever, at any time, now or in the future, they become strong. I invoke opposing shores against their shores, the sea against their sea, and arms against their arms. May they and their descendants always be at war."

THE SUICIDE OF DIDO

Thus she spoke and turned her mind in every direction, wishing to break away as soon as possible from the hated light of day. Then briefly she addressed Barce, the nurse of Sychaeus, for her own nurse had died long since in the old country:

"Dear nurse, have sister Anna come here to me. Tell her

that she should quickly sprinkle her body with river water and bring the animals and the offerings of atonement with her. Let her come in this way, and you yourself bind your temples with a holy wreath. I have a mind to finish the sacrifice to Stygian Jove—the proper beginning I have prepared—to put an end to my troubles, and to set fire to the pyre of this Trojan person."

Thus she spoke. The nurse hurried away as eagerly as an old woman could.

But Dido, trembling and frantic because of her unnatural design, her eyes rolling and bloodshot, her cheeks trembling and blotched with color, and pale at the thought of future death, rushed into the interior rooms of the palace, stealthily ascended the high pyre, and unsheathed the Trojan sword, a gift which she had not asked from Aeneas for this use. Then after she viewed the Ilian garments and the familiar bed, delaying a little to weep and think, she lay upon the couch and said these very last words:

"Relics, so dear as long as the Fates and Heaven allowed, receive this spirit and free me of this anguish. I have lived and I have run the course which fortune allotted me; now my renowned shade will go beneath the earth. I have founded a famous city; I have seen my buildings rise. I avenged my husband and I punished my wicked brother. I would have been happy, alas too happy, if only the Trojan ships had never touched our shores!"

Thus she spoke and, pressing her lips to the couch, cried out: "I shall die unavenged, but let me die; in this way, in this way it is my pleasure to go to the abode of the dead. Let the cruel Trojan see this fire from the deep, and let him carry with him the omens of my death."

As she finished speaking, her companions saw that she had fallen upon the sword in the midst of her words, that the sword was running with blood and her hands were stained. A shout rose in the high-vaulted halls; Rumor wildly ran through the shocked city. Homes were filled with laments and weeping and the shrieking of women. The air resounded with great cries of grief, just as if all Carthage or ancient Tyre were falling before onrushing enemies and raging flames were rolling out through the roofs of the homes of men and the temples of the gods.

The startled sister heard, and frightened, rushed through the crowd with frantic speed, tearing her face with her nails and beating her breast with her fists, while shouting to Dido by name:

"So this was what you planned, sister? Were you deceiving me? Was this what your pyre, was this what the fires of these altars were preparing for me? What shall I, now deserted, complain of first? Have you not spurned your faithful sister by dying? Would that you had called me to the same fate. Would that the same pain and the same hour had ended both our lives with the sword. Did I even erect this pyre with my own hands and with my own voice invoke our ancestral gods only to be cruelly absent when you placed yourself upon it? Sister, you have destroyed yourself and me, your people, the elders of Sidon, and your city. Bring me water so that I may wash her wounds, and if any breath still lingers, I shall breathe it in with my mouth."

After speaking these words, she went up the high steps and, pressing her dying sister to her breast, fondled her and dried up the dark blood with her garment. Dido, trying to open her heavy eyes, again failed; the deep wound gurgled in her breast. Raising herself three times, she sat leaning upon her elbow; three times she fell back on the couch and sought with her wandering eyes the light in the high heavens and groaned when she found it.

Then all-powerful Juno, taking pity on her long suffering and her difficult death, sent Iris, the rainbow, down from Olympus to free her struggling soul from the body to which it was joined. For since she was perishing not by the decree of fate nor by a death she deserved but miserably before her day when she was fired by sudden madness, Proserpine had not yet taken a lock of golden hair from her head and sentenced her to Stygian Orcus. Therefore, dewy Iris flew down on saffron wings through the heavens, drawing behind her a thousand varying colors opposite the sun, and she stood above her head and spoke thus: "Obedient to command, I bear this sacred lock to Dis and I free you from this body of yours."

With her right hand she cut the hair; immediately all warmth left Dido, and her soul vanished into the air.

Book Five

HERCULES

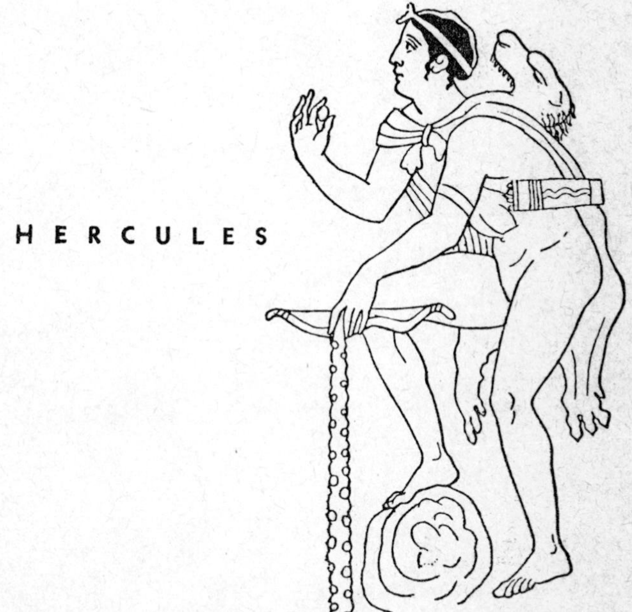

Book Five

A STORM DRIVES AENEAS TO SICILY

Meanwhile Aeneas was steadily sailing over the deep with his fleet and cutting waves rough with the north wind, when he looked back at the buildings, now alight with the flames set by the unhappy Elissa. The cause of this great blaze was unknown to the Trojans. But they did know how bitter is the anguish arising from a great love that is betrayed, and what a furious woman can do, and this knowledge filled their minds with sad forebodings.

When the ships were sailing the deep and there was no longer sight of land but only sea and sky on all sides, a dark rain cloud appeared overhead. This brought on a stormy night. The waves grew rough in the darkness.

Palinurus, the pilot, from his high stern, cried out: "Ah! why have such huge rain clouds filled the heavens? What are you preparing, father Neptune?"

Then, after speaking thus, he ordered them to reef the sails and to bend to the strong oars. As he tacked into the wind, he uttered these words:

"Stout-hearted Aeneas, I should not hope to reach Italy in such weather as this, even if Jupiter were to pledge me his assurance. The changed winds wail across our bow and rise out of the dark west, and the air is turned into clouds. We are not able to head into the wind or even to keep our course. Since Fortune has the upper hand, let us follow where it calls, and let us change our course. I think that the safe shores of your brother Eryx and the Sicilian ports are not far distant, if with correct memory I now survey the stars I observed before."

Then dutiful Aeneas agreed: "Indeed I see that it is vain for you to pray to the winds and to sail against them. Turn your course with the sails. Could any land be more pleasing to me, any land where I should prefer to beach my battered ships than the one that preserves Trojan Acestes and embraces in its bosom the bones of my father Anchises?"

After these words they sought the port, and favorable winds filled their sails. The swift fleet was borne over the deep and finally they came with joy to the familiar shore.

Afar off, from a mountain's lofty peak Acestes gazed in wonder at the approaching friendly ships. He ran to meet them, carrying bristling spears and wearing the shaggy skin of a Libyan bear. His mother was Trojan and had born him to the river god Crinisus. Not unmindful of his ancient ancestors, Acestes congratulated them on their return, joyfully received them with rural splendor, and consoled the weary men with friendly assistance.

ANNOUNCEMENT OF THE GAMES

At the break of the morrow's dawn when the light of day had put the stars to flight, from all along the shore Aeneas called his comrades together in a group and addressed them from the top of a mound:

"Great sons of Dardanus, race sprung from the noble blood of the gods, a year is ending, its months having passed since we buried in the earth the mortal remains of my divine parent and dedicated altars of mourning. And now, unless I am mistaken, the day has come which I shall always remember—it was your will, O gods—with sorrow and with pride. Even if I were to pass this day an exile on the African shoals, if I were caught in the Argolic Sea or in the city of Mycenae, nevertheless I would duly carry out my annual vows and the solemn processions, and I would lade the altars with their proper gifts.

Now unexpectedly we are present at the very ashes and the bones of my parent—it seems to me not without the powerful intent of the gods—and after being carried along by the winds, we have entered a friendly port. So come now! Let us all celebrate the happy feast. Let us pray for favorable winds. May it be my father's will that after the city has been founded, I offer sacrifices each year in temples dedicated to him. Trojan-born Acestes gives you two head of cattle for each ship. Invite our ancestral household gods to the banquet and the gods our host Acestes adores. Moreover, if the ninth dawn ushers in a favorable day for mortals and covers the earth with its rays, first I will set up for the Trojans a contest among the swift ships. Then whoever is good at foot racing, whoever, courageous in his strength, comes forward superior with the javelin and light arrows, or dares to fight with the rough gauntlet of leather and lead, should be present and expect prizes for victories won. Speak words of good omen, all of you, and bind your temples with wreaths."

MEMORIAL SERVICE TO ANCHISES

After speaking thus, he bound his temples with myrtle, sacred to his mother. Helymus did the same, and Acestes, advanced in age, and the boy Ascanius; the rest of the young men followed them. Aeneas went from the council to the tomb with many thousands, in the midst of a great accompanying crowd. Here, making a libation, he duly poured out upon the ground two bowls of pure wine, two of fresh milk, two of sacred blood, and scattered purple flowers. Then he spoke these words:

"Hail, holy father! Hail, once again, ashes rescued in vain, spirit and shade of my father! It was not permitted me to reach the borders of Italy and its destined fields, nor in company with you to seek the Italian Tiber, wherever it is."

After he had finished speaking, a huge, sleek snake from the depths of the shrine dragged his seven coils, his seven folds, gently encircling the tomb and creeping over the altars. Its back was spotted with blue markings, and the light reflected from its golden scales, as a rainbow throws a thousand varying colors upon the clouds when the sun is opposite. Aeneas was stupefied at the sight. At length, gliding with its long train between the tureens and polished cups, it ate of the food and harmlessly went down to the bottom of the tomb, leaving the altars whose offerings it had tasted. All the more eagerly he renewed the sacrifices begun to his father, uncertain whether to consider it the guardian of the place or the attendant spirit of his parent. He slaughtered, as was the custom, two sheep, as many hogs and bullocks with black backs; he poured forth wine from the bowls and kept calling upon the soul of great Anchises and the spirits freed from Acheron. His companions, too, happily brought forth gifts, whatever each one happened to have, and they laded the altars and sacrificed the bullocks. Others placed kettles in a row and lying on the grass, put live coals under the spits and roasted the meat.

THE GAMES BEGIN

The expected day arrived, and the horses of Phaëthon were already bringing on the ninth dawn with its clear light. The fame and the name of illustrious Acestes had enkindled curiosity among his neighbors. Anxious to see the companions of Aeneas, they filled the shores with a happy throng, some of whom were prepared to compete. The prizes were placed before their eyes in the middle of the circular track: sacred tripods, green crowns, and palms as rewards for the victors, arms and garments dyed with purple, and a quantity of silver and gold. From a mound in the center a trumpet announced that the games were beginning.

THE BOAT RACE

Four equally matched ships from the whole fleet entered the first contest for heavy oars. Mnestheus—soon to be Italian Mnestheus, from which name came the house of Memmius—

managed the rapid Shark with swift oars. Gyas captained the huge Chimaera, towering like a city building, driven forward by Trojan youths in triple rows with three banks of oars rising together. Sergestus, from whom the house of Sergius takes its name, rode the great Centaur, and Cloanthus, from whom your family, Roman Cluentius, sprang, entered the race with the dark blue Scylla.

Far out in the sea opposite the foaming shores there is a rock which is submerged and beaten by the swelling waves when the winter winds from the northwest blow clouds that hide the stars. In calm weather it is tranquil, and its land rises out of the motionless wave, a most pleasant spot for sun-loving sea birds. Here father Aeneas set up a green goal of leafy oak as a sign to the sailors so that they would know at what point they should return and circle back in their long course. They then received their places by lot. The captains themselves on the ships gleamed from afar in purple and gold; the rest of the youths wore poplar wreaths, and their naked shoulders glistened with oil. They took their places at the rowing benches, their arms tensely gripping the oars. They eagerly awaited the signal; throbbing anxiety and ardent desire for praise inspired their exulting hearts.

Then when the clear trumpet gave the sound, all the ships without delay surged forth from their starting lines. The noise of the sailors reached the heavens, and the disturbed waters foamed as their arms pulled back the oars. Together they plowed the waves, and all the sea yawned, churned by the oars and the triple-pointed breaks of the ships. Not so headlong in a horse race do chariots, leaving the starting pole, take the field and rush forth; not so headlong do drivers shake their streaming reins over the racing teams and, bending forward, poise themselves to lash the horses. Then all the grove sounded with the applause and shouts of the men showing their enthusiasm for their favorites, and the surrounding shores rolled the sound upward and the reverberating hills re-echoed the clamor.

Gyas dashed out and glided over the tops of the waves amid confusion and shouting, and then Cloanthus, better with the oars, followed him, but his boat of pine was slow because of its weight. After them the Shark and the Centaur at an equal distance strove to take the lead. Now the Shark was out in front, now the great Centaur passed ahead of it, now both were borne along together, beak to beak, and they plowed the salt water with their long keels.

They were just approaching the cliff and were nearing the turning point when Gyas, leading the race and victor in the midst of the flood, called to Menoetes, the pilot of his ship:

"Why are you going so far right? Turn this way! Keep to the shore and graze the rocks on your left without using the oars! Let the others sail the deep waters."

So he ordered, but Menoetes, fearing the hidden rocks, turned his prow to the waves of the deep water.

"Where are you going off course? Head toward the rocks, Menoetes!" cried Gyas, again calling him back with a shout.

Then looking over his shoulder, Gyas saw Cloanthus pressing along the inside, taking the course to the left between the ship of Gyas and the sounding reefs. Suddenly Cloanthus passed the ship ahead of him and leaving the turning point behind, was out in the safe sea. Then indeed a great passion flared up in the soul of young Gyas. His cheeks were wet with tears and forgetting his self-control and the safety of his companions, he threw his pilot Menoetes from the high stern headlong into the sea. The captain himself went up to the helm to be the pilot, and he urged the men and twisted the helm toward the shore. When the elderly Menoetes, now weighed down with wet garments, eventually came to the surface from the very depths, he swam toward the top ledge of the reef and sat down upon the dry rock. The Trojans laughed at the slipping, swimming man, and made sport of him as he spat salt water from his mouth.

At this point the last two, Sergestus and Mnestheus, were fired with the joyful hope of defeating the lagging Gyas. Sergestus took the lead and approached the reef, though he was not ahead by the full length of his ship but only by a fraction, for the straining Shark overlapped a part with its beak.

Mnestheus, walking among his comrades in the middle of the ship, urged them on: "Now pull on the oars, O companions worthy of Hector, whom I chose as comrades in the final disaster of Troy. Now show that strength, that spirit which you displayed amid the African shoals and the Ionian Sea and the treacherous waves about the Malean headlands. I, Mnestheus, am not seeking the first prize, nor am I striving to win, although— But no! may those win to whom you have granted this joy, O Neptune. It would be a shame to come in last. Win this, comrades, and prevent that disgrace." They bent to the oars in a supreme effort; the bronze-covered ship trembled from their heavy blows, and the surface of the sea swept under it. Their chests heaved with rapid panting, their mouths were parched, and they were drenched with sweat from head to foot.

Chance itself brought the wished-for honor to the crew, for while Sergestus on the inside, in a fit of anger turned his prow toward the rocks and entered the narrow space, he was unfortunately grounded on the protruding rocks. They struck the crags, the oars crashing against the sharp ridge were splintered, and the rammed prow was held fast. The sailors rose up and loudly shouted about the delay; they seized their iron poles and their sharp-pointed pikes, or gathered up their broken oars in the waves.

But Mnestheus, more on the alert now because of his very success, with swift sweep of his oars and full sails sought the quiet sea and sailed into the open deep. Just as a dove, suddenly startled from a cave where it has its home and dear nestlings in hollowed-out pumice stone, flies over the fields and, frightened from its shelter, beats its wings violently, but soon, falling from the quiet air, glides over its watery way without moving its swift wings: so Mnestheus and his Shark in last place cut through the seas in flight. Its very impetus sent it flying and left Sergestus, who had been ahead of him, struggling on the high reef and in the shallow waters, vainly calling for help and trying to row with broken oars. Then he came alongside Gyas and his massive Chimaera, which fell behind because it was robbed of its pilot. Then only Cloanthus remained between him and the goal, and after him Mnestheus raced. Striving with all his might, he pressed onward.

Then indeed a great shout arose, and all urged on the pursuer with their cheers, and the air resounded with wild shouts. Cloanthus' sailors despised their own honor and the glory they had gained unless they could hold it, and they were ready to barter their lives for victory. Success inspired Mnestheus' men; they could because they thought they could. Perhaps the race would have ended in a tie had not Cloanthus, stretching both hands to the sea, poured out these prayers and called upon the gods to hear his vows:

"O gods, whose rule is over the deep and on whose seas I sail, I will gladly offer you before the altars a white bull, once we are on the shore, and keeping to my vow, I will throw the entrails into the salt sea and pour out liquid wine."

He finished speaking, and from the depths of the waves all Phorcus' chorus of nymphs and the virgin Panopea heard him, and father Portunus himself impelled the moving ship with his great hand. Swifter than wind or flying arrow it raced to the shore and was safe in the deep port.

Then the son of Anchises, summoning all together as was the custom, declared by the great voice of the herald that Cloanthus was the victor, and placed upon his temples the green laurel and he gave as gifts to the crew of each ship the choice of three bullocks, together with wine and a heavy silver talent to carry away. He added special honors for the captains themselves: to the victor a golden cloak, around which thick Meliboean purple runs in two borders. Woven into it the royal boy, Ganymede, on leafy Ida is speedily pursuing swift deer with a spear, clearly portrayed as if panting; the armed eagle of Jove has borne him aloft from Mount Ida with hooked claws; in vain his aged guardians stretch their hands to the heavens, and the barking of dogs sounds savagely upon the air. Then to the man who because of his performance held second place he gave for his very own, as an honor and a defense in battle, a coat of mail woven together with polished rings and three plies of gold, which he himself as victor had taken away from Demoleos near the rapid Simois under the walls of high Troy. The slaves Phegeus and Sagaris could hardly carry this heavy armor, though straining their shoulder muscles. But once upon a time, Demoleos, wearing this armor as he ran, drove the scattered Trojans before him. Aeneas made the third prize two cauldrons of brass and cups wrought from silver, embossed with relief work.

Then after a time, all the winners, proud of their treasures, were going about, their brows bound with purple bands, when Sergestus, barely freed from the savage rock by much skill, and crippled by the loss of one bank of oars, came steering his dishonored ship, an object of derision.

Often a serpent is caught on the crown of a road and crushed by a bronze wheel, or left wounded and half dead by a traveler because of a heavy blow from a rock when it was vainly trying to escape. As it coils its body, fierce in one part, its eyes burning and its neck rising high as it hisses, while the other section, paralyzed from the wound, holds it back, though it struggles with its coils and doubles itself upon its own members, in like manner the ship slowly moved itself with its oars. It hoisted its sails, however, and entered the bay under full canvas. Aeneas gave Sergestus the promised reward and was happy over the saving of the ship and the return of his comrades. He gave him a slave woman, Pholoë, gifted in the arts of the loom, a Cretan by race, with twin sons at her breast.

THE FOOT RACE

When this contest was finished, noble Aeneas moved toward a grassy plain, surrounded on all sides by forests with sloping hills. In the midst of this valley was a circular theater. To this place amid many thousands the hero strode and seated himself upon an upraised platform. Here with prizes he excited the minds of those who wished to compete in a foot race, and he offered rewards. From all sides the Trojans and the Sicilians, mingling together, assembled. First of all, Nisus and Euryalus came forward—Euryalus, of handsome physique and fresh youth, Nisus attached by a chaste love to the boy. Then they were followed by royal Diores, from the noble race of Priam, and after him by Salius and Patron at the same time—the former, an Acarnanian, the latter from the Arcadian blood of the Tegean tribe. Then came two Sicilian youths, Helymus and Panopes, accustomed to the forest, companions of the elderly Acestes, and many others, too, whose fame is lost in obscurity. In the midst of these men Aeneas thus began:

"Listen to these words I speak and attend with joyful mind. No one of this number shall go unrewarded by me. To each one I will give two shining Cretan spears of polished iron and an ax with silver engravings to carry as his own. All shall have this reward. The first three shall receive prizes, and their heads shall be crowned with the pale-green olive. The first winner shall have a horse with magnificent trappings; the second, an Amazonian quiver full of Thracian arrows, around which runs a broad golden belt, fastened by a buckle with a glistening gem; the third shall go away happy with this Greek helmet."

After these words, they took their places. On hearing the signal, they suddenly dashed onto the course and left the starting line, pouring out like a rain cloud. At the same time they marked the location of the goal. Nisus was away first and dashed out far ahead of all the others, faster than the winds and the wings of lightning. Nearest to him, but still at a very great distance, Salius followed. Then Euryalus came third in the space behind. He was followed by Helymus, after whom Diores flew, even stepping on Helymus' heels and rubbing against his shoulder. Indeed, if the course had been longer, he would have crossed the line before him, or the race would have been a tie at least.

They were wearily coming almost into the last stretch in front of the goal when Nisus unfortunately lost his footing on the slippery blood from slaughtered bulls, which happened to cover the ground and had moistened all the green grass. Here the joyous victor did not keep his footing, but unsteady once he touched this spot, he fell prone upon the unclean slime and the sacred blood. However, he was not forgetful of his dear friend Euryalus, for, rising on the slippery ground, he blocked the path of Salius, who, rolling over, lay on the packed sand. Euryalus darted forward and won the first place, thanks to his friend, and sped along amid applause and favoring shouts. Afterward Helymus came in, and the third prize went to Diores.

Thereupon Salius filled the assembly of the large theater and the first rows of the elders with great shouts, and demanded that the honor unfairly snatched from him be returned. Partiality for Euryalus, his pretty tears, and his merit, more pleasing in a handsome body, gained favor for him. Diores, who won a place, helped by shouting in a loud voice, for he would hold the last prize in vain if the first honors were returned to Salius.

Then father Aeneas said: "Your prizes are definitely yours, lads, and nobody is moving the order of the winners. Let me express sorrow for the mishap of my blameless friend." So saying, he gave Salius the huge skin of an African lion, heavy with fur and gilded claws.

Here Nisus cried out: "If such great prizes are given to the vanquished and you take pity on those who slip, what worthy gift will you give to Nisus? I would have merited the first crown with honor had hostile Fortune not mistreated me, as she did Salius."

While he spoke, he kept showing his face and his limbs, foul with moist slime. The kindliest of princes smiled upon him and ordered a shield to be brought forth, the artistry of Dydymaon, which had been taken by the Greeks from the sacred door of Neptune's temple. With this splendid gift he rewarded the noble youth.

THE BOXING MATCH

Afterward when the races were finished and the gifts distributed, Aeneas said: "Now if anyone has the courage and the spirit present in his heart, let him come forward and raise up his arms with his hands bound with leather."

So he spoke and proposed two prizes for the fight: for the victor a bullock crowned with gilded wreaths, for the loser a sword and an ornamented helmet as a consolation.

There was no delay. Straightway Dares, a man of vast powers, presented himself and boasted of his prowess amid the great applause of the men. He alone, accustomed to contend against Paris even at the tomb where great Hector lies, had struck down the champion Butes of huge frame and stretched him out, a dying man, on the yellow sand—Butes, who boasted that he came from the Bithynian race of Amycus. This Dares raised his head high, awaiting the first contest, and he showed his broad shoulders. Extending his arms alternately, he struck out and beat the air with his blows. An opponent was sought for him, but nobody from that huge throng dared to approach the man and put on the gauntlets. Therefore, thinking that everyone was yielding the prize to him, he joyfully stood before Aeneas and without any further delay, held the bull by a horn with his left hand, and spoke as follows:

"Goddess-born, if nobody dares to trust himself to the fight, what is the purpose of my standing here? How long is it fitting that I be detained? Order me to take the prize away."

At the same time, all the Trojans kept shouting their demand that the promised gifts be handed over to the man.

Thereupon Acestes severely berated Entellus as he reclined nearby on the green couch of grass: "Entellus, in vain bravest of heroes once upon a time, will you so meekly allow such great gifts to be carried away without a fight? Where now is that divine teacher Eryx, of whom we have idly boasted?

Where now is your fame in all Sicily, and those spoils hanging in your house?"

In reply to these words, Entellus said: "Neither the love of praise nor glory has yielded through craven fear, but with slowing age the chilled blood is sluggish and the worn-out powers of the body are cold. If I now had that youthfulness I once had, in which this braggart so confidently exults, I would have come forth without thought of the prize and the handsome bullock, nor do I now consider the gifts."

After speaking these words, he threw into their midst two gauntlets of immense weight with which fierce Eryx was accustomed to engage in conflict and to bind up his arms with tough hide. All were amazed at the seven great pieces of oxhide, stiff with lead and iron sewn into them. Most of all, Dares himself was astonished and shrank far back, while the greathearted son of Anchises turned the heavy, immense windings of the gauntlets over and over.

"What would anyone here think," the aging man exclaimed with feeling, "if he had seen the gauntlets and weapons of Hercules himself and that disastrous fight on this very shore? Your brother Eryx once bore these arms—you see they are still stained with blood and scattered brains—and with these he withstood the great Hercules. I was accustomed to these weapons as long as better blood gave me strength and envious old age had not scattered gray hairs along my temples. But if Trojan Dares refuses these weapons of mine, if dutiful Aeneas likes the plan, and Acestes, the sponsor of the games, approves, let us make the fight equal. For your benefit I lay aside the weapons of Eryx. Dismiss your fears and take off the Trojan gauntlets."

So saying, he threw from his shoulders his cloak of double thickness and revealed the great muscles of his limbs and his huge bones and arms. A mighty man he stood in the middle of the arena.

Then the son of Anchises brought forth matched gauntlets and wrapped their hands with equal weapons. Both, suddenly raising themselves, stood on their toes and fearlessly raised their arms up high. They drew back their proud heads far from the blows; they sparred with their hands and provoked to battle. Dares, overflowing with youth, was better at his footwork; Entellus was powerful because of his massive limbs, but his slow legs were weak and trembling, and his labored breathing shook his huge body. The men vainly exchanged many blows and struck many a time on their opponent's hollow-sounding sides. They pounded heavily on each other's chests, and frequent blows fell about their ears and temples, and their jaws chattered under hard knocks.

Grave Entellus stood unmoved in the same position, avoiding blows simply by his shifting body and his vigilant eyes. Dares, like one who attacks a high-lying city with siege machinery or camps around an armed mountain fortress, now tested this approach and that, and skillfully ranged over the whole place, vainly attacking with varying assault. Entellus, rising, held forth his right hand and raised it aloft. Dares was swift to see the blow coming from above and dodged, stepping aside with his lithe body. Entellus struck the air with full force and, off balance, his great mass fell to the earth with a heavy thud, as at times a hollow pine, torn up from its roots, falls on Mount Erymanthus or on great Ida. The Trojans and the Sicilian youths anxiously jumped up. A shout rose to the heavens. First Acestes ran forward and in pity raised up his friend, the same age as himself, from the ground, but the hero, not at all hurt or terrified by the fall, returned with more spirit to the fight and anger roused his energy. Then shame and conscious courage kindled his strength, and on fire, he drove Dares headlong over the whole plain, redoubling his blows now with his right hand and now with his left. There was no delay or rest. As clouds filled with hail rattle upon the roofs, so the hero again and again with repeated blows battered Dares and drove him about with both his fists.

Then father Aeneas, unwilling that Entellus' wrath should continue longer and that he should rage in the bitterness of his spirit, put an end to the fight and rescued the fagged Dares.

Calming him with words, Aeneas spoke as follows: "Unhappy man, what great madness has taken possession of your mind? Do you not perceive that there are other powers and that the will of heaven has changed? Yield to the god."

He spoke and with a command stopped the fight. Then the faithful companions of Dares led him to the ships, his weak knees buckling and his head lolling from one side to the other as he spat from his mouth thick gore and teeth mixed with blood. His friends were called back and received the helmet and the sword for him; they left the palm and the bull to Entellus.

The latter, gloating in spirit and proud over the bull, exclaimed: "Goddess-born, and you, O Trojans, realize what these powers of mine were when my body was young, and from what death you saved the rescued Dares."

He spoke and stood in front of the bull, which was standing nearby as a prize for the fight. Drawing back his right hand and raising himself up, with his rough gauntlets he dealt it a mighty blow between its horns and crashed into its bones, dashing out its brains. The animal was struck down; lifeless and trembling, it fell to the ground. Standing above it, he poured forth these words from his heart:

"O Eryx, to you I offer this better soul in place of the death of Dares. Here, as champion, I lay aside my gauntlets and my art."

THE ARCHERY CONTEST

Straightway Aeneas invited whoever might wish to enter the contest of the swift arrow, and he set up prizes. With his mighty hand he raised a mast from the ship of Serestus, and from that high mast he hung by a cord twisted about its leg a swift dove, at which they should aim their weapons. The men assembled, and the bronze helmet received the lot that was to be cast out. Amid favoring applause the first place of all came out for Hippocoön the son of Hyrtacus; Mnestheus, recently the victor in the naval contest, followed him—Mnestheus crowned with green olive. The third was Eurytion, your brother, famed Pandarus, who once ordered by Minerva to break the truce, first hurled a weapon into the midst of the Greeks. The last to remain in the bottom of the helmet was the lot of Acestes, who dared to assay the youthful exercise with his own hands.

Then each one of the men bent his curved bow with all his might, and they drew arrows from their quivers. The first arrow from the twanging bowstring of the youthful son of Hyrtacus cut through the swift breezes in the heavens; it struck and buried itself in the wood of the opposing mast, which trembled while the wings of the startled bird fluttered. There was great applause on all sides. Then keen Mnestheus, having drawn back his bow, took his position, and looking up, directed his gaze and his weapon at the same time. But the unlucky man was not able to touch the bird itself with his arrow. He did sever the strands of the flaxen cord by which its leg was held to the high mast, and the bird, flying on the winds, escaped into the dark clouds. Then holding his drawn weapon against his ready bow, Eurytion quickly breathed a prayer to his brother, and sighting the happy dove already beating its wings in the clear heavens under a black cloud, he transfixed it. It fell dead, leaving its life in the ethereal stars and bringing back the arrow that had pierced it in its fall. Having lost the prize, Acestes alone remained; nevertheless, the aged man shot his arrow into the airy breezes, showing his art with the twanging bow. Hereupon a marvel that was to be a famous portent suddenly appeared before their eyes; a great event later revealed this, but the frightening soothsayers foretold their omens too late. For, flying in the liquid clouds, the reed burned and marked its course with flame, and being consumed, disappeared into thin air, as falling stars often dart across the heavens and leave a trail as they shoot. In their astonishment the Sicilians and the Trojans froze where they stood, and prayed to the gods; nor did great Aeneas deny the omen, but after embracing joyful Acestes, loaded him down with valuable gifts and spoke as follows:

"Take them, father, for by such omens the great king of Olympus has willed that you receive these honors outside the competition. You shall have this gift of the aged Anchises himself to keep as a memento and a pledge of his love, an engraved bowl which Thracian Cisseus had once given to my father Anchises."

Thus speaking, he bound Acestes' temples with green laurel and called him the first winner, ahead of all the others. Nor was good Eurytion jealous of the honor to the one preferred before him, although he alone brought down the bird from high heaven. Next, the one who cut the restraining cord came forth for his gifts, and last, the one who struck the mast with his swift reed.

THE EQUESTRIAN GAMES

Now, before the contest was over, father Aeneas summoned to his side Epytides, the guard and companion of the youthful Julus, and spoke these words into his faithful ear: "Go now and tell Ascanius, if he has already lined up his troop of boys and arranged the running of the horses, that he should lead the bands in memory of his grandfather and display himself armed."

Aeneas himself ordered all the crowd that had poured out over the oval arena to move back and leave the fields wide open. The boys advanced and in straight lines glittered upon their bridled horses in the presence of their fathers, and as they rode along, all the youths of Sicily and Troy admired and cheered them. As was the custom, all wore their hair pressed down with a clipped wreath, and each bore two spears of cornel wood tipped with iron. Some carried upon their shoulder smooth quivers; a collar of flexible, twisted gold circled each neck at the top of the chest. There were three companies of horses, and each had three leaders who rode to and fro; following each one, twelve boys gleamed as the line parted behind an equal number of drill masters. The leader of one joyous line of youths, little Priam, named after his grandfather, was your famous son, Polites, destined to increase the number of Italians—Priam who rode a two-colored Thracian mount with white spots, which proudly displayed its white front feet and its white forehead. Another leader was Atys, from whom the Atian tribe of Latins took its origin, little Atys, a boy beloved by the boy Julus. The last, Julus, more beautiful in form than all the others, was mounted on a Sidonian horse which fair Dido had given him as a memento and pledge of her love. The rest of the youths rode on the Sicilian horses of the elder Acestes.

The onlooking Trojans received the timid boys with applause and rejoiced as they recognized the features of their family ancestors. After they joyfully paraded on horseback before all the assembly and the eyes of their own kin, Epytides from afar signaled to them with a shout and cracked his whip when they were ready.

They rode apart in equal units, and after the bands separated, the three groups each broke up their lines. When they were summoned back, they wheeled around and leveled their hostile lances. After this, in spaces opposite to one another, they advanced and retreated, and intermingled alternate circles with circles and staged a sham battle; now they bared their backs in flight, again they leveled their shafts in a hostile manner, and later, after making peace, rode along side by side. Just as the Labyrinth on mountainous Crete, so the story goes, had an intricate system of tunnels with blind walls and a perplexing maze of a thousand passages whereby involved and untraceable windings would prevent all signs of pursuit, by just such a course the sons of the Trojans made complicated maneuvers and worked retreats and battles into their games, like dolphins that in swimming cut through the liquid Carpathian and African seas [and sport through the waves]. Ascanius revived this custom of exercises on horseback and these contests when he surrounded Alba Longa with walls, and he taught the ancient Latins to celebrate them as he himself and the Trojan youths with him had done. The Albans taught their children; from them great Rome straightway received and kept this ancestral honor; this game of the boys is now called *Troy* and the troop *Trojan.* Thus far the contests were celebrated in honor of holy father Anchises.

THE BURNING OF THE TROJAN SHIPS

Then Fortune changed and failed them. While they were carrying out the solemn rites at the tomb with various games, Juno the daughter of Saturn, plotting many schemes—for her old grief was not appeased—sent Iris, the rainbow, down from heaven to the Trojan fleet, breathing winds upon her as she went. Swiftly making her way on her arc of a thousand colors, she came down in her rapid course as a maiden, unobserved by anyone. She viewed the huge crowd and wandered along the shores, noting the deserted port and the abandoned fleet.

Now far away, apart on a lonely shore, the Trojan women were mourning for lost Anchises and all were tearfully gazing at the deep sea. "Alas, what weariness to have come over so much water and so much sea!" was the one word on the lips of all. They prayed for a city; they were weary of suffering the labor of the sea. Therefore, Iris, skilled in troublemaking, threw herself into their midst, putting aside the face and dress of a goddess. She became Beroë, the aged wife of Doryclus of Tmaros, a man of noble birth who once had a name and offspring. In this guise she mingled among the Trojan mothers and said:

"O miserable women, you whom the Greek band did not drag down to death in the war under the walls of the fatherland! O unhappy race, for what ruin is Fortune preserving you? The seventh summer after the destruction of Troy is already returning since we have traveled over all the seas and lands, passing by so many treacherous rocks and under so many stars, while tossed on the waves, pursuing a fleeing Italy through the wide sea. Here is the friendly territory of Eryx, here our host, Acestes. Who forbids us to build walls and give our people a city? O fatherland and household gods, snatched in vain from the enemy, will no walls ever be called Trojan? Shall I never see the rivers dear to Hector, the Xanthus and the Simois? Come now! Burn with me these ill-omened ships. For as I slept, the image of the prophetess Cassandra seemed to hand me burning torches, saying: 'Here seek Troy: here is your home.' Now is the time for action, nor must there be a delay after such great portents. Behold four altars to Neptune; the god himself furnishes the torches and the spirit."

Saying these things, she first seized the fatal fire with vigor and raising her hand aloft, she brandished the flame with all her might and threw it. The minds of the Trojan women were aroused and their senses stunned. Hereupon, one of the throng, Pyrgo, the oldest, the royal nurse of so many sons of Priam, cried out: "Mothers, this is not your Beroë, nor is she the Trojan wife of Doryclus. Note the signs of her divine beauty and her gleaming eyes. Mark what spirit she has, what features; note the sound of her voice and her gait as she walks. I myself have just now left Beroë; she was ill and indignant because she alone would be absent from this ceremony and would not perform the rites due Anchises."

Thus she spoke. But the mothers, at first wavering, were gazing at the ships with spiteful eyes, torn between an unfortunate love of the land where they were sojourning and a kingdom calling with the voice of fate, when the goddess ascended to the heavens on balanced wings and cut a great arc under the clouds in her flight. Then, indeed, the women, astonished at this portent and driven by madness, shouted out and seized fire from the hearths within the homes. Some despoiled the altars and threw together foliage and brush and torches. Vulcan, the god of fire, raged in unbridled fury through the rowers' benches, the oars, and the painted sterns of fir.

Eumelus brought word to the tomb of Anchises and the assembly at the theater that the ships were on fire, and they themselves looked back to see the dark ashes rising in a cloud of smoke. And first Ascanius just as quickly sought the disturbed camp on horseback as he had gladly led the equestrian games, nor could the breathless instructors hold him back.

"What madness is this?" he cried. "What now—what do you mean? Ah, wretched women, you are not burning an enemy and a hostile camp of the Greeks but your own hopes. Look! I am your Ascanius!"

He threw at their feet his empty helmet, which he had worn while carrying out the maneuvers of the sham war. At the same time, Aeneas and the Trojans hurried to the scene, but the fearful women scattered in different directions along the shore and stealthily sought refuge in the forest or wherever there was a hollow place in the rocks. They were ashamed of their deed and loathed the light of day; being themselves once again, they recognized their own people, and the spell of Juno was cast from their hearts. But the flaming fires did not lessen their fierce fury on that account. Beneath the damp oak, hemp smoldered, pouring forth slowly rising smoke; a creeping fire consumed the timbers, and the ruin spread down through the whole framework. Nor were the efforts of the heroes or the drenching water of any avail.

Then devout Aeneas tore his garment from his shoulder and stretching forth his hands, called on the gods for help:

"All-powerful Jupiter, if as yet you do not hate the Trojans to the last man, if your former mercy pities human suffering at all, grant now that the fleet may escape the fire, O father, and save the few possessions of the Trojans from ruin; or else —the only thing that remains—send me, if I deserve it, to my death with a deadly bolt of lightning and destroy me here with your right hand." Hardly had he said this when a dark storm with a downpour of rain raged in unusual fury, and the hills and the plains trembled with thunder. From the whole sky a storm broke, whirling with rain and black with dense clouds driven by the south winds. The ships were filled with water, the half-burned oak was soaked until all the fire was extinguished. All the hulls, except four that were lost, were saved from destruction.

Now father Aeneas, crushed by this bitter disaster, turned

over these great worries in his mind, changing from this view to that, whether, unmindful of fate, he should reside in the fields of Sicily or try to reach the Italian shore. Then the elder Nautes, the sole man whom Pallas the daughter of Triton taught and made outstanding in many an art—she used to give replies explaining what the great anger of the gods foretold or what the order of the Fates demanded--began to speak, consoling Aeneas with these words:

"Goddess-born, let us follow whither the Fates call us again and again; no matter what happens, all misfortune must be overcome by patience. You have Trojan Acestes of divine origin. Take him into your counsel and make him a willing ally. Commit to him those left over because of the loss of the ships and those who have regretted taking part in your great undertaking and your designs. Choose those advanced in age and mothers tired of the sea, those who are weak and fearful of danger, and let these wearied ones have their city on this land. They shall call the city Acesta, once Acestes has granted his permission."

Roused by such words as these from his elderly friend, his mind was indeed distraught by every sort of care. Dark Night, borne aloft by her chariot, held the center of the heaven. Then the image of his parent Anchises, coming down from heaven, seemed suddenly to pour forth these words:

"My son, dearer to me than life itself when I was alive, O son harassed by the fate of Troy, I come here at the command of Jove, who drove off fire from the fleet and at length has shown pity from his high heaven. Obey the most wise commands which the aged Nautes is now giving you. Take chosen youths, the stoutest hearts, to Italy. A tough race and one fierce in its way of life you must fight in Latium. But before that, go to the home of Dis in the lower world and seek a meeting with me, my son, through deep Avernus. For impious Tartarus of gloomy shades does not hold me, but I dwell in Elysium amid the pleasant councils of the virtuous. To this place the chaste sibyl will lead you after you have sacrificed much blood from black cattle. Then you will learn about your whole race and what city will be given you. And now, farewell! Midway in her course dewy Night turns back, and cruel East has breathed upon me with his panting horses."

He finished speaking and like smoke he fled into thin air.

"Where are you rushing now?" Aeneas exclaimed. "Where are you hastening? From whom are you fleeing? Who forbids you to embrace me?" Saying these things, he roused the ashes of the smoldering fires and suppliantly venerated with blessed meal and a cloud of incense the protective deity of Troy and the sanctuary of aged Vesta.

He at once approached Acestes first and then his comrades, and he revealed both the command of Jove and the precepts of his dear father, making clear what decision he had reached in his mind. There was no delay in the planning, nor did Acestes reject the order. They enrolled the mothers in a city and left behind those who wished to stay and those who were not eager for great fame. They renewed the rowers' benches and replaced the ships' timbers, half burned by the flames, and they fitted the oars and the ropes. The crew was small in number but had courage ready for war. Meanwhile Aeneas marked off the city with a plow, and casting lots, gave out the sites for homes. He ordered that the place be called Ilium and the region, Troy. Trojan Acestes rejoiced in this kingdom and set up a court and gave laws to the assembled senators. Then close to the stars on the peak of Mount Eryx, a shrine was built to Venus of Idalia, a priest was added for the tomb of Anchises, and a grove dedicated to him, to be held sacred far and wide.

Now the whole tribe feasted and paid honors at the altars for nine days; placid waves calmed the seas, and the rising South Wind called them again to the deep. A great wail rose along the curved shore; while bidding their last farewells, they lingered for a night and a day. Now even the mothers and those men to whom once the very sight of the sea seemed repulsive and the name unbearable wished to go and to endure all the labor of voyaging. These good Aeneas consoled with friendly words and commended with tears to his kinsman Acestes. Then he ordered that a sacrifice of three bullocks to

Eryx and a lamb to the Tempests be offered, and that the moorings be loosened in their proper order. He himself, his brow bound with leaves clipped from the olive tree, standing high on the prow, held a drinking bowl and cast the sacred parts of the entrails into the salt waves and poured out the flowing wine. The wind, rising from the stern, pursued them as they went; his comrades struck the sea eagerly and swept over the deep.

VENUS APPEALS TO NEPTUNE

But in the meantime, Venus, deeply troubled, addressed Neptune and poured such complaints as these from her heart:

"The deep anger of Juno and her insatiable revenge compel me, O Neptune, to lower myself to every kind of petition, for neither time nor any show of piety melts her, nor does she rest quiet, obedient to the will of Jove and the Fates. It is not enough to have swallowed up with impious hatred the city from the midst of the Trojan race, nor to have dragged them through every kind of suffering; she even pursues the remains of Troy, the ashes and bones of the destroyed city. Let her try to explain the causes of such great madness. You yourself are my witness as to what a great storm she suddenly started not long ago on the Libyan waves; with the heavens she mingled all the seas, vainly relying on the storms of Aeolus, and she attempted this in your kingdom. See too, how, after wickedly rousing the Trojan mothers, she shamefully burned the ships, and once the fleet had been lost, forced Aeneas to leave some of his companions in an unknown land. As to the rest, I beg that by your leave they may be allowed to sail safely through the waves and to reach the Laurentian Tiber, if I seek what has been agreed upon and if the Fates permit these walls."

Then Neptune, the master of the deep sea, said: "It is altogether right, goddess of Cythera, for you to trust my kingdom, from which you take your origin. Moreover, I have merited your trust; often I have suppressed the great fury and madness of the heavens and the sea. Nor have I less care—I call to witness Xanthus and Simois—for your Aeneas on earth. When Achilles in pursuit pushed the frenzied battle lines against the walls and was killing many thousands, when the swollen rivers were groaning, and Xanthus could not find a way to pour itself into the sea, then I snatched Aeneas away from combat in a hollow cloud, since neither the gods nor the strength of the warriors was equally matched, although I wished to overturn from their very foundations the walls of perjured Troy, built by my own hands. Now my will remains the same; put aside your fear. He shall enter the port of Avernus, as you wish. There shall only be one whom you shall seek, lost in the flood; one life shall be given for many."

After calming and gladdening the heart of the goddess with these words, father Neptune harnessed his horses with a golden yoke and put foaming bits into their fierce mouths and loosened all the reins from his hands. Lightly he skimmed over the surface of the sea in his dark blue chariot; the waves subsided, the sea, swollen with billows, was laid low beneath his thundering chariot, and the clouds fled from the vast heavens. Then various faces of his companions appeared on the right, huge sea monsters, and the aged chorus of Glaucus, and Palaemon the son of Ino, and the swift Tritons, and all the army of Phorcus; on the left were Thetis and Melite, and the virgin Panopea, Nesaeë, Spio, Thalia, and Cymodoce.

THE DEATH OF PALINURUS

Then calm joy in turn filled the troubled mind of father Aeneas. He quickly ordered all the masts to be hoisted and the sails to be stretched on the arms. All the ships set the sheets together and as one, loosened now the left, now the right sail; together the high horn-tipped yards turned to and fro; favorable winds bore the fleet along. Ahead of all, Palinurus led the closely sailing line of ships; the others followed the course as he directed.

And now the dewy night had almost reached the middle

point in the heavens. The sailors, sprawled over the hard seats beneath the oars, were relaxing in peaceful calm, when gentle Sleep, gliding down from the stars of heaven, moved aside the murky air and dispelled the shadows, looking for you, Palinurus, carrying dire dreams for you, although you were guiltless.

The god in the shape of Phorbas sat upon the high deck and poured forth these words from his mouth: "Palinurus son of Iasius, the seas themselves are carrying along the fleet. Fair blow the winds; an hour for rest is given you. Lay your head down and relieve your tired eyes from weariness. I myself will perform your duties for you."

Palinurus, hardly raising his eyes, said to him: "Are you ordering me to ignore the surface of the placid sea and the quiet waves and to entrust myself to this monster? Why indeed should I entrust Aeneas to the deceiving winds, having been so often fooled by the wiles of a serene sky?"

He kept talking in this way, and clinging tightly, he never let go of the tiller, but kept his eyes fixed on the stars. Behold, the god pressed upon both his temples a branch wet with leafy dew and drugged with Stygian power, and overcame his drowsy eyes, although he resisted. Hardly had unexpected sleep relaxed his body when, bending over him, the god threw him headlong into the liquid waves with a part of the ship that was torn away together with the tiller. Often he called to his companions in vain. The god himself, flying on wings, rose into thin air. Nonetheless, the fleet ran its course safely over the sea, and suffering no harm, sailed on, as father Neptune had promised.

And now the fleet, wafted along, was approaching the cliffs of the sirens, once dangerous and white with the bones of many men, when afar off the noisy rocks resounded from the pounding of the sea. When father Aeneas realized that he was sailing off course and that his helmsman was lost, he himself guided the bark through the dark waves, grieving much and crushed in spirit at the death of his friend.

"O Palinurus, relying overmuch on a quiet heaven and sea, you shall lie naked on an unknown strand."

Book Six

PLUTO

Book Six

THE TEMPLE OF APOLLO

In tears Aeneas uttered these words, and giving the fleet full sail, at length he glided along the shores of Euboean Cumae. They turned the prows toward the sea; then the anchor with its clinging fluke held the ships, and the curved sterns were lined up along the shores. An eager band of youths leaped out upon the Hesperian shore; some sought the sparks of hidden fire in the veins of flint, while others scoured the dense forests, the lairs of wild animals, or pointed out the streams they had found.

But dutiful Aeneas sought the citadel, over which great Apollo presided, and at some distance the secret haunt of the dreaded sibyl, a vast cave. Into her the Delian prophet breathed his great mind and soul and to her he revealed the future. Soon they entered the groves of Hecate and the golden temple.

THE ART OF DAEDALUS

Daedalus, as the story goes, fleeing the kingdom of Minos and daring to take to the air on swift wings, flew to the cold north by this unusual route and at length gently landed upon the Chalcidian citadel. First touching earth there, he consecrated to you, Phoebus, his wings and established a great temple. Upon the doors were pictured the death of Androgeos and next the Athenians ordered to pay the penalty—a dreadful sight!—seven youths each year; the urn stood with the lots already drawn. On the opposite door the land of Gnossus, rising from the sea, balanced the work. Here Daedalus depicted the bull's cruel love, stealthily mated Pasiphaë, and the mixed race of the two-formed offspring, the Minotaur, recalling an unspeakable lust. Here was pictured that famed labor of the palace and its maze—inextricable had not Daedalus, taking pity on the great love of Princess Ariadne, solved the puzzling windings of the Labyrinth by guiding the blind course of Theseus. You also, Icarus, would have had a great part in this stupendous work if only grief had allowed it. Twice Daedalus tried to depict your mishap in gold; twice the father's hand fell limp.

THE SIBYL OF CUMAE

Indeed, they would have continued examining everything if Acates, who had been sent ahead, had not come up with Deiphobe the daughter of Glaucus, the priestess at once of Phoebus and Hecate. She spoke these words to Prince Aeneas:

"This is not the time to be looking at such sights as these. Now it would be better to sacrifice seven bullocks, as yet unyoked, and just as many sheep according to the custom."

Having addressed Aeneas with these words—nor did the men delay in performing the rites she commanded—the priestess summoned the Trojans into the lofty temple. The huge side of the Euboean cliff was a hollowed-out cave, to which a hundred passages and a hundred doors led and from which just as many voices, the replies of the sibyl, rolled.

They had come to the threshold when the virgin cried out: "It is time to supplicate the oracles; lo, the god!"

As she stood speaking before the entrance neither her face nor her color was the same, nor did her hair stay arranged, but her breast panted and her heart swelled in uncontrolled frenzy. She became larger, nor was her voice human, since she was breathed upon by the power of the god, now closer to her.

"Do you delay your vows and your prayers, Trojan

Aeneas?" she asked. "Do you delay? The great doors of this trembling dwelling shall not open until you comply." After these words she became silent.

A cold chill ran through the powerful frames of the Trojans, and Prince Aeneas poured forth these prayers from the bottom of his heart:

"Phoebus, always pitying the heavy trials of Troy, who directed Trojan weapons from the hands of Paris into the body of Achilles, under your guidance I have sailed so many seas touching on great lands, the land of the Massylians far and remote and the fields bordering on the Syrtes, and now at length we are reaching out for the fleeing shores of Italy. May Trojan misfortune follow me thus far and no farther. It is right that you, too, all gods and goddesses, spare the race of Pergamus, you to whom Troy and the great glory of the Dardanian land has been an object of displeasure. You, most sacred priestess, knowing the future, grant—I do not ask for a kingdom that is not due me by the will of the Fates—that the Trojans and the wandering gods and the storm-tossed divinities of Troy may settle in Latium. Then I will set up a temple of solid marble to Phoebus and Hecate, and ordain festive days named after Phoebus Apollo. Great shrines await you, too, in our realm, for there I will store your oracles and secret fates spoken to my race, and I will dedicate chosen men to your service, dear priestess. Only do not commit your verses to leaves lest, when disturbed, they fly about, the sport of the rapid winds. I beg that you yourself prophesy." Then he finished speaking.

But the prophetess, not yet yielding to the power of Phoebus, raged wildly in the cave in an effort to put the great god out of her breast; so much the more did he weary her frenzied mouth, overcoming her wild heart and forcing her to his will. Now the hundred great doors of the abode opened unaided and carried the responses of the priestess through the air:

"O you who have finally come through great perils of the sea, still greater dangers remain on land. The Trojans shall come into the kingdom of Lavinium—free your heart of this worry—but they shall wish that they had not come. I see wars, fearful wars, and the Tiber foaming with streams of blood. Another Simois shall not be missing, nor a Xanthus, nor Greek camps. Another Achilles has already been born in Latium, he, too, the son of a goddess; nor shall Juno, hating the Trojans still, relax her efforts anywhere, when you, a suppliant in dire need, ask help of so many Italian tribes, of so many cities! Again the cause of such a great evil for the Trojans is a foreign bride, again an alien marriage. Do not yield to evil, but go on even more bravely than your Fortune will allow you. The first road to safety shall be opened up by a Greek city—a thing you would least expect."

With such words the sibyl of Cumae prophesied fearful mysteries from the shrine, and her voice resounded from the cave as she mingled truth with obscurities; Apollo shook his reins over her as she raved, and turned his goads into her breast.

As soon as the madness ceased and her frenzied mouth was still, the hero Aeneas began: "O virgin, no new or unexpected aspect of trouble rises up before me; I have divined and considered everything in my own mind. One thing I ask: since the portal of the king of Hades and the dark swamp formed from the overflow of Acheron are said to be here, grant that I may go to see the face of my dear father. Show me the way and open the sacred doors. Upon these shoulders I bore him through the flames and a thousand flying weapons, and I rescued him from the midst of the enemy. Accompanying me on my voyage over all the seas, he bore all the perils of wave and sky, though suffering beyond the strength and proper lot of old age. Nay more, with a prayer he ordered that as a suppliant I should seek you and approach your threshold. Dear prophetess, I beg of you, have mercy on a son and a father—for you can do everything, nor has Hecate vainly put you in charge of the groves of Avernus. If Orpheus, carrying his Thracian harp with tuneful strings, was able to approach the shade of his wife, if Pollux redeemed his brother by dying at intervals for him, going and returning along the route so often—why should I mention Theseus, why recall Hercules? —remember that my origin, too, is from supreme Jove."

These were the words of his prayer, and he still was holding the altar when the prophetess began to speak thus:

"O you who are born of the blood of the gods, Trojan son of Anchises, easy is the descent to Avernus; the door of dark Dis stands open day and night. But to retrace your steps and come out to the air above, that is work, that is labor! A very few of divine origin, whom impartial Jupiter has loved or outstanding virtue raised to the heavens, have been able to do it. Forests occupy all the middle space, and the Cocytus, gliding along, surrounds it with a black winding stream. But if in your mind there is such a great love, such a great desire twice to cross the Stygian lake, twice to see dark Tartarus, and it pleases you to indulge in this insane toil, attend to what must be done in advance. A bough, considered sacred to Proserpine, golden its leaves and pliant stems, is hidden in a certain tree with heavy foliage; all the grove covers it, and shadows enclose it in a dark valley. But the right to enter the hidden regions of the earth is not given until one plucks the golden sprig from the tree. Beauteous Proserpine has ordained that this very gift of hers must be brought along. When the first bough is plucked, a second golden bough appears in its place, and a branch of like metal blooms. Therefore, look with your eyes aloft, and once you have rightly found it, seize it in your hand: for it will come off naturally and easily if the Fates are summoning you; otherwise, you shall not be able to overcome it with any force or to wrench it away with hard iron. Moreover, the lifeless body of your friend lies in death —alas you do not know it!—and the whole fleet is defiled because of his body, while you seek oracles and linger upon our threshold. First, place him in his last resting place and bury him in a tomb. Lead forth black cattle; let these be the first purifying sacrifice. Only in this way shall you see the groves and the kingdom of Styx, untrod by the living." She spoke and remained silent, her lips tightly pressed together.

LAMENT FOR MISENUS; HIS PYRE

Leaving the cave, Aeneas, with downcast eyes and sad face, walked along, turning over these mysterious happenings in his mind. With him went his faithful companion, Achates, revealing a like worry as he trod the ground. They discussed many things in their varied talk, what companion the prophetess told them was dead and what body ought to be buried. As they proceeded, they saw on the dry shore Misenus, swept away by a premature death, Misenus the son of Aeolus. There was no one more gifted than he in rousing men with the trumpet and stirring the spirit of Mars with his notes. Distinguished for his trumpet and his spear, he had been the companion of great Hector, and at his side had gone into battle. After victorious Achilles deprived Hector of his life, the great hero Misenus enlisted as a companion in arms with Trojan Aeneas, following just as renowned a leader. But once when he happened to make the sea ring by blowing on his hollow shell and —insane fellow!—challenged the gods to a competition in trumpeting, then jealous Triton seized the man, if we can believe the story, and drowned him in foaming waves among the rocks.

Thereupon, all, especially devout Aeneas, lamented with a great shout. Then without delay, they mournfully hastened to carry out the commands of the sibyl, and strove to build a funeral pyre with trees, and raised it heavenward. They went into the ancient forest, the lofty dens of wild animals, and felled pine trees. The holm oak, struck by axes, resounded; they split beams of ash and straight-grained oak with wedges, and rolled down great ash trees from the mountains. Aeneas was the first to urge on his comrades amid such work, handling like tools himself.

THE GOLDEN BOUGH

He turned over these matters in his sad heart, as he looked about at the immense forest, and uttered aloud this prayer: "If only now that golden bough would show itself to us in this great grove, since the prophetess has spoken everything truly, alas too truly about you, Misenus."

He had hardly uttered these words when two doves by chance came flying down from heaven before his very face and rested upon the green sward. Then the great hero recognized his mother's birds and prayed with joyful heart: "Be my leaders, and if there is a path, direct through the air my course into the grove where the rich bough shades the fertile earth. Dear mother, do not fail me in this moment of doubtful issue."

Having spoken thus, he slackened his pace, observing what signs they brought and what direction they took. While feeding, they flew ahead as far as the eyes of the men following could keep them in sight. When from there they came to the mouth of ill-smelling Avernus, they rose up quickly and, gliding through the liquid air, came to rest upon the double-natured tree in the desired spot, whence a variegated sheen gleamed through the golden branches. As in the wintertime, mistletoe in the forests usually breaks out with new leaves, which its own stock does not produce, and surrounds smooth trunks with a yellow growth; such was the beauty of the leafy gold on the dark ilex, thus the gold leaf rustled in the gentle wind. Though the bough resisted, Aeneas suddenly seized it and eagerly pulled it off. Then he bore it into the dwelling of the prophetic sibyl.

THE BURIAL OF MISENUS

Meanwhile the Trojans continued to weep for Misenus, as they performed the last rites over his unfeeling ashes. First, they constructed a huge pyre heavily laden with pitch pine and cut oak, into whose side they worked black leaves. In front of this they placed funereal cypresses, and above they adorned it with gleaming weapons. Some took care of the warm water and the kettles boiling over the flames, and washed and anointed the cold body of the hero. A great wail arose. Then they placed his lamented body on the couch and thereon they threw purple garments, the usual dress. Some advanced toward the great bier—a sorrowful ministry—and turning their gaze aside, applied the torch, as parents do. Offerings of incense, victims, and bowls, after the oil had been poured out, were heaped high upon the fire. After all was reduced to ashes and the flame had subsided, they sprinkled the remains of the thirsty ashes with wine, and Corynaeus placed the collected bones in a bronze urn. He likewise blessed his comrades three times, sprinkling over them a light dew with a fruitful olive branch, purifying them as he spoke the last words of farewell. In addition, devout Aeneas erected a tomb of great size and set up as emblems the oar and trumpet alongside the hero at the foot of a mountain, which is now called Misenus after him, holding that name forever, throughout the ages.

SACRIFICES TO THE GODS OF THE NETHER WORLD

When this was done, he quickly carried out the commands of the sibyl. There was a deep cave, frightful with a vast, yawning mouth, rocky and protected by a black lake and the darkness of the groves. Over this opening hardly any birds could wing their way without harm, such was the vapor pouring from the dark throat and rising to the vault above. [For this reason the Greeks called the place by the name *Birdless*.] Here first he offered four black-backed bullocks. The priestess poured out wine upon their foreheads and seizing the ends of the long hairs between the horns, she put them in the sacred fires as the first offerings, calling aloud to Hecate, powerful in heaven and in the lower world. Some plunged daggers into the throats of the animals and caught the warm blood in bowls. Aeneas himself slew with his sword a black-fleeced lamb as an offering to Night, the mother and great sister of the Furies, and a sterile cow to you, Proserpine. Then he consecrated to Pluto, the king of the Styx, altars to be used at night, and placed upon the flames whole carcasses of bulls, pouring rich oil upon the burning entrails.

Behold, however, just at the first light of the rising sun, the earth began to rumble under their feet and the forest ridges to move, and dogs seemed to howl through the darkness as the goddess came.

"Go far away, O far away, profane men," the priestess cried. "Depart from the entire grove. But you, Aeneas, take up the course, draw your sword from its sheath. Now there is need for courage, now there is need for a firm heart."

Saying no more, under the influence of a divine frenzy, she plunged into the open cave; with steps not at all timid he kept up with his guide ahead of him.

DESCENT TO HADES

O gods, whose rule is over souls, and you, silent shades, and Chaos and Phlegethon, places silent far and wide during the night, may I be allowed to say what I have heard, and with your blessing lay bare secrets hid in the darkness of the deep earth. Scarcely visible in the lonely night, they went along through the shadows by the phantom houses in the barren realm of Dis. It was such a trip as one takes in the forest under the treacherous light of a feeble moon, when Jupiter has hid the heavens in shadow, and the dark night has taken away color from nature.

Before the very entrance and in the very jaws of Orcus, Sorrow and avenging Cares set up their couches. There dwelt pale Disease and sorrowful Age, Fear, Hunger that persuades to evil, and squalid Poverty—forms terrible to behold—and Death and Toil; there also Sleep, the kinsman of Death, and the sinful Joys of the mind, deadly War on the opposite threshold, and the iron chambers of the Furies, and insane Strife, whose viper hair is bound with blood-stained fillets. In the middle of the court a huge shadowy elm spreads its gnarled branches, around which, they say, a swarm of vain Dreams dwells, clinging under all the leaves. In addition there are many monstrous shapes of various wild animals. Centaurs have their stalls at the doors, as do shapes like the two-formed Scylla, hundred-handed Briareus, the hydra of Lerna, wildly shrieking, the Chimaera armed with flames, Gorgons and Harpies, and the shape of a triple-bodied shade. Hereupon Aeneas, panic-stricken with sudden fear, seized his sword and presented its drawn edge to these advancing shapes. Had not his wise companion advised him that they were thin bodiless spirits flitting about under the shadowy image of a form, he would have attacked them and vainly beaten the air with his sword.

From here there was a road that led to the waves of hell's Acheron. Here a stream churning with slime from a vast whirlpool boiled up and threw all its sand into the Cocytus. The horrifying toll collector Charon, frightfully squalid, guarded the waters of these rivers. His chin had a great growth of unkempt gray hair, his eyes were aflame, and from his shoulders there hung a foul garment, held up by a knot. He himself pushed along the boat with a pole, managed the sails, and carried bodies across in his iron-colored skiff. Though he was old, his age had the vigor and freshness of a god.

All the crowd kept rushing in a stream to this point on the banks—mothers and husbands and greathearted heroes deprived of life, boys and unmarried maidens and youths, placed upon their pyres before the eyes of their parents—even as many fluttering leaves fall in the forests at the first cold of autumn or as many birds gather on the land from the deep flood when the cold year puts them to flight across the sea and sends them to lands of sunshine. They stood, praying to be the first to make the journey across, and stretched forth their hands in their desire for the farther shore. But the grim boatman received now these spirits, now those, but pushed others far back from the beach.

Aeneas, astonished and moved at the tumult, asked: "Tell me, virgin, what does this gathering at the river mean? What do these souls want? Why do these remain on the shores while those sweep over the murky waters with oars?"

The aged priestess thus addressed him briefly: "Son of Anchises, undoubted offspring of the gods, you see the deep pools of Cocytus and the Stygian swamp by whose power the gods fear to swear falsely. All this crowd which you see is poor and unburied. The toll collector is Charon; these are buried people whom he carries across on the wave, nor is he allowed to transport over the noisy flood those on the banks until their bones have rested in the tomb. For a hundred years they wander about and flit around these shores. Then finally, when permitted, they revisit these wished-for pools."

The son of Anchises stood still and slowed his pace, pitying in thoughtful mood their unhappy lot. There he saw Leucaspis and the leader of the Lycian fleet, Orontes, sad men, lacking the honors of burial. The South Wind fell upon them as they were sailing together from Troy over the windy sea, overwhelming the men and their ship in the flood.

MEETING WITH PALINURUS

Suddenly the helmsman Palinurus approached, who, while observing the stars some time before on the voyage from Libya, had fallen headlong from the ship into the midst of the waves. When Aeneas with difficulty recognized this gloomy man amid the heavy shadows, he first addressed him thus:

"Which of the gods snatched you from us, Palinurus, and drowned you in the midst of the seas? Come, tell me. For though never found false before, Apollo, who prophesied that you would be unharmed by the sea and that you would come to the borders of Italy, deceived me in this one revelation. Is this his promised fidelity?"

But he replied: "My leader, son of Anchises, the oracle of Phoebus has not deceived you, nor did the god drown me in the sea. For as I fell headlong, I dragged along the tiller, which by chance was wrenched away by a great force, to which as its appointed guard I was clinging, and with which I was guiding the course. By the rough seas, I swear that, as far as I was concerned, I feared nothing so much as that your ship, deprived of its rudder and its helmsman tossed overboard, would capsize amid such great billows. For three wintry nights the wind, whipping up the waves, bore me through the measureless seas. Just at the dawn of the fourth day, riding the crest of a wave, I saw Italy. Slowly I swam toward the land. Soon I would have been safe if a cruel people, ignorantly thinking me a rich prize, had not attacked me with swords when I was weighed down by wet clothes and was seizing with grasping hands the rough edges of the cliff. Now the waves possess me, and the winds blow me about on the shore. For this reason, I beseech you, unconquered hero, by the pleasant light and the air of heaven, by your father, by your hope in growing Julus, snatch me from these evils. Either throw earth upon me, for you can, and seek the port of Velia, or if there is any way which your goddess mother shows you—for I do not believe that you are preparing to cross such great rivers and the Stygian swamp without the help of the gods—aid a miserable man and take me with you over the waves so that at least in death I may rest in a peaceful abode."

Thus had he spoken when the prophetess began with these words: "How, Palinurus, has such an impious desire as this entered your mind? Although unburied, you wish to see the waters of the Styx and the awful river of the Furies, and unbidden you would approach its bank? Cease hoping to turn aside the will of the gods by your prayers. But keep this well in mind as a solace for your dire mishap. Indeed, neighbors, induced by heavenly prodigies far and wide through the cities, shall take pity on your bones, and they shall erect a tomb and there conduct solemn rites. The place shall have the everlasting name of Palinurus."

Because of these words, his worries were quieted, and for a short time grief left his sorrowing heart as he rejoiced in the naming of the land.

CHARON

Then they continued the journey they had begun and approached the river. When the boatman, even from that distance on the Stygian wave, saw them coming through the silent grove and directing their footsteps to the shore, he addressed them first with these words and even scolded them:

"Whoever you are who come armed to our shore, speak up and tell from where you are, why you come, and advance no farther. This is the place of ghosts, of Sleep and drowsy Night. It is sacrilegious to carry living bodies in this boat. Indeed, I did not rejoice ferrying Hercules when he came to this lake, nor Theseus and Pirithous, although they were born of the gods and had never been conquered by any power. With his bare hands Hercules sought to chain the watchdog of hell and dragged it trembling from the throne of King Pluto himself; the other two attempted to carry off Queen Proserpine from the bedchamber of Pluto."

In reply to these words, the Amphrysian prophetess spoke briefly: "Here there is no such stratagem—do not be alarmed—nor do these weapons have any force. Let the great doorkeeper, barking in his cave, forever terrify the pale ghosts; let chaste Proserpine stay within her uncle's home. Trojan Aeneas, outstanding for his reverence and military exploits, descends to see his father amid the dark shades of Erebus. If the picture of such great piety does not move you, then recognize this branch."

She showed the stem that was hidden in her garment. Then the swelling anger in the heart of Charon subsided, and he said no more. Marveling at the sacred gift of the fated bough, seen now after so long a time, he turned his dark ship and made for the shore. Then he scattered other ghosts that were sitting on the long benches, and he cleared the gangways. At the same time he received huge Aeneas. The ship, made from sewed leather, groaned under his weight, and being full of cracks, let in a flood of water from the swamp. At length Charon landed the prophetess and the hero across the river on the foul slime and the dark sedge.

CERBERUS

Great Cerberus, with his triple-throated barking, thundered through this domain, a monstrous beast lying in a cave in front of them. The prophetess, seeing its necks already bristling with snakes, threw it a cake, drugged with honey and sleep-producing grain. Opening its three mouths with ravenous hunger, it seized the food thrown it, and sprawling on the ground, relaxed its great frame and extended its huge body through the whole cave. Once the watchdog was buried in sleep, Aeneas entered the cave and quickly left the shore of the waters that may not be recrossed.

THE ABODE OF INFANTS, THE FALSELY ACCUSED, AND SUICIDES

Immediately at the very entrance voices were continuously heard and a great wailing of infants and weeping spirits whom a dark day had carried off and buried in bitter death, depriving them of sweet life and snatching them from their mothers' breasts. Near these were spirits condemned to death on false accusations. Indeed these places are not given out without a judge's casting lots: the magistrate Minos moves the urn; he summons the council of the silent shades and discovers the crimes of men's lives. Then the next places are occupied by those sad people who, being guiltless, committed suicide, and hating the light of day, threw away their lives. How they would now wish to be in the world above and to bear poverty and hard labor! But the divine law forbids this, and the hated pool with its gloomy waters holds them, and the Styx, encircling them nine times, confines them.

THE FIELDS OF MOURNING

Not far from here the Fields of Mourning—by this name they are called—came into view, extending in every direction. Here secret paths conceal those whom harsh love destroyed with cruel pining, and a forest of myrtle trees protects them. Their cares do not leave them even in death. In this place he made out Phaedra and Procris and sad Eriphyle, showing the wounds received from her cruel son, and Evadne and Pasiphaë; Laodamia goes along as their companion and Caeneus, once changed to a youth but now a woman again, returned by fate to her original form.

MEETING WITH DIDO

Among these, Phoenician Dido with a fresh wound was wandering about in the great forest. As soon as the Trojan hero stood nearby and faintly recognized her through the shadows—as one who at the first of the month sees or thinks he has seen the moon rising through the clouds—he began to weep and addressed her with words of sweet love:

"Unhappy Dido, then the message that reached me was true, that you had taken your life by the sword? Alas, was I the cause of your death? I swear by the stars, my queen, by the gods above and whatever faith there is here in the lower regions, that I departed unwillingly from your shore. But divine commands, which now compel me to go through these shadows and this rough wasteland of utter darkness, drove me by their orders. I could not believe that by leaving I was bringing such great sorrow as this upon you. Check your steps and do not withdraw from my sight. From whom are you fleeing? This is fated to be the last word that I may speak to you."

With such pleas Aeneas kept trying to calm the angry spirit of Dido, who glared at him fiercely, and he began to weep. Her gaze averted, she kept her eyes fixed on the ground, nor from the time he began to talk did her expression change any more than if she were made of the hard flint of a Marpesian crag. At length she darted away and in hostile mood fled into the thick-shaded grove where her former husband, Sychaeus, sorrowed with her in her sorrow and returned her love with love. Nevertheless, Aeneas, crushed by her unjust misfortune, in tears followed her afar off and pitied her as she departed.

MEETING WITH TROJAN WARRIORS

From then on, the road they were permitted to travel became more difficult. Already they were coming to the most remote fields where famed warriors lived apart. Here Tydeus, here Parthenopaeus, renowned for his deeds in arms, and the ghost of pale Adrastus met him. Here were Trojans fallen in war and much lamented on earth. For all of them he mourned as he saw them in a long line: Glaucus, Medon, Thersilochus, the three sons of Antenor, Polyboetes the priest of Ceres, and Idaeus, still gripping his chariot, still holding his weapons. Numbers of ghosts crowded around him on the right and left; nor were they satisfied when they had seen him once. It was pleasing to them to delay him further, to walk along with him and learn the cause of his coming. But when the chieftains of the Greeks and the battle lines of Agamemnon saw the hero and his shining arms through the shadows, they trembled with great fear. Some turned their backs, just as they once did when they fled to their ships; some raised a squeaking voice, but the shout they began failed as they opened their mouths.

And here he saw Deiphobus the son of Priam, whose entire body was lacerated, whose face and hands were cruelly mutilated, whose ears were torn from his temples, and whose nose was disfigured by an unsightly wound. Aeneas hardly recognized him, trembling thus and covering his grim wounds, and he addressed him first with familiar words:

"Deiphobus, powerful in arms, sprung from the noble blood of Teucer, who wanted to wreak such cruel punishment upon you? Who was allowed to do you so much harm? The story reached me that on the last night, worn out from slaughtering many Greeks, you had fallen upon a mass of unrecognizable carnage. Then I set up an empty tomb on the Rhoetean shore and with a loud voice I thrice called upon your spirit. Your name and arms mark the place. Friend, since I was departing, I was unable to find you and bury you in your fatherland."

"You left nothing undone," the son of Priam answered. "You have carried out all the rites for Deiphobus and the shade of his dead body. But my fate and the foul crime of Helen overwhelmed me with these evils; she left me these tokens. For you know how we passed the last night amid false rejoicing. One can remember it only too well. When the fateful horse overleaped high Pergamus and, weighted down, carried armed soldiers in its hollow, Helen, simulating a religious procession, led the Trojan women about, celebrating the rites to Bacchus. She herself in their midst held a great torch and signaled to the Greeks in the high citadel. At that time, I was in my ill-fated bedroom, overcome with worry and buried in sleep. A sweet and deep repose, very much like placid death, lay upon me. Meanwhile, that exemplary wife had removed all the weapons from the house and taken away my faithful sword from under my pillow. Into the house she called Menelaus and opened the doors, hoping, of course, that this would be a great service to her loving husband and that thus she could erase the ill repute of her former wickedness. But why do I delay? They rushed into the bedroom. The son of Aeolus, that inciter to crime, joined him as his companion. O gods, repay the Greeks for such crimes, if I demand their punishment devoutly! But pray tell in turn what chance has brought you alive to this place. Do you come driven over the sea in your wanderings, or at the admonition of the gods?

What ill fortune goads you to approach these sad, sunless homes, these dismal places?"

At this point in their talk, Dawn with her rosy chariot had already crossed the middle of the heavens in her ethereal course. They might have spent all the allotted time in this way, but his companion, the sibyl, admonished him, speaking briefly:

"The night is rushing on, Aeneas; we are passing the hours in weeping. This is the place where the road parts in two directions: on the right is the one that leads up to the very walls of great Dis, and by this route we go to Elysium. But the left road inflicts punishment upon the wicked and sends them to the hell of the damned."

Deiphobus replied: "Do not be angry, great priestess. I will depart. I will join the other ghosts and return to the darkness. Go, go, glory of Troy; enjoy a better fate." Having said so much, he turned away as he spoke.

TARTARUS

Aeneas looked off to the side and suddenly saw under a cliff to the left a far-scattered castle surrounded by a triple wall. Around this, Phlegethon, the rapid river of hell, flows with rolling flames and hurls up sounding rocks. Straight ahead, there is a great gate and columns of adamant so solid that no human power, not even the gods themselves, could destroy them with engines of war. An iron tower rises heavenward, and seated Tisiphone, clothed in a blood-stained mantle, tirelessly guards the entrance night and day. From here are heard groans and the sounding of savage lashes, then the crunching of iron and the dragging of chains. Aeneas halted, and frightened at the noise, stood still.

"Maiden, say what kind of crimes have they committed; with what punishments are they being tortured? What great lamentation is born on the breeze?"

Then the prophetess began to speak thus: "O famed leader

of the Trojans, it is right for no innocent man to set foot on this wicked threshold; but when Hecate put me in charge of the groves of Avernus, she explained the punishments meted out by the gods, and led me through all this region. Here Rhadamanthus of Gnossus maintains his harsh rule. He chastises; he hears the recital of crimes and forces a confession from everyone who, rejoicing in his foolish deception while among the living, deferred the atonement of his crimes until death, when it is too late. Immediately, vengeful Tisiphone, armed with a whip, tramples and lashes the guilty, and wielding the fierce snakes with her left hand, summons the savage band controlled by her sisters. Then finally the dreadful gates with screeching, harsh-sounding hinges lie open. Do you see what guard sits at the entrance, what form keeps watch over the thresholds? A still more savage hydra, fierce with fifty black mouths, has its den inside. Then, too, hell itself extends twice as far down into the shadows as the view to the peak of airy Olympus.

"Here the ancient race of Earth, the offspring of the Titans, struck down by a thunderbolt, turned over and over in the deep abyss. Here I saw the savage bodies of the twin sons of Aloeus, who tried to tear down with their hands the great heavens and to unseat Jove from his high kingdom. I saw Salmoneus suffering cruel punishments because he imitated the lightning of Jove and the thunder of Olympus. Drawn by four horses and waving a torch, he went joyously through the lands of the Greek people and through the city in the center of Elis, demanding divine honors for himself, insane man to simulate thunder clouds and inimitable lightning with bronze and the beating of horn-footed horses! But the all-powerful father hurled his weapon among the dense clouds. Jupiter did not hurl firebrands nor flash lights from smoking torches, but he drove Salmoneus with the fierce onrush of the thunderbolt. One could see Tityus also, a child of the all-producing Earth, whose body is stretched out over nine full acres. A huge vulture with a hooked beak, plucking the ever-growing liver and the vitals, tears at the feast and lives under the high breast of Tityus; nor is any rest given the constantly renewed tissue. Why should I talk of the Lapiths, of Ixion, and of Pirithous, over whom hangs a dark stone, already on the point of falling and actually appearing to fall? The golden supports of high festive couches shine brightly, and a banquet of royal splendor is prepared before their eyes. The oldest of the Furies reclines nearby and forbids them to touch the table with their hands, and brandishing a torch, she rises and growls at them.

"Here are those who in life envied their brothers or struck a parent or plotted treachery against a client; those who hoarded up money that they found, without giving some to their relatives; these last make up the largest crowd. Here, too, those who were slain because of adultery and those who followed treasonable arms without fearing to break their agreements with their masters, await punishment, shut up in prison. Do not ask to be told what punishment they await or what kind of misfortune has buried them in the abyss. Others roll along a huge stone or hang spread out on the spokes of wheels. Unfortunate Theseus sits there and will sit forever; Phlegyas, a most miserable man, admonishes all and loudly proclaims through the shadows: 'Being warned, learn justice and do not scorn the gods.' For money one man sold his fatherland and set over it a powerful master, and he passed and annulled laws for a price; another entered into the chamber of his daughter and a forbidden marriage. All dared to do some barbarous wickedness and accomplished what they dared. If I had a hundred tongues and a hundred mouths and an iron voice, I could not list all the types of crimes or run through all the names of the tortures."

After the aged priestess of Phoebus had spoken these words, she said: "But come now! Begin the trip; finish the duty you have begun. Let us hurry. I see the bastion built by the forges of the Cyclopes and the arched doors in front of us where we are directed to place these ordered gifts."

She finished speaking, and moving along the dark route side by side, they covered the intervening space and approached the doors. Aeneas crossed the threshold, sprinkling his body with fresh water, and placed the branch on the doorstep in front of him.

THE ELYSIAN FIELDS

When these requirements were finally carried out and the rite to the goddess was performed, they came to the happy region and the pleasant green of the happy groves and the blessed seats. Here a freer air clothed the fields with brilliant light, and the shades enjoyed their own sun and their own stars. Some exercised their bodies on the grassy turf, contended in sports, or wrestled on the yellow sand; some beat out dances with their feet and sang songs. The Thracian priest Orpheus in his long robe swept in accompaniment the seven strings of his lyre, now striking them with his fingers and now with his ivory pick. Here was the ancient race of Teucer, a most illustrious progeny, great heroes born in better years, and Ilus, Assaracus, and Dardanus, the founder of Troy. Afar off he gazed at the weapons and the empty chariots of the heroes. Their spears stood fixed in the ground, and their horses freely grazed here and there through the field. The same pleasure they had during life in chariots and arms, the same interest they had in pasturing their sleek horses followed them when they went to their death. On the right and left he saw other men feasting as they lay on the grass and singing in chorus the joyful song of victory in the fragrant laurel grove, from which the great river Eridanus rose through the forest to the upper region. Here were bands of those men who suffered wounds fighting for the fatherland, those who were chaste priests when life was theirs, those who were devout poets and who spoke what was worthy of Phoebus, or those who spent their lives in artistic invention or who by reason of their merit caused men to remember them. The temples of all these men were bound with a snowy crown.

The sibyl addressed these assembled men, especially Musaeus, for he was in the center of the largest group, and she looked up at him, a man head and shoulders over the others:

"Tell us, happy spirits, and you, O best of poets, in what region, in what place is Anchises? Because of him we have crossed over the great rivers of Erebus."

And the hero thus replied to her in these words: "No one has a definite house. We live in the dark groves and dwell on soft banks and fresh meadows by the rivers. But if this is your desire, climb this ridge, and I will soon put you on the easy path."

He spoke and walking ahead, pointed out the shining fields from above. From here they left the lofty heights.

AENEAS MEETS ANCHISES

Now father Anchises, deep in the green valley, was looking with thoughtful interest at the imprisoned spirits that were to go to the light of the world above, and he happened to be reviewing all the host of his kinsmen and his dear descendants, the fates and fortunes of these men, their customs and mighty deeds. When he saw Aeneas coming toward him over the grass, he joyously stretched forth his arms, and as tears streamed down his cheeks, these words came from his lips:

"Have you come at last and has your devotion, long awaited by your parent, conquered the rough journey? Am I permitted to look upon your face, my son, and to hear and answer your familiar voice? Thus indeed I calculated and thought it would be, as I reckoned the time, nor did my hopes deceive me. I welcome you, my son, borne over how many lands and what vast seas, and tossed about by what perils! How I feared that the kingdom of Libya might harm you!"

"Your sad ghost," Aeneas replied, "appearing so often to me, forced me to set out for these regions: the fleet is anchored on the Tuscan Sea. Give me your right hand, father, please, and do not withdraw from my embrace."

Thus he spoke, as tears coursed down his face. Three times he attempted to put his arms around his neck, and three times the image, vainly grasped, escaped his hands, like gentle breezes or a fleeting dream.

Meanwhile, in a remote valley, Aeneas saw a secluded grove and the murmuring thickets of a forest and Lethe's stream, which flows past quiet dwellings. About this river, races and peoples without number were flitting; as when bees in the peaceful summer rest in the meadows on various flowers and swarm about white lilies, so over all the plain their murmuring was heard. Aeneas was startled at the sudden sight and asked the cause, not knowing what those rivers in the distance were and what men covered the banks in such a dense mass.

ANCHISES EXPLAINS REBIRTH OF SOULS

Then father Anchises replied: "These are souls destined by fate to have second bodies; at the wave of the river Lethe they drink the care-banishing waters of long forgetfulness. Indeed, for a long time I have been desiring to tell you about these spirits, to show them to you face to face, and to list my numerous progeny so that you may rejoice the more with me when you have found Italy."

"O father, is it possible that any souls go from here to the light of day above and again return to sluggish bodies? What a fierce desire for the light of day these miserable beings must have!"

"Indeed I will tell you and not hold you in suspense, my son." Anchises began and explained everything in order. "First of all, a spirit within sustains the heavens, the earth and the seas, the shining moon and the sun; mind, infused through the various parts, moves the whole mass and mingles itself with the great body of the universe. From this mind come the race of men and beasts, the life of birds, and the monsters that the sea produces under its smooth surface. But these seeds have a fiery force of celestial origin insofar as harmful bodies do not retard them nor earthly limbs nor mortal parts weaken them. For this reason they fear and desire, they grieve and rejoice. These souls do not discern the light of day, enclosed as they are in the darkness of the windowless prison of the body.

"Even when life departs from the body on the last day, all evil does not straightway leave miserable souls, nor do all bodily ills entirely disappear. Indeed it must necessarily be that many impurities, intermingling for so long a time, take deep root in a marvelous way. Therefore, they are punished and pay the penalty for their former wrongs. Others are hung up and exposed to the unseen winds; from others the stain of crime is washed away by torrents of water or burned out by fire. We each suffer our own expiation; then we are admitted into the vast region of Elysium. A few of us keep to these happy fields until that far-off day, after the circle of time has been completed, takes away the stain of impurity and leaves the ethereal sense purified, a spark of pure spirit. When they have completed the cycle of a thousand years, the god summons all of them in a dense throng to the river Lethe in order that they may visit again the vaulted world above and begin desiring to return to bodies."

ANCHISES POINTS OUT FUTURE HEROES OF ROME

After Anchises finished speaking, he drew his son and with him the sibyl into the midst of the assembly and the murmuring throng, and occupied a mound whence he could survey everybody in a long line opposite him and examine the features of those approaching.

"Now come, and I will explain what glory shall later follow Trojan progeny, what descendants shall stem from the Italian race, illustrious souls destined to bear our name, and I will tell you your fate. Look! That youth leaning upon the headless spear has by lot the place closest to the light above, and he shall be the first mixed with Italian blood to rise to the upper region—Silvius, an Alban name, your posthumous offspring, whom Lavinia your wife shall bear you in your old age, a king over the forests and a parent of kings. From him our race shall rule over Alba Longa.

"That next one is Procas, the glory of the Trojan race, and then Capys and Numitor and the one who shall bear your name, Silvius Aeneas, outstanding equally for his piety and arms, if he ever comes into the rule of Alba. What youths they are! Look, what strength they show! They bear on their brows garlands of civic oak! They shall set up for you Nomentum, Gabii and the city Fidenae; they shall set up Collatine citadels in the mountains, Pometii, and the fort of Inuus, Bola, and Cora. These shall be their names then; now they are nameless lands.

"Indeed Romulus, a child of Mars, whom his mother Ilia, from the race of Assaracus, shall bring forth, shall join his grandfather as a companion. Do you see how the twin crests rise from his head and how his father marks him with the honors of divinity? Lo, my son, Rome, famed by his auspices, shall extend her rule over the world and her spirit to Olympus; for her own protection she shall surround the seven hills with a wall. She shall be happy in her male offspring, just as the Berecinthian mother, borne, turret-crowned, in her chariot through the Phrygian cities, is happy in her divine offspring, possessing a hundred descendants, all dwellers of heaven, all with their homes in high heaven.

"Now turn your gaze here. Look at this race, your Romans. Here is Caesar and all the progeny of Julus that shall rise to the great world above. Here is the hero, here is the man whom you have often heard promised to you, Caesar Augustus of the race of the divine Julius, who shall again establish the golden age through the land once ruled by Saturn of Latium, who shall extend his rule over the Garamantes and the Indians—a land that lies beyond the stars, beyond the path of the year and the sun, where Atlas the heaven-bearer turns the firmament, studded with gleaming stars, upon his shoulders. At the thought of his coming, already the Caspian kingdom and the Scythian land shudder at the oracles of the gods, and the Nile of seven mouths is troubled with fear. Indeed, Hercules did not cover so much of the earth, although he shot the bronze-footed deer, pacified the groves of Erymanthus, and caused Lerna to tremble with his bow. Nor did Liber travel so far, who victoriously manages his team with vine-wreathed reins, driving his tigers from the high peak of Nysa. And do we still hesitate to display our courage in action, or does fear hold us back from settling on Ausonian land?

"But who is that man afar off, carrying sacred objects, distinguished by his olive branch? I recognize the gray locks and beard of a Roman king who shall set up laws for the growing city, a man sent from the poor land of little Cures to great dominion. Then Tullus shall succeed, who shall destroy the ease of the fatherland and rouse slothful men to arms and battle lines long unaccustomed to triumphs. Next to him follows the rather arrogant Ancus, who even now is too ready to court popular favor. And do you wish to see also the Tarquin kings and the proud soul of the avenger Brutus and the recovered fasces? He shall be the first to receive the power of the consul and the fearful axes, and as a father, he shall condemn to punishment his sons, instigating revolution in defense of sweet liberty. Unhappy man, no matter how future generations shall record these facts. Love for the fatherland and man's immense desire for praise are bound to prevail. But look now at the Decii and the Drusi afar off and cruel Torquatus with his ax and Camillus, bringing back the standards.

"But those spirits yonder that you see shining in identical armor, in agreement now while they are captive in the realm of night, alas! what a great war between themselves and what great battle lines and slaughter they shall cause if they reach the light of day. The one, a father-in-law, descending from the Alpine mountains and the height of Monoecus, the other, a son-in-law in battle array with forces from the East! Do not, my children, foster such great wars in your minds nor turn such strong powers against the heart of the fatherland. You, the more noble, who take your origin from Olympus, hold back! Cast your weapons from your hand, my offspring!

"Yonder famed victor Mummius shall drive his chariot to the lofty capital of Corinth in recognition of his defeat of the Greeks. That other shall destroy Argos and Agamemnon's Mycenae, and Perseus, descendant of Aeacus himself, of the race of Achilles and powerful in arms, thus avenging his Trojan ancestors and the violated temple of Minerva.

"Who could pass you over in silence, great Cato, or you, Cossus? Who could pass over the race of the Gracchi or the two Scipios, two thunderbolts of war, the ruin of Libya, or you, Fabricius, powerful though poor, or you, Serranus, planting your furrows? Why do you hurry me along in my weariness, you Fabians? Are you that famous man, Maximus, who unaided restores the state to us by delaying? Others with more graceful art, I suppose, will beat out lifelike bronze, or form living features from marble, plead cases more effectively, mark with a pointer the motion of the heavens, and foretell the rising of the stars. But you, Roman, remember to rule over peoples with your government. This will be your art: to impose conditions of peace, to spare the conquered, and to crush the proud."

Thus spoke father Anchises, and as they marveled, he added these words: "Look how noble Marcellus advances, laden with princely spoils, ranking as victor above all men! He shall stabilize the Roman state when a great tumult arises, and as a knight, he shall lay low the Carthaginians and the rebellious Gauls, and shall hang these trophies, the third time they shall ever be taken, in the temple of father Quirinus."

And here Aeneas spoke, for he saw a youth walking along with Marcellus, a youth of splendid build and gleaming arms, but his brow was sad and his eyes were downcast:

"Father, who is that youth who so nobly accompanies the hero as he walks ahead? Is he his son or one of the descendants from a great race? What great acclaim he receives from his companions around him! What great dignity is in him! But the darkness of night envelops his head with a gloomy cloud."

Then father Anchises began, as tears started from his eyes: "O son, do not inquire into the great sorrow of your kinsmen. The Fates shall only show this youth to the earth, nor shall they permit him to be there for a long time. The Roman progeny would seem too powerful to you, O gods, if these gifts were to be lasting. What great groanings from men shall the Field of Mars carry to the great city! What a funeral you shall see, Tiber, when you flow by the recently built tomb! Nor shall any boy of Trojan race raise so high the hopes of his Latin ancestors, nor shall the land of Romulus ever boast so much over any foster son. Alas for piety, alas for ancient faith, and bravery unconquered in war! No one ever would have crossed his path with impunity when he was armed, or when as a foot soldier he would go against the enemy, or dig his spurs into the sides of a foaming horse. Alas, O pitiful boy, if in any way you can break your harsh fate, you shall be Marcellus. Scatter handfuls of lilies and let me strew beautiful flowers. Let me heap upon the spirit of my descendant these gifts at least, even though I shall perform a vain service."

Thus they wandered in every direction over the broad, airy fields of the whole region and observed the entire scene. After Anchises had led his son through every part and roused his spirit with love of coming fame, he then recounted to the hero the wars which must be fought thereafter, and showed him the Laurentian peoples and the city of Latinus and how he might either escape or bear each burden.

There are twin gates of Sleep: the one by which an easy exit is given true shades is said to be made of horn; the other, smooth and shining, is of white ivory, but by this ivory gate the gods of the lower world send false dreams to the world above. When with these words Anchises had accompanied both his son and the sibyl and sent them forth from the ivory gate, Aeneas made his way back to the ships and came once more to his comrades.

Then along the straight coast he sailed to the port of Caieta. The anchor was thrown from the prow; the ships were beached on the shore.

Book Seven

MARS

Book Seven

THE TROJANS SAIL TO THE TIBER RIVER

Caieta, nurse of Aeneas, in your death you, too, gave to our shores eternal fame, and now your honor preserves your tomb, and your name marks the resting place of your bones in great Hesperia, if that glory is anything. Now after duly performing the rites of burial and erecting a mound of earth, devout Aeneas set sail when the deep sea grew calm, and left the port. The breezes blew him into the night; the bright moon did not deny her rays for the course, and the sea shone under her trembling light. They skirted very close to the shores of the land of Circe where that rich daughter of the Sun makes the inaccessible groves resound with endless song, and fragrant cedar burns in her proud halls for light in the darkness, while she runs over the thin threads on her loom with a clear-sounding sley. From here could be heard the angry groans of lions fighting their chains and roaring late into the night; bristle-bearing swine and caged bears raged, and great wolves howled. These the savage goddess Circe had changed, by means of powerful herbs, from the appearance of men into the features and bodies of wild animals. So that the reverent Trojans might not be blown into the port and suffer such terrors, or approach these grim shores, Neptune filled their sails with favorable winds and let them escape, carrying them beyond the boiling waters.

And now the sea was growing red with light, and from high heaven the saffron Dawn was gleaming in her rosy chariot, when suddenly the winds died down and all their blowing ceased, and the oars beat in a windless sea. Here Aeneas sighted from the wave a large grove. In the midst of this, the lovely stream of the Tiber with rapid whirlpools carrying much yellow sand rushed into the sea. Around and above, different kinds of birds native to the river and its banks were charming the air with song and flying in the grove. He ordered his companions to change their course and to turn their prows to the land, and he joyfully entered the shaded river.

INVOCATION OF THE MUSE

And now, Erato, with your aid I will explain who the kings were, what turn events took, and what was the condition in ancient Latium when a foreign army first sailed its fleet to the Ausonian shores, and I will recall the very beginning of the struggle. O goddess, counsel your poet. I will tell of horrible wars, I will tell of battle lines and kings driven in anger to their death, and of the Tuscan band and all Italy, mustered to arms. A greater series of events is being planned in my mind, and I am attempting a greater work.

KING LATINUS AND THE ORACLES

King Latinus, already an old man, was ruling over the calm fields and cities of Latium in a long peace. It is handed down that he was born of Faunus and the Laurentian nymph Marica. The father of Faunus was Picus, who claimed, O Saturn, that you were his father and the very fountainhead of his race. By the fate of the gods he had no male offspring, for his son had been snatched away in early youth. Only a daughter, already ripe for a husband, having reached the full age for marriage, preserved the home and kept alive this great line. Many men from great Latium, even from all Ausonia, sought her hand. Among them was Turnus, more handsome than all the others, and powerful because of his long line of ancestors. The queen with a great show of affection was eager to have him for a son-in-law, but divine portents of varying terror stood in the way. There was in the midst of the palace, in the very shrine, a laurel with sacred foliage, preserved in reverence through many years, which, it was said, father Latinus himself consecrated to Phoebus when he found it on establishing the first citadel, naming the colonists Laurentians from that laurel. A dense swarm of bees—a marvelous tale!—settled upon the very top of this tree. Flying through the clear air with great buzzing, and clinging, feet to feet, the sudden swarm hung from the leafy branch. Straightway the prophet said:

"I see a foreign hero coming and a battle line verging on the same spot from the same direction as these bees, seizing control from the very top of the citadel."

Moreover, as the maiden Lavinia stood beside her father while he kindled the altars with holy torches, her long hair, it seemed, took fire—a fearful omen—and all her adornments burned with a crackling flame, and her royal hair and her tiara, bright with gems, were lighted up; then she was wrapped in smoke of a yellow hue and scattered fire through the whole palace. This sight, horrible and astonishing to behold, was noised about. Indeed the prophets were predicting that she would enjoy a distinguished fame and fate but would bring a great war upon her people.

Now the king, disturbed by these omens, approached the oracle of Faunus, his prophet-ancestor, and consulted the grove beneath the cascade of Albunea, which, the largest in the woods, thunders from its sacred source and exhales a poisonous vapor in the shade. From this place the Italian tribes and all the land of Oenotria sought oracles in their doubts. When the priest had brought gifts and in the silent night had lain on the outspread skins of slaughtered sheep and had fallen asleep, he saw many images flitting about in marvelous guise. He heard various voices and enjoyed conversation with the gods and addressed Acheron in the depths of Avernus. Here, too, father Latinus himself, consulting the oracle, duly sacrificed a hundred wool-bearing sheep. Supported by their hides, he was lying on the outspread fleece when suddenly a voice was heard from the depths of the grove: "Do not seek to join your daughter in a Latin marriage, my offspring, nor trust in the nuptials already arranged. Foreign sons-in-law are coming, whose blood shall raise our name to the stars. From their line your descendants shall see everything subject to the control of their rule where the returning Sun looks upon both oceans." Latinus himself did not reveal these replies of father Faunus and the advice given him in the silent night, but Rumor, flitting far and wide, had already spread the news throughout the Ausonian cities when the Trojan youths moored the fleet by the grassy steep along the bank of the river.

THE TROJANS "EAT THEIR TABLES"

Aeneas and the chief leaders and handsome Julus reclined under the branches of a high tree, and began their banquet. They placed on the grass wheatcakes for their food—this they did under the inspiration of Jupiter—and heaped wild fruits upon their wheat cakes. Their slight rations drove them to cut into the little wheat they had and to break with their hands and strong jaws the fateful, round crust and the flat cakes marked with squares. Since their other food was consumed, Julus declared in jest, "There, we are even eating our tables!" He said no more.

The end of their trials first came with the hearing of these words. As soon as he spoke, his father snatched the remark from his lips and amazed at the divine manifestation, fixed it in his mind. Immediately he said:

"Hail, land granted me by the Fates, and you, O household gods of Troy, hail! Here is our home, here our fatherland. Indeed, as I now recall, my father Anchises bequeathed me such secrets from the Fates:

" 'When, my son, after you have been driven to unknown shores, hunger compels you to eat your tables once you have consumed your meal, then in your weariness remember to hope for a home and there to locate your first dwelling with your own hand and to build up ramparts.'

"This was that hunger: this awaited us as the last hunger, putting an end to our trials. Wherefore, come now and joyously at the first light of dawn, let us seek to find what place this is, what kind of men inhabit the land, and where the city of this race is, and let us search in diverse directions from the port. Now pour out bowls of wine to Jupiter and call upon father Anchises in prayer and put back the wine upon the tables."

As he spoke these words, he placed a green wreath upon his brow and called upon the guardian deity of the place, and Earth, first of all the gods, and the nymphs. He prayed to the yet unknown rivers; then in succession he invoked Night and the rising constellations of Night, and Jupiter of Mount Ida and the Phrygian mother, Cybele, and his two parents, Venus in heaven and Anchises in the underworld. Hereupon the all-powerful father clearly thundered thrice from high heaven and shaking out a cloud with his hand, displayed it aloft as it gleamed with rays of golden light. Then a rumor spread through the Trojan line that the day had come when they were to found the promised city. They eagerly renewed the banquet and rejoicing at the great omen, they set up the drinking bowl and wreathed the wine cups.

THE ENVOYS TO KING LATINUS

When the following day began to illumine the earth with its first light, in different directions they sought the city and the borders and the shore line of this people. They discovered that the pools of the fountain of Numicius were there, that the river was the Tiber, and that brave Latins dwelt there. Then the son of Anchises ordered a hundred envoys, chosen from every rank, all shaded with branches sacred to Pallas, to go to the walls of the king, to bring gifts to the hero, and to ask for peace. Without delay they hurried as they were ordered and hastened along with rapid steps. He marked off walls with a shallow ditch and built up the place and, as if it were a camp, surrounded the first settlement on the shore with battlements and a rampart.

On completing the journey, the youths began to make out the towers and the lofty buildings of the Latins, and they went up to the wall. Before the city, boys and youths in the first bloom of life were exercising on horseback and driving their chariots in the dust, stretching fierce bows or hurling pliant javelins with their arms, or vying with one another in racing and boxing, when a messenger, riding up on horseback, brought to the ears of the aged king the news that mighty men had come. He ordered them summoned within the temple and seated himself in the middle upon the ancestral throne.

On the citadel of the city there was a great, august temple, supported by a hundred columns, the palace of Picus of Laurentum, an awe-inspiring place because of the nearby forests and the honors shown there to the ancestors of the Latins. Here kings auspiciously began their rule by receiving the scepter and assuming the fasces; this temple was their court, this their hall for sacred banquets. Here after sacrificing a ram, the elders were accustomed to dine together at long, connected tables. Moreover, the effigies of their ancient ancestors, carved from old cedar, ranged in order in the vestibule—Italus and father Sabinus, the vine planter, represented as holding the curved sickle, and aged Saturn and the image of two-faced Janus, and other kings from the beginning, and those who suffered wounds in war while fighting in defense of the fatherland. In addition, upon the doorposts there hung many weapons, captured chariots, curved axes, crests of helmets, great bars of doors, javelins, shields, and beaks seized from ships. Picus himself, a tamer of horses, holding his augur's wand and clothed in a short toga, sat bearing his shield in his left hand. His lover Circe, smitten with passion, once struck him with a golden rod and after drugging him, changed him into a bird, scattering colors upon his wings. In this temple of the gods, Latinus, sitting upon the throne of his father, called the Trojans to him inside the palace. The first to speak, he calmly uttered these words as they entered:

"Say, sons of Dardanus—for we are not ignorant of your city or race and not unheard of do you sail over the sea—what do you seek? What cause, what need has brought your ships to the shore of Ausonia through so many dark seas? Whether you have entered the banks of the river and are anchored in port because you lost your course, or were driven by storms or experienced whatever numerous mishaps sailors suffer on the deep sea, do not flee our welcome nor ignore the Latins, a race from Saturn, upright without prisons or laws, restraining themselves of their own free will in the manner of the ancient god. And indeed I remember—the story has become obscured with the passing of the years—that the elder Auruncans used to tell how Dardanus, reared in these fields, penetrated to the Idaean cities of Phrygia and Thracian Samos, which is now called Samothrace. From here he set out from the Etruscan settlement at Corythus. Now the golden palace of the star-studded heaven receives him upon a throne, and another is added to the altars of the gods."

Latinus finished speaking, and Ilioneus replied with these words: "O king of the glorious race of Faunus, no dark storm has driven us by its waves to turn to your land, nor have the stars or the shore deceived us in the direction of our journey. With set purpose and willing minds we sailed to this city, after having been driven from our kingdom, which once was the greatest that the sun rising over Olympus ever looked upon. From Jove was the beginning of the race; the Dardan youths rejoiced in their ancestor Jove. Our king himself, Trojan Aeneas, from the supreme race of Jove, sent us to your borders. If the ends of the earth, where the ocean flows back, hold any mortal, if the zone of the torrid sun, stretched in the middle of the four zones, isolates any man, even he has heard what a great storm from savage Mycenae swept over the Idaean plains. He has heard, too, of the fate that drove both the continents of Europe and Asia into battle. Borne from that destruction over so many vast seas, with harmless intent we ask for our ancestral gods a small settlement and a shore line and the water and the sky that is free to everybody.

"We will not bring disgrace upon your rule. Your fame shall not be considered light, nor shall the favor of such a great deed fade away, nor the Ausonians regret having taken Troy to their bosom. I swear by the fate of Aeneas and his mighty right arm, whether the test has been of loyalty or with the weapons of war, that many peoples, many tribes—do not scorn us because we freely bear these garlands in our hands and speak humble words—have sought us out and wished to be leagued with us; but the will of the gods drove us by their commands to seek your land. From here Dardanus sprang; to this place he calls us back. Apollo urges us with stern commands to return to the Etruscan Tiber and the sacred waters of the fountain of Numicius. Aeneas, moreover, gives you these trifling gifts from his former fortune, remnants saved from burning Troy. From this gold cup Anchises poured out wine at the altars; these were the regalia of Priam when he used to give laws to the assembled populace—his scepter, his sacred tiara, and his garments, the work of Trojan women."

At these words from Ilioneus, Latinus, with face cast down, sat motionless upon the throne, rolling his eyes intently. Neither the embroidered purple garments nor the scepter of Priam moved the king as much as his thought of the marriage and the nuptials of his daughter. He turned over in his mind the oracle of ancient Faunus. He reflected that this must be that son-in-law, foretold as setting forth from a foreign place, the one that was to be called to rule under equal auspices; that from him that progeny, outstanding for courage, would come, destined to rule the whole world with its power.

At length Latinus spoke joyfully: "May the gods favor our beginnings and their augury! Trojan, what you wish shall be granted, nor do I spurn the gifts. While Latinus is king, the abundance of rich fields and the wealth of Troy shall not be lacking to you. Only let Aeneas himself come, if he desires our friendship so much, if he is eager to be joined with us in hospitality and to be called an ally, and let him not fear friendly faces. It shall be a part of the terms of peace that I should touch the right hand of your ruler. Now in turn bear back my message to your king. I have a daughter whom neither the oracles from our ancestral shrine nor numerous portents from heaven allow to be joined in marriage with a man of our race. They prophesy that this lot awaits Latium: that sons-in-law, who by their nobility are to raise our name to the stars, shall come from foreign shores. I think that this is the man that the Fates demand, and if my mind has any presentiment of truth, I wish it so."

So saying, the king selected horses for the whole group—three hundred sleek ones stood in their high stalls—and he ordered that these wing-footed animals, covered with purple and embroidered trappings, be led forth at once in a line for all the Trojans. Golden ornaments hung suspended from their chests; they were covered with gold, and bit on yellow gold with their teeth. To the absent Aeneas he gave a chariot and a twin team from a heavenly line, breathing fire from their nostrils, of the race of those whom crafty Circe, deceiving her father, had bred as spurious from a substituted mare. With such gifts and such words from Latinus, the followers of Aeneas, mounted on the horses, returned and announced the peace.

THE VENGEANCE OF JUNO

But lo, the vengeful wife of Jupiter was returning from Inachian Argos, and borne along in her chariot, was holding to her course, when high in the air she sighted afar off, even from Sicilian Pachynus, joyful Aeneas and the Trojan fleet. She saw that they were already building houses, already trusting to the land after leaving their ships. She stood motionless in her deep sorrow. Then shaking her head, she poured out these words from her heart:

"Alas, hated race and fate of the Trojans opposed to my fate! Could they not have died on the Sigean fields? Could they not, once captured, remain captured? Did burned Troy reduce its men to ashes? No! Through the midst of the battle lines and the fire they made their way. But, I suppose, my powers finally lie exhausted or, glutted with hatred, I have begun to rest. Indeed, as a foe I dared to follow these exiles from their fatherland over the waves and to oppose the refugees over the whole sea. The powers of the heavens and the deep have been used up against the Trojans. Of what profit to me were the Syrtes or Scylla or ravaging Charybdis? They are anchored on the longed-for waters of the Tiber, safe from the sea and me. Mars was able to destroy the savage race of the Lapiths; the founder of the gods himself handed over ancient Calydon to the anger of Diana. What great punishment for crime did the Lapiths or Calydon deserve? But I, the great wife of Jupiter, who was able in my unhappiness to leave nothing untried and to turn my power in every direction, am vanquished by Aeneas. But if my powers are not sufficiently great, indeed I will not hesitate to petition whatever power there is anywhere. If I cannot bend the gods to my purpose, I will move Acheron. Granted that it shall not be permitted me to prevent the Latin kingdom and that Lavinia unalterably remains his bride by the will of the Fates, nevertheless I am still permitted to drag out and to delay such great undertakings, to destroy the races of both kings. Let the son-in-law and the father-in-law unite at this cost to their people. Maiden, you shall be dowered with Trojan and Rutulian blood, and the goddess of war awaits you as a bridesmaid. Not only Hecuba, dreaming that she was to give birth to a firebrand, brought forth nuptial torches; nay, even Venus produced a like offspring, a second Paris, and deadly marriage torches again for a rebuilt Troy."

After speaking these words, the dreadful goddess descended to earth. From the seat of the grim sisters and the darkness of hell she summoned the grief-bearing Alecto, whose delight is in sorrowful wars, discord, stratagems, and dreadful crimes. Even her father Pluto, even her sisters in Tartarus hate the monster. She turns herself into so many shapes, with faces so savage and black all over! She is alive with so many serpents! Juno aroused her with these words and spoke as follows:

"Maiden, born of Night, perform this special labor, this work for me, lest my honor and reputation, being tarnished, yield place, or the followers of Aeneas be able to entrap Latinus by marriage or settle within the Italian borders. You can arm your like-minded brothers for battle and distract their homes with hate; you can bring scourges and the torches of death to their houses, for you have a thousand names and a thousand harmful stratagems. Look into your fertile breast, disrupt the agreed peace, and sow the seeds of war. Let the youths desire weapons and demand and seize them at the same time."

ALECTO ROUSES QUEEN AMATA AND TURNUS

Then Alecto, poisoned by the venom of the Gorgon, first alighted upon Latium and the palace of the ruler of Laurentum and settled on the silent threshold of Amata, who, burning with womanly anxiety and anger, was aroused over the coming of the Trojans and the marriage with Turnus. The goddess thrust a serpent from her black hair into the queen, and it buried itself in the very deepest spot in her breast so that through this monster she might in her rage disturb the whole house. The serpent, slipping between her clothes and her smooth breasts, crept along without burying itself and deceived the frenzied woman, who breathed in the viper's spirit. The huge snake became the twisted gold about her neck. As the band of her long garland, it caught up her hair and subtly glided over her. The first infection, spreading its dank poison, attacked her senses and breathed fire into her bones, but as yet her spirit did not feel the flame in her entire breast. She spoke rather gently, as is the custom with mothers, weeping a flood of tears over her daughter and the Trojan marriage:

"Is Lavinia to be given in marriage to an exiled Trojan, father? And have you no pity on your daughter or yourself? Have you no pity on her mother, whom, when the first north wind blows, the treacherous robber will desert, seeking the deep sea with the abducted maiden? Was it not in this way that the Trojan shepherd penetrated Lacedaemon and carried off Helen the daughter of Leda to the Trojan cities? What about your sacred promise? What about your former interest and your pledge, so often given to your kinsman Turnus? If a son-in-law is being sought for the Latins from a foreign race and that decision is unchangeable, if the commands of your parent Faunus weigh on your mind, then indeed I think that every land that is separated and free from our rule is foreign, and that this is the intent of the gods. Turnus, if the very first origin of his line is sought, had Inachus and Acrisius as ancestors and came from the heart of Greece."

When, after vainly speaking these words, she saw that Latinus was obdurate, and felt the maddening poison of the serpent make its way deep into her vitals and through her whole being, then indeed the unhappy woman, excited by these great terrors, madly raged, flouting convention, throughout the length and breadth of the city. As at times a top, which boys in a wide ring in an empty hall eagerly spin at play, whirls from the twisted cord—driven by the lash, it moves in circles while a puzzled band of youths stands in amazement about it, marveling at the humming boxwood, as the whip gives life to the top: so, with no less rapid movement, Amata rushed through the midst of cities and their brave peoples. Nay, she even flitted into the forest, beginning a greater impiety and a greater madness under the feigned influence of Bacchus. She hid her daughter in the forested mountains to save her from the Trojan nuptials and delay the marriage, wailing "Hail, Bacchus!" proclaiming that you alone, Bacchus, were worthy of the virgin; that for you she was taking up the pliant, soft staffs; that she was dancing about you and growing the sacred lock of hair for you.

The story traveled, and at the same moment a like ardor drove all the mothers whose hearts were enkindled with madness to seek new dwellings. They deserted their homes, some baring their necks and their hair to the winds, while others filled the air with tremulous howling, and clothed in skins, carried vine-wreathed wands. She herself in their midst excitedly raised aloft a burning pine torch and chanted the nuptials of her daughter and Turnus, as she rolled her bloodshot eyes and of a sudden wildly shouted:

"Come, you Latin mothers, wherever you are, hear me! If there is any favor left in devout souls for unfortunate Amata, if interest in a mother's rights rouses your concern, loosen your garlands from your hair and perform these orgies with me."

From all sides Alecto, using the goads of Bacchus, drove the queen among the forests and the lairs of wild animals. After it seemed to Alecto that she had sufficiently aroused the first madness and that the order of the whole house of Latinus was upset, straightway the gloomy goddess rose on her dark wings and, borne by the swift South Wind, was carried from there to the walls of the bold Rutulian, to the city which Danaë is said to have founded with Acrisian colonists. The place was once called Ardea by our grandfathers. Now the great name of Ardea remains, but its glory has passed. Here Turnus was already deep in the midst of sleep in the dark night. Alecto put aside her fierce face and furious aspect; she transformed her features into those of an old woman and furrowed her horrible forehead with wrinkles. She put on white hair with a garland and then intertwined a sprig of olive. She became Calybe, the aged servant of Juno and priestess of her temple, and presented herself before the eyes of the young man, saying these words:

"Turnus, will you suffer so many of your labors to be expended in vain and your rule to be handed over to Trojan colonists? The king is refusing you marriage and the dowry you won in blood, and is seeking a foreign heir for the kingdom. Go now, offer yourself to thankless dangers, laughingstock! Go, lay low the Tyrrhenian battle lines! Protect the Latins with peace! Even all-powerful Juno herself clearly ordered me to speak this message to you when you were calmly sleeping. Wherefore, up now, and joyfully order the youths to be armed and led through the gates to war. Burn the painted ships of the Phrygian leaders settled on the beautiful river. The great power of heaven orders this. Unless King Latinus himself confesses that he is willing to keep his word by giving his daughter in marriage, let him at length experience the feeling of meeting Turnus in arms."

Hereupon the young man, scoffing at the priestess, in turn began to speak in this way: "The news that the fleet has reached the waves of the Tiber has not, as you think, escaped my ears. Do not invent such terrors. Royal Juno is not unmindful of me. But old age, overcome by dotage and incapable of truth, troubles you to no good end, old woman, and deceives the prophetess with baseless fear in matters concerning the arms of kings. Your business is to guard the images and temples of the gods. Men, by whom wars must be carried on, shall manage the affairs of war and peace."

At such words the anger of Alecto was enkindled. Now a sudden trembling seized the limbs of the young man as he spoke and his eyes began to stare. The Fury hissed from many serpents, and her great shape revealed itself. Then rolling her flaming eyes, she scorned him, as he hesitated in spite of his desire to say more. She caused twin snakes to rise from her hair, and cracked her whips, while adding these words from her raging mouth:

"Behold me, overcome by dotage, whom old age, incapable of truth, deceives with baseless fear about the arms of kings! Look at these weapons! I come from the seat of the grim sisters; I carry wars and death in my hand!"

Thus speaking, she hurled a torch at the man and fixed the brand smoking with dark fire in his breast. Terror ended his deep sleep, and sweat, oozing from his whole body, bathed him from head to foot. Madly he clamored for arms; for arms he searched near his couch and throughout the palace. Love for the sword, the criminal insanity of war, and above all, madness were now turned loose, just as when a loud, crackling brush-flame is placed under the sides of a boiling caldron and the water bubbles up with the heat, while the steaming water within boils and tosses high its spray and the liquid contains itself no longer but as dark vapor rises into the air. Therefore, since the peace was violated, he commanded the leaders of the youth to march against King Latinus and gave them the order to prepare their arms, to defend Italy, and to expel the enemy from its borders. He declared that he would come ready to meet both Trojans and Latins. After he had said these words and invoked the gods in prayer, the Rutulians eagerly urged one another to arms. The outstanding build of the youthful body of Turnus moved some men; others were impressed by his kingly ancestors, and still others by his famous exploits in arms.

THE OCCASION FOR WAR: ASCANIUS WOUNDS A PET STAG

While Turnus was infusing into the Rutulians a spirit of boldness, Alecto on Stygian wings flew against the Trojans. With a new stratagem in mind, the virgin from Cocytus, looking at the spot on the shore where handsome Julus was trapping and running down wild animals, suddenly roused the dogs and blew into their nostrils a familiar scent so that they would hotly pursue a stag. This was the prime cause of the conflict, and it roused the minds of the country folk to war.

There was a stag of outstanding beauty with high antlers, which Tyrrhus and his sons—he was in charge of the royal stables and the trusted guard of the broad fields—had snatched from its mother's udders and raised. Silvia, the sister, used to decorate the stag, obedient to her commands, by intertwining its antlers with soft garlands, and she curried the animal and washed it in pure water. Tame to her hand and freely fed at the table of its master, it wandered about in the forests and again returned home to the familiar threshold, even though it might be late at night.

The raging dogs of the hunter Julus scented afar off the deer when it happened to be floating downstream with the current and cooling itself on the grassy bank. Ascanius, especially fired with a love for honor and distinction, directed a shaft from his curved bow. Alecto did not fail to guide his right hand, aimed wide of the mark, and the reed, driven with a great sound, pierced the deer's belly and flank. Thereupon the wounded animal fled to its known refuge. Groaning, it entered the stables, and streaming with blood, filled all the place with its cries as if begging for help.

First, the sister, Silvia, striking her arms with her hands, called for help and shouted for the rough woodsmen. They were unexpectedly present—for the fierce pest, Alecto, was hidden in the silent forests—some armed with fire-hardened brands, others with heavy, knotted clubs. Everyone in his anger used whatever weapon he found in his search. Tyrrhus, as he was splitting sections of oak into four parts with wedges, picked up his ax and, breathing revenge, summoned a troop of men.

Now the savage goddess, having won time to do harm, from her watchtower sought the steep roofs of the stable and from the very top sounded the shepherd's signal, and on a curved horn she blew a Tartarean blast, whereat all the grove straightway trembled and the deep forests re-echoed. Afar off, the lake of Trivia heard; the river Nar, white with sulfurous water, and the springs of Velinus heard, and trembling mothers pressed their children to their breasts.

THE WAR BEGINS

Then, indeed, at the blast given by the signal from the grim bugle, the impetuous farmers, seizing their weapons, quickly rushed from all sides, and the Trojan youth brought help to Ascanius from the unprotected camp. The battle lines were formed. Not as in a rustic encounter was the battle fought with hard clubs or fire-hardened stakes, but this was, they realized, a fight with two-edged swords. The dark land bristled far and wide with drawn swords, and bronze weapons, struck by the sun, gleamed, throwing their light to the clouds, as when waters at first begin to whiten on the deep and the sea rouses itself little by little and tosses the waves higher and then surges to heaven from the lowest depths. Here, in front of the first battle line, the youth Almo, the oldest of the sons of Tyrrhus, was slain by a whistling arrow. The wound was deep in his throat and shut off with blood the passage of his liquid voice and the thin stream of breath. The bodies of many heroes lay about, among them the aged Galaesus, the only just man and once the richest in the Ausonian fields, who took up a position between the lines in the interest of peace. Five flocks of sheep had he, five herds of cattle returned to his barns, and he turned his land with a hundred plows.

While the indecisive fighting was taking place in the fields, the goddess, having kept her promise, deserted Italy when blood was shed in the war and death took place in the first fighting, and flying through the winds of heaven, victoriously addressed Juno with proud words:

"Behold, discord has been worked up for you by means of a sorrowful war! Tell me now if they will enter into friendship and conclude pacts. Inasmuch as I have stained Trojans with Ausonian blood, I will also add this torment to them, if I have your definite order: by means of rumors I will rouse up the nearby cities to war and kindle their minds with a love for insane Mars so that they may bring aid from all sides. I will scatter arms in their fields."

"Now there is enough terror and deceit," Juno replied. "The causes for war are set up, and hand-to-hand fighting is in progress; the arms which chance first offered have been stained with fresh blood. Let the noteworthy race of Venus and King Latinus himself celebrate such a marriage and such nuptials! The father of all, the ruler of lofty Olympus, would hardly wish you to wander too freely in this ethereal air. Depart from this region. If there is any further crisis in these troubles, I myself will take control."

With these words Juno finished speaking. Then Alecto raised her wings, hissing with serpents, and sought the region of Cocytus, leaving the steep heights. At the foot of high mountains in central Italy, there is a place, famous and renowned on many shores, the valley of Amsanctus. On both sides a sloping forest, dark with dense foliage, encloses this valley, and in the middle a crashing torrent resounds amid rocks and swirling whirlpools. Here a fearful cave and the door to dreadful Pluto are pointed out, and a great abyss opens its poisonous throat from a cleft in Acheron. In this the hated and powerful Fury hid herself and relieved heaven and earth of her presence.

Nonetheless, Juno meanwhile placed the final touch on the war. The whole band of shepherds rushed from the battle line into the city carrying their slain, the boy Almo and Galaesus, wounded about the face, and they implored the gods and called Latinus to witness. Turnus was present and in the midst of the criminal murder and the anger it aroused, he redoubled their frenzy, saying that the Trojans had been called into the government, that Phrygian blood was being intermingled with theirs, and that he was being expelled from the country. Then the relatives of those matrons who under the spell of Bacchus were leaping in dances through the trackless groves—for the name of Amata carried no little weight—came together from all sides, clamoring for war. In spite of the omens and the fates of the gods, all, under the influence of a perverse power, immediately demanded unspeakable war. In hostile mood they surrounded the palace of King Latinus. He resisted like a cliff along the sea when a great crash comes, holding its position by reason of its mass while many waves roar about; in vain they wail around the foaming stones of the cliff, and the driven seaweed is washed back from its side. Indeed when no power was at hand to overcome the senseless plan, and matters were progressing according to the will of savage Juno, after calling many times upon the gods and the empty air, he said:

"Alas, we are crushed by fate and are set adrift by the storm! Miserable men, you shall pay for these crimes with your impious blood. A dreadful penalty awaits you, Turnus, a sorrowful punishment, and you shall reverence the gods with tardy prayers. For I have won rest and am entering unharmed into port; yet I am deprived of a happy burial." Without saying more, he left the palace and gave up the reins of government.

JUNO OPENS THE TEMPLE OF JANUS

There was in Hesperian Latium a custom which thenceforth the Alban cities held sacred and which Rome, the heart of the world, now cherishes—a custom followed when they moved toward the first hostile acts, whether they were preparing to declare war, disastrous for the Getae, the Hyrcanians, or the Arabs, or to push toward the Indians and, continuing to the East, to demand back the standards from the Parthians. There are twin gates of War—so they are named—sacred because of the religious fear in which savage Mars is held. A hundred bronze bolts and the everlasting strength of iron bar the portal, nor does Janus, the guard, leave its threshold. When the senators definitely make up their minds in favor of war, the consul himself, resplendent in the toga of Quirinus and the Gabine cincture, unlocks the creaking doors and himself issues the call to battle. Then the rest of the youth raises the cry, and the bronze horns blow in raucous unison.

By reason of this custom, Latinus was urged to declare war against the sons of Aeneas and to open the gloomy gates. The father refrained from touching them and averting his gaze, fled that vile office and hid himself in utter darkness. Then Juno herself, the queen of the gods, gliding down from heaven, forced the gates with her own hand and swinging the hinge, broke the iron jambs of the doors of war. Ausonia unexcited and quiet before, now seethed. Some prepared to take to the fields on foot; others spiritedly dashed about in the dust on high chargers. Everybody sought weapons. Some cleaned their shields with tallow fat until they glistened, and their javelins until they gleamed, and they put their axes on the whetstone. It was thrilling to bear the standards and to hear the sounds of the trumpets. As many as five great cities set up anvils to make weapons: powerful Atina, proud Tibur, Ardea, Crustumeri, and turret-crowned Antemnae. They beat out safe protection for their heads, and they shaped willow wickers for their shields. Some forged bronze breastplates or shining greaves from pliable silver. All thought of the plowshare and the sickle yielded to this employment; to this all love for the plow gave way. They melted their fathers' swords in furnaces. Then the trumpets sounded, and the password, the signal for war, traveled along. One man hastily seized his helmet from his home; another drove his whinnying horses to the chariot, armed himself with his shield and his coat of mail of triple gold, and buckled on his faithful sword.

LISTING OF THE ALLIES OF TURNUS

Throw open wide the gates of Helicon, goddesses, and inspire me to sing what kings were roused to war, what troops following each leader took to the field, what heroes the dear land of Italy even then produced, and with what weapons it raged: for you remember, goddesses, and can name them. The faint whisper of their fame hardly reaches our ears.

First Mezentius, that fierce despiser of the gods from the Tyrrhenian shores, entered the war and armed his battle lines. Near him was his son Lausus—no man more handsome than he, save Turnus of Laurentum. Lausus, the tamer of horses and the conqueror of wild beasts, in vain led forth from the city of Agylla the thousand men who followed him, a worthy son who deserved a happier fate in his father's kingdom, who deserved a worthier father than Mezentius.

After these, handsome Aventinus, the son of handsome Hercules, displayed his prize-winning chariot and his victorious horses on the meadow, and he bore his father's device on his shield, a hundred snakes and a hydra surrounded by serpents. In the forest of the Aventine hill the priestess Rhea, a woman who had united with a god, had secretly brought forth her child upon the shores of light, after Hercules, the victor from Tiryns, on slaying the monster Geryon, had come to the field of Laurentum and bathed his Iberian cattle in the Etruscan river. The followers of Aventinus bore in their hands javelins and dreadful pikes for use in war, and they fought with a smooth spear and the Sabellian lance. He himself on foot, wrapped about with the huge skin of a lion—shaggy with terrible mane and showing white teeth—which he drew over his head, thus entered the royal palace, a grisly man, his shoulders covered with the mantle of Hercules.

Then the twin brothers, Catillus and fierce Coras, Greek youths, left the walls of Tibur, a city named after their brother Tiburtius, and they advanced before the first battle line where the weapons fell thickest, as when two cloud-born centaurs descend from the lofty peak of a mountain, leaving Homole and snowy Othrys in their rapid course; the great forest gives place to them as they rush along, and the groves yield with a great crashing. Nor was Caeculus, the founder of the city of Praeneste, absent. Every age has believed the story that this king, the son of Vulcan, was born among rural flocks and found at a hearth. A rustic legion from far and wide accompanied him: the men who inhabited high Praeneste, the fields of Gabinian Juno, the cold Anio, the Hernican rocks, wet from brooks, all the people whom rich Anagnia feeds, and you, father Amasenus. Not all these men had arms or shields or sounding chariots. A very great number slung pellets of dark-colored lead, while some carried a pair of spears in their hands. They wore, as head covering, a yellowish cap of wolf skin. Their footprints showed that their left feet were bare and that their right were shod with a rough, rawhide boot.

Now Messapus, the trainer of horses and the offspring of Neptune, whom neither fire nor sword might destroy, suddenly called to arms throngs of sluggards and bands unaccustomed to war, and he seized his sword once more. These made up the Fescennine battle lines and those of Aequi Falisci; they held the heights of Soracte and the Flavinian fields, the lake and mountain of Ciminus, and the groves of Capena. They marched along in even ranks and praised their king in song, as when at times snowy swans return through the clear clouds after feeding and sing tuneful strains from their long throats while the river Cayster and the far-off Asian swamp resound. Nobody would think that bronze-clad battle lines were being formed from that great crowd, but rather that a cloud of hoarse birds was being driven from the deep sea to the shores.

Look at Clausus, leading a great battle line of the ancient blood of the Sabines, himself a veritable battle line! From him the Claudian tribe and clan is now spread through Latium, for Rome was shared with the Sabines. With him came a great cohort from Amiternum, the ancient people from Cures, and all the band of Eretum and olive-bearing Mutusca; those who inhabited the city of Nomentum, the Rosean countryside of Lake Velinus, the cliffs of rough Tetrica, Mount Severus, Casperia, Foruli, and the banks of the river Himella; those who drank from the Tiber and the Fabaris; those whom the cold town of Nursia sent, the hosts of Hortina, and the Latin peoples; and those whom the rushing Allia, ill-omened word, separated with its waters. They were as numerous as the waves that roll in the Libyan Sea, where savage Orion hides in the wintry waves, or as many as the full ears of corn that are heated by the warm sun either on the plain of Hermus or on the yellow fields of Lycia. Their shields resounded, and the earth was terrified by the beating of their feet.

Thereupon, Halaesus, the enemy of the Trojan name, who had been allied with Agamemnon, hitched his horses to his chariot and hurried along a thousand fierce clans for Turnus' side: those who tilled with their hoes the Massic soil, fruitful in wine; those whom the Auruncan fathers sent from their high hills and the nearby plains of Sidicinum; those who left Cales; the inhabitants along the shallow river Volturnus; likewise the rough men from Saticulus; and the band of Oscans. They had as weapons smooth javelins, usually fitted with a pliant thong. Bucklers protected their left hands, and they used curved swords in hand-to-hand fighting.

Nor will you go unmentioned in our song, Oebalus, whom, according to the story, Telon begot of the nymph Sebethis when at an advanced age he ruled Capreae, the kingdom of the Teleboans. But his son, not contented with his father's fields, even then subjected to his sway the Sarrastian people and the plains which the Sarnus waters, and those who held Rufrae and Batulum and the fields of Celemna, and those upon whom the fortifications of fruitful Abella looked down. They were accustomed to hurl javelins in the Teuton manner; their head protection was bark, torn from the cork tree; their shields gleamed with bronze and their swords with gold.

Mountainous Nersae sent you into battle, Ufens, noted for your fame and fortune in arms, whose race, the Aequian, was accustomed to rough land and much hunting in the forest. Under arms they tilled the soil and always found pleasure in rounding up fresh booty and living by plunder.

And, too, the priest from the Marruvian race, brave Umbro, with a rich olive garland decorating his helmet, came at the command of King Archippus. By incantation and the motion of his hands he was accustomed to scatter sleep upon the race of vipers and hydras that breathed forth deadly poison, and he softened their rage and skillfully healed their bites. But he was not able to cure a blow from a Trojan's spear, nor did his sleep-bearing incantation and his herbs, picked on Marsian mountains, help him against wounds. The grove of Angitia wept for you as did Fucinus' glassy wave and liquid lakes.

Virbius, too, famed in war, the handsome son of Hippolytus, marched along, sent by his mother Aricia. He was reared in the groves of Egeria around the damp shores of the lake, where there is a rich and generous altar to Diana. For the story goes that Hippolytus, after he died by the artifice of his stepmother and paid for his father's crimes with his blood, though mangled by the frightened horses, came again beneath the ethereal stars into the air of the upper world, having been revived by the herbs of Apollo and the love of Diana. Then the all-powerful father, indignant that any mortal should rise from the shades of hell to the light of life, with his thunderbolt hurled down to the Stygian wave Aesculapius, the Apollo-born discoverer of such healing arts. But gracious Trivia hid Hippolytus in a secret place and consigned him to the nymph Egeria and her grove where, alone and unknown in the Italian forests, he spent his life, living under the name of Virbius. For this reason, too, horn-footed horses were kept away from the temple of Trivia and the sacred groves because on the shore they had upset, when frightened by sea monsters, the youth and his chariot. Nonetheless, the son drove the spirited horses across the level field and rushed into war with his chariot.

Among the leaders Turnus moved, holding his weapons, a man of outstanding build, a head taller than the others. His high-tasseled helmet with triple crest bore the Chimaera, breathing forth fires of Aetna from her jaws—the more raging and savage with dreadful flames as the battle grew fiercer with the shedding of blood. Moreover, stamped in gold on his polished shield was Io with uplifted horns, already a heifer covered over with stiff hair—a famous story—and Argus, the guard of the maiden, and father Inachus, pouring forth his river from an engraved urn. A crowd of foot soldiers followed Turnus, and armed battle lines were thick over the whole plain, Greek youths, Auruncan bands, Rutulians, old Sicanians, Sacranian ranks, and men from Labicum with colored shields. There were those, too, who plowed your woodland pastures, Tiber, and the sacred bank of the river Numicius, and those who furrowed with a plow the Rutulian hills and the ridge of Circeii, over whose fields preside Jupiter of Anxur and Feronia, rejoicing in her green grove, where the dark pool of Satura lies and the cold river Ufens makes its way through the depths of the valley and is lost in the sea.

After these came Camilla, a warrior maiden of the Volscian race, leading a band of horsemen and squadrons gleaming with bronze. Although a woman, her hands were not used to the distaff and the wool basket of Minerva; rather she was accustomed to bear grim battles and to outstrip the winds as she ran on foot. She would flit over the top of the harvest without touching it, nor would she harm the tender wheat as she raced along; perched on the swelling flood, she would make her way through the midst of the sea, without dipping her swift feet in the water. All the youths, pouring out from homes and fields, and the crowd of mothers marveled at her. They looked at her as she walked along, and they gazed in astonishment at how her garment of royal purple veiled her smooth shoulders, how a clasp of gold intertwined her hair, and how she bore her Lycian quiver and shepherd's shaft of myrtle, tipped with a spear point.

Book Eight

VULCAN

Book Eight

THE LATINS SEEK THE HELP OF DIOMEDE

When Turnus raised the war standard from the citadel of Laurentum and the horns blared with a raucous blast, when he spurred his spirited horses and clashed his arms, the minds of all were suddenly roused, and at the same time the whole of Latium united in a disorderly uprising, and the temper of the wild youths ran high. The principal leaders, Messapus, Ufens, and Mezentius, that despiser of the gods, recruited troops from all sides and took the tillers from the broad fields. Venulus was sent to the city of great Diomede to seek help and carry the news that the Trojans had settled in Latium; that Aeneas had come with his fleet and was bringing his conquered household gods, maintaining that he was designated by the Fates to be king; furthermore, that many tribes were allying themselves with the Trojan hero and that his name was spreading far and wide in Latium. How Aeneas would follow up these first advances, what he would wish the outcome of the battle to be, if Fortune favored him, should certainly be clearer to Diomede than to King Turnus or King Latinus.

Such was the state of affairs in Latium. As the hero Diomede, descendant of Laomedon, considered all these troubles, he tossed on a great tide of worry. Now his swift mind grasped at this solution, now at that. He forced his thought in various directions and turned over every idea, just as when a tremulous light, reflected by the sun or the radiant moon from bronze bowls of water, flits over everything far and wide and even is tossed into the air and strikes the ceiling of the high roof.

TIBER APPEARS TO AENEAS

It was night, and throughout the whole earth weary animals, birds and beasts, were wrapped in deep sleep when father Aeneas, his heart troubled by the deplorable war, lay down on the shore under the cold sky and surrendered his body to tardy slumber. It seemed to him that Tiber, the old god of the place, rose from the beautiful river among the poplar trees—a thin garment of sea-green linen covered him, and shady reeds protected his hair—and addressed Aeneas, stilling his worries with these words:

"O descendant of the race of the gods, you who are rescuing the Trojan city from the enemy and preserving eternal Troy, long awaited upon the soil of Laurentum and the fields of Latium, here is your secure home, here your household gods are safe. Do not retreat or be terrified by the threats of war: all the indignant anger of the gods has quieted down. Lest you think that these words are the vain imagining of sleep, under the ilexes along the shore you shall find, lying spread out upon the ground, a great white sow with her litter of thirty white sucklings around her teats. [This shall be the location of the city, this the certain surcease of your labors;] in conformity with this omen, after thirty revolving years Ascanius shall found Alba, a city of famous name.

"Indeed I am not prophesying what is uncertain. Now listen, and I will explain in a few words how you may victoriously carry out the work at hand. The Arcadians, a race descended from Pallas, as comrades following King Evander's banners, chose a spot on these shores and established in the mountains a city Pallanteum, named after their ancestor Pallas. They wage unceasing war with the Latin race. Add them as allies to your camp and join in a treaty. I myself will lead you along my banks by a direct course so that, though rowing upstream, you shall overcome the current with your oars. Rise now, goddess-born, and as the first stars disappear in the dawn, duly offer your prayers to Juno and overcome her angry threats with pleading vows. Once victorious, you shall pay honor to me. I am the dark, full-flowing Tiber, a stream most pleasing to heaven, which you see gliding along the banks and cutting through rich fields. Here is my great home; my source rises amid high-lying cities."

He finished speaking, and then the god of the river hid himself in the deep bed of the stream, seeking the bottom. Aeneas awakened and it was dawn. He arose and looking at the light of heaven's sun in the east, piously raised up water from the river in his cupped palms and poured out such words as these upon the air:

"O nymphs, nymphs of Laurentum, from whom comes the race of rivers, and you, father Tiber with your holy river, receive Aeneas and pray guard him from danger. No matter in what waters or in what fountain you dwell, no matter through what land you flow in all your beauty, you, who pity our troubles, shall always be honored by me and my gifts, horned river, ruler of Italian waters. Only be present and confirm your powers more openly."

Thus he spoke and choosing two biremes from the fleet, he fitted them out with oarage. At the same time he equipped his companions with arms.

But behold, a sudden, startling omen appeared before their eyes. A white sow of the same color as its white litter was seen lying in the forest along the green shore. Even to you, great Juno, devout Aeneas, bearing the sacred emblems, sacrificed this sow and placed it with the litter on the altar.

AENEAS SEEKS HELP FROM EVANDER

Throughout that long night Tiber quieted the swelling stream and, flowing backward, with his silent wave he tarried so that the level surface of the water stretched out like a quiet pool or a placid marsh, offering no opposition to the oars.

Therefore, amid favorable cheers, they hastened the journey

they had begun. The keels of pitched fir slipped into the water and the waves marveled; the unaccustomed grove was startled at the shields of men shining afar and the painted ships moving in the river. They toiled at the oars through the night and the day. They rounded the long bends in the river and were covered by different kinds of trees as they cut through the green forest along the placid plain. The fiery sun had already climbed midway in the heavens when they saw in the distance the walls and the citadel and the roofs of a few homes which now the power of Rome has raised to the heavens. But then Evander had a poor state. Quickly they turned their prows and approached the city.

By chance on that day the Arcadian king was offering solemn sacrifice to great Hercules and the gods in a grove in front of the city. Together with him, Pallas, his son, all the leaders of the youths, and the poverty-stricken senate were offering incense, and warm blood was steaming at the altars. Seeing the high ships gliding through the dark grove and the men silently pulling on the oars, they were terrified at the sudden sight, and all rose and left the tables. Bold Pallas forbade the interruption of the sacred ceremonies, and seizing his weapon, rushed to meet them and shouted afar off from a mound:

"Men, what reason has driven you to explore an unknown course? Where are you going? Of what race are you? From what home? Do you bring peace here or war?"

Then father Aeneas spoke these words from his lofty ship, holding out in his hand a branch of the peace-bearing olive tree: "You see men born at Troy and weapons hostile to the Latins. They repelled us, though we were refugees, in an unrighteous attack. We are seeking Evander. Bear this news and say that chosen leaders of Dardania have come, asking for an alliance in arms."

Pallas was struck dumb at the sound of such a great name and exclaimed: "Disembark, whoever you are, and speak to my father face to face. Enter our home as a guest."

He extended his hand in welcome and embracing Aeneas,

clung to his right hand. Walking along they entered the grove and left the river.

Then Aeneas addressed the king with friendly words: "Best of the Greeks, to whom Fortune willed I should make my petition and extend this branch adorned with a garland, indeed I had no fear because you were an Arcadian leader of the Greeks and related to the line of the twin sons of Atreus. But my courage, the sacred oracles of the gods, our related parents, and your fame spread over the earth have joined me to you and have driven me, the willing tool of fate. Dardanus, the first father and founder of the Trojan city, born, as the Greeks say, of Electra, the daughter of Atlas, sailed to the Trojans; great Atlas, who holds up the world upon his shoulders, was the father of Electra. Your father was Mercury, whom bright Maia brought forth on the cold peak of Mount Cyllene. But Atlas, the same Atlas who bears aloft the stars of the heavens, was the father of Maia, if we can believe what we have heard. Thus our race springs from one blood. Relying on this, I did not send ambassadors to you or arrange a clever approach in advance. I risked my very life and came as a suppliant to your threshold. This is that same race of Turnus that pursues *you* in cruel war. If they expel us, they feel that nothing will prevent their completely subjugating all Italy and dominating the sea that washes the shores above and below. Receive our promise and give yours. We have stout hearts in war and a spirited youth, tested by trials."

Aeneas finished speaking. For a long time Evander observed the speaker's face, his eyes, and his whole body. Then he answered briefly as follows:

"How gladly I welcome you and recognize you, bravest of the Trojans! How well I remember the words, the voice, and the features of your great parent Anchises! For I recall that Priam the son of Laomedon came to Salamis to visit the kingdom of his sister Hesione and the cold country of Arcadia. Then my first beard was covering my cheeks. I kept gazing at the leaders of the Trojans, I kept gazing at Priam himself. But taller than all walked Anchises. My mind was aflame with youthful desire to address the hero and to join my right hand with his. I approached and eagerly led him to the walls of Pheneos. At his departure he gave me a splendid quiver, Lycian arrows, a cloak interwoven with gold, and two golden bits which my Pallas now has. So, then, the pledge you seek I have already given by that treaty, and as soon as tomorrow's light returns, I will order out men happy to aid you, and I will help you with supplies. Meanwhile, since you have come here as friends, graciously celebrate with us these yearly sacred rites, which we cannot postpone, and at once become acquainted with the tables of your allies."

After saying this, he gave orders that the banquet and the goblets that had been removed should be brought back. He seated the men on a grassy plot, especially welcomed Aeneas on a couch overspread with the skin of a shaggy lion, and invited him to the maple throne. Then the priest at the altar and chosen youths eagerly carried the roasted sides of bulls and piled bread in baskets and served the gift of Bacchus. At the same time, Aeneas and the Trojan youths ate from the long sides of beef and the expiatory parts.

THE ORIGIN OF THE SACRIFICE TO HERCULES

After their hunger was relieved and their desire satisfied, King Evander said: "Vain superstition and ignorance of the ancient gods have not imposed upon us these solemnities, this customary banquet, this altar to such a great power. Preserved from savage dangers, Trojan guest, we perform these merited honors.

"Now first look at that crag, overhung with rocks. See how masses are scattered far and wide, how that mountain home stands deserted, and how great ruin is spread over the cliffs. Here was a cave where the cruel-faced semihuman Cacus dwelt deep in a vast recess, inaccessible to the rays of the sun. The ground was always warm with fresh blood; fixed to the cruel doors hung human heads, ghastly with awful gore. Vulcan was the father of this monster. Pouring forth dark fires from his mouth, he carried his great mass along. Finally, in answer to our prayers, time brought help and the presence of the god. For Hercules, the greatest of avengers, came, boasting over the slaughter of the three-bodied Geryon and his other spoils. Victoriously he drove great bulls along here, and the cattle filled the valley and the river bank.

"But the wild-minded Cacus—lest his madness should leave any crime or deceit undared or untried—turned four bulls of splendid form and just as many heifers of surpassing beauty aside from the cattle camp. So that there would be no trace of their true tracks, he dragged each into the cave by the tail, and when the direction of their course had been changed, he enclosed the stolen animals in the dark with a boulder. Anyone seeking them would find no hoofprints leading to the cave.

"Meanwhile, when the son of Amphitryon was moving the satisfied herd from the feeding grounds and was preparing to leave, the cattle lowed. They filled all the grove with their complaints and bellowed as they left the hills. A cow, returning the call, lowed in the vast cave, and though kept under guard, ruined the hopes of Cacus. Then indeed, the temper of Hercules flared up with fury and deadly wrath. He seized arms and an oak club heavy with knots, and ran to the top of a high mountain.

"Then for the first time our men saw Cacus in terror, with a look of fear in his eyes. Straightway he fled, faster than the wind, and sought his cave; fear added wings to his feet. As he shut himself in and let down, after breaking its chains, a huge rock suspended by his father's skillful iron work, thus blocking the firm-set entrance with this obstacle, lo! Hercules came raging, trying every approach, turning his gaze in all directions as he ground his teeth. Furious with anger, three times he ranged about the mount of the Aventine; three times he vainly tried the stony threshold; three times in his weariness he sat down in the valley. There was a steep crag rising from the back of the cave with sharp rocks on all sides, a lofty sight, a fitting home for the nests of wild birds. Leaning with his right hand in front of him, he pushed this rock hanging from the ridge over the river to the left, and tore it loose from its deep roots; thereupon he suddenly thrust it forward. At this impact the wide heavens thundered, the banks sprang apart, and the frightened river flowed backward.

"Now the cave and the great palace of Cacus were uncovered, and the shaded caverns lay open far within, much as if the earth, split by some force, were to disclose the nether regions and reveal the ghastly realm hated by the gods, as if the wild abyss were viewed from above and the spirits trembled at the admitted light. Thereupon with weapons from above, Hercules harassed Cacus, who was caught suddenly in the unexpected light and enclosed in the hollow cave while he bellowed strange sounds. Calling into play all his weapons, Hercules attacked with heavy timbers and huge stones. But the monster, for now no flight from danger was left him, poured forth from his throat—a marvelous tale—a great cloud of smoke and filled his home with blinding darkness, making clear vision impossible, and he massed in the cave a smoky night whose blackness mingled with fire. Hercules was not disposed to bear this and leaped headlong through the flame where most of the fumes were billowing and where the great cave smoked with a black cloud.

"He seized Cacus, who was belching forth vain fires in the darkness and, tying him in a knot, forced out his bulging eyes, after shutting off the blood in his throat. When the doors were torn away, the dark lair was suddenly laid bare; the disavowed theft of stolen cattle lay open to the heavens. The shapeless corpse was dragged forth by its feet. We could not satisfy our desire by gazing at the terrible eyes, the face, the hairy, bristling chest of the half-wild being, and the throat from which had come the fires, now extinguished.

"From that time honor was shown Hercules. The happy descendants, and the first founder, Potitius, and the house of Pinarius, the guardian of the temple of Hercules, have kept the day alive. In this grove the god set up this altar, which shall always be called The Greatest and which shall always be the greatest. Wherefore, come now, youths, in appreciation of such praiseworthy deeds, garland your hair with leaves and hold up your bowls in your right hand, and calling upon our common god, offer a libation."

Evander finished speaking. A garland made from the two-colored poplar tree in the shadow of the temple of Hercules veiled his hair and hung entwined with leaves, and a sacred goblet filled his right hand. All in joyous mood quickly poured out wine upon the table and prayed to the gods.

Meanwhile, evening approached closer as the heavens revolved. And now the priests and noble Potitius, clad in skins, as was the custom, and carrying torches, formed a procession. They renewed the banquet, bringing pleasing gifts for the second feast and piling the altars high with laden platters. Then the Salian priests, one a chorus of youths, another of old men, their temples bound with poplar wreaths, circled the smoking altars to the accompaniment of song, chanting praises of the deeds of Hercules: how, gripping with his hand, he strangled the first monsters of his stepmother, Juno, the twin snakes; how he laid waste in war the beautiful cities, Troy and Oechalia; how he suffered a thousand hard labors under King Eurystheus because of the decrees of unjust Juno.

"Unconquered one, you killed by your own hand the cloud-born centaurs, Hylaeus and Pholus, the Cretan monster, and the huge Nemean lion under the cliff. The Stygian lakes feared you, as did the guard of the gate of Orcus, lying upon half-gnawed bones in his bloody cave. No face terrified you, not even Typhoeus himself as he brandished his weapons aloft; nor did Lerna's serpent, attacking you with its numerous heads, find you without a plan of attack. Hail, true offspring of Jove, splendor added to the gods. Benignantly approach us and your sacred mysteries with auspicious tread."

They celebrated these exploits in song; last of all they ended with the tale of the cave of Cacus and the monster himself breathing out fire. All the grove resounded with the noise, and the hills gave back the echo.

Then when the divine services were ended, they returned to the city. The king, weighed down with years, walked along with Aeneas as his companion while holding to his son Pallas, and lightened the way with varied discourse. Aeneas looked about and cast rapid glances at everything. Enchanted by the place, in happy mood he asked and heard about each monument to former heroes.

Then King Evander, the founder of the Roman citadel, said: "These groves were held by the native fauns and nymphs and the race of men born of trunks of rough oak, who had neither customs nor culture. They did not know how to yoke bulls or to store up their resources or sparingly use their savings, but branches were their shelter and crude hunting supplied their livelihood. First, fleeing the weapons of Jupiter, Saturn came from airy Olympus, an exile after his kingdom had been taken from him. He organized the intractable race that was scattered over the high mountains, gave them laws, and wished the place to be called Latium, since he had been sheltered in safety upon these shores. Men call the age under that king golden. Thus he ruled the people in calm peace until little by little a corrupt and debased age and the madness of war and the love of possessing followed. Then the Ausonian throng and the Sicanian races appeared, and the land of Saturn changed its name rather often. Then came kings and rough Thybris of huge body, for whom we Italians afterward called the river by the name Tiber; thus the ancient Albula lost its true name. All-powerful fortune and unavoidable fate placed me in this region, an exile from my fatherland who sailed to the farthest rim of the ocean. I was driven by dreadful admonitions of my mother, the nymph Carmentis, and my guide, the god Apollo."

Hardly had Evander said these words when, walking along, he pointed out the altar and the Carmental Gate, as the Romans call it, the first honor shown the nymph Carmentis, the prophetic priestess who first prophesied that the sons of Aeneas would be great and the city of Pallenteum noble. Then he showed the great grove which brave Romulus proclaimed the Asylum and the Lupercal under the cold cliff, named in the Arcadian style after Lycaean Pan. He also pointed out the grove of the sacred Argiletum and called on the place to witness his innocence as he told of the death of his guest Argos. From here Evander led him to the Tarpeian seat and the Capitol, golden now but once rough with wooded thickets.

Even then a religious dread of the spot terrified the fearful rustics; even then they trembled at the sight of the forest and the rock.

"This grove," he said, "and this hill with its wooded top are inhabited by a god—which god is not certain. The Arcadians believe that they have seen Jupiter himself striking the dark-clouded shield with his right hand and stirring the rain clouds. Moreover, you see these two towns with their scattered walls, all that remains of the monuments of ancient men. Father Janus founded this citadel, Saturn that one; Janiculum was the name of the one, Saturnia that of the other."

Chatting thus with each other, they approached the home of poor Evander and saw, as they went along, the cattle lowing in the Roman Forum and in the magnificent quarter of Carinae. When they arrived at the seat of power, he said:

"Victorious Hercules deigned to cross this threshold; this palace received him. Dare, guest, to despise wealth and make yourself worthy of the god, and do not come with a feeling of disdain toward poverty."

Thus he spoke, and he led the great Aeneas under the roof of the narrow house and placed him on a bed of outspread leaves and the skin of a Libyan bear.

VULCAN MAKES ARMOR FOR AENEAS

Night rushed on and embraced the earth with its dark wings. But Venus, a mother deeply disturbed in mind and roused by the threats and the rough tumult among the Laurentians, spoke to Vulcan. In the golden chamber of her husband she began her plea and breathed divine love with her words:

"While the Greek kings were laying waste in war the walls

of Troy and the citadel was on the point of being destroyed by enemy fire, I asked no help for the stricken Trojans nor any of your skillfully wrought arms. I did not wish that you, dear husband, should labor in vain, although I owed much to the children of Priam and often wept over the hard trials of Aeneas. Now at the commands of Jupiter, Aeneas has landed on the shores of the Rutulians. Therefore, I now come as a suppliant and ask your godhead, sacred to me, for armor; a mother pleads for her son. Thetis, the daughter of Nereus, and Aurora, the wife of Tithonus, could bend your will with their tears. Look at the tribes that are assembling, the towns that behind closed doors are sharpening their swords for the destruction of me and mine."

After speaking thus, the goddess in various ways fondled her reluctant husband in the soft embrace of her snowy arms. Suddenly he felt the usual flame, and the familiar passion pierced his marrow and ran through his weakened body, just as when a jagged cleft of fire flashes with a bright light through the rain clouds. His wife, happy in her plot and conscious of her beauty, perceived this change. Then her husband, bound by everlasting love, spoke:

"Why are you looking for far-fetched excuses? What has become of your confidence in me, goddess? If you had shown similar concern before, then indeed it would have been lawful for me to arm the Trojans. Neither the all-powerful father nor the Fates forbade that Troy should stand and that Priam should survive for ten more years. And now, if you are prepared and determined to make war, cease mistrusting your powers by begging for whatever skill I can promise in my art, for anything that can be made from iron and molten electrum, for as much as fire and bellows can fashion."

After speaking these words, he gave her the longed-for embrace and resting on the bosom of his wife, he yielded to placid sleep.

Then when the first calm of Night, past its midway course, had driven sleep away, when first the wife, whose task it is to make a frugal living by her spinning and sewing, stirs the ashes of the slumbering fires, beginning her work while it is still night and keeping her slaves busy at their long tasks near the grate so that she can preserve her husband's pure home and rear the young children—at that hour in just the same way Vulcan with no less energy rose from his soft couch to the work of the forge.

Near the Sicilian coast and Aeolian Lipare there rises a steep island, the home of Vulcan, a land named Vulcania. This burns with smoking rocks, at the foot of which a cavern and the caves of Aetna, burned out by the forges of the Cyclopes, thunder. Powerful blows heard from the anvils re-echo the noise, and the hot iron bars give off a hissing sound in the caverns, and the fire roars in the furnaces. Then to this place the powerful god of fire descended from high heaven. The Cyclopes with naked bodies—Brontes, Steropes, and Pyracmon—were working iron in the vast cave. They held in their hands a rough, partly finished thunderbolt, many of which father Jupiter hurls from the whole heaven upon the earth. A part of it had yet to be completed. They had put on it three shafts of whirling hail, three of rain clouds, three of red fire, and the winged south wind; now they were mixing into their work terrifying lightning, fearful sounds, and angry, darting flames. In another spot they were making for Mars a swift-wheeled chariot in which he rouses men and cities. They were eagerly polishing the weapons of angry Pallas, the breastplate dreadful with golden serpent scales, the intertwined snakes, and, on the breast of the goddess, the Gorgon herself, rolling her eyes, though her head was severed.

"Take away everything," he said, "and carry off the work you have begun, you Cyclopes of Aetna, and turn your attention to this: arms must be made for a brave man. Now you must employ your strength, now your quick hands, now all your masterful art. Away with delay."

He spoke no more; but they all, dividing the work equally, quickly bent to the task. The bronze and the gold metal flowed in rivers; deadly steel turned liquid in the vast furnace. They fashioned a huge shield, one to equal all the weapons of the

Latins, joining seven layers to one another. Some drew in and forced out the air from the windy bellows; others dipped the hissing bronze in water. Once the anvils were set in place, the cave resounded. With great force they raised their arms in turn and handled the mass with tight-gripping tongs.

EVANDER AND AENEAS COUNSEL TOGETHER

While Vulcan, the lord of Lemnos, was speeding up this work on the Aeolian shores, the blessed light and the morning songs of the birds under the roof roused Evander from his humble home. The king rose, put a tunic about his body, and bound up his feet with Tyrrhenian sandals. Then to his side and shoulders he fastened an Arcadian sword, throwing back the skin of a panther that fell to his left. Twin watchdogs from the high threshold preceded and accompanied their master's footsteps. The hero, mindful of their conversation and the promised favor, sought out the quiet retreat of his guest Aeneas. In the early morn he, too, walked abroad. With him went his companion Achates; with Evander, his son Pallas. On meeting, they clasped their right hands and seating themselves in the middle of the building, finally enjoyed the opportunity of conversing. The king spoke first as follows:

"O great leader of the Trojans, while you are alive, I shall never admit that the state of Troy and its kingdom are conquered. We have slight strength to aid in war, considering our great name: on the one side we are shut off by the Etrurian river, on the other the Rutulians press us and surround our wall with arms. But I am preparing to ally you with a great people and a camp rich in kingdoms, a source of safety which a sudden stroke of luck offers. You come here at the command of the Fates. Not far from here is the seat of the city of Agylla, founded upon an ancient rock, where once the Lydian race, outstanding in war, settled on the Etruscan ridges. Then Mezentius, a king of haughty rule, cruel in arms, kept it in a flourishing state for many years. Why repeat his unspeakable slaughters, the wild acts of that tyrant? May the gods hold the same in reserve for him! In fact, he even used to bind dead bodies to the living, placing them hands to hands and face to face as a kind of torture, and thus in this miserable embrace he killed his victims, reeking with foul blood and gore, in a slow death. But at length the wearied citizens, resorting to arms, surrounded the unspeakably mad tyrant and destroyed his home and his companions by hurling fire to the roof. Amid the slaughter he escaped and fled to the territory of the Rutulians, where he is protected by the arms of his host Turnus.

"For that reason, all Etruria has risen in righteous wrath; under the threat of war it is demanding back its king for punishment. At the head of these thousands I will put you, Aeneas, as leader. For the ships massed along the entire shore are straining and ordering the advance, but the aged soothsayer holds them back with this prophetic utterance:

" 'O chosen youths of Maeonia and you, the flower of courageous old men, whom a just grief drives against the enemy and Mezentius enkindles to a well-deserved resentment, it is not right for any Italian to conquer so great a race: choose foreign leaders.'

"Since then, the Etruscan army, startled by the commands of the gods, has settled down on this plain. Tarchon himself sent ambassadors to me with the royal crown and the scepter, entrusting these insignia to me that I might take over the camp and assume the rule of the Etruscans. But old age, sluggish with its cold blood and worn out by the years, begrudges me the rule, and my powers are slow to brave deeds. I would urge my son were it not for the fact that, born of a Sabine mother, he partly claims this country as his fatherland. You, to whose years and race the Fates are kind, you whom the gods demand, take up the task, bravest of all leaders of the Trojans and the Italians. Moreover, I will attach Pallas, my hope and solace, to you. Let him under you, his teacher, become accustomed to endure military service and the heavy labors of war and to observe your deeds. In his tender years let him admire you. To him I give two hundred Arcadian horsemen, the chosen strength of our youth, and Pallas shall give you just as many in his own name."

Aeneas the son of Anchises and faithful Achates kept their heads bowed down and would have thought of many hardships in their sad hearts had Venus not given a sign in the open sky when Evander had scarcely finished speaking. For lightning, flashing in the heaven, unexpectedly came with the sound of thunder. Suddenly everything appeared to tremble, and an Etruscan blast of a trumpet seemed to rumble through the sky. They looked up in wonder: again and again the great crashing resounded. Though the weather was clear, they saw in a cloud in a serene region of the heavens gleaming arms that sounded when struck. The others were startled in their minds, but the Trojan hero recognized the sound and the promises of his divine mother.

Then he said: "Do not ask, my host, do not ask what peril these portents bring. I am commanded by Olympus. My divine mother prophesied that she would send this sign, if war were to assail me, and that she would bring arms from Vulcan through the air to aid me. Alas, what great slaughter is in store for the miserable men of Laurentum! What satisfaction shall you render me, Turnus! O father Tiber, how many shields and helmets of men and brave bodies shall roll along under your waves! Let them issue their challenge to war and let them break treaties!"

When Aeneas finished speaking, he rose from his high throne and stirred the banked fires on the altar of Hercules and joyously approached the lar worshiped the day before and the little household gods. Evander and the Trojan youths each offered sheep chosen in the customary way. Later he left this spot for the ships and visited his allies. From their number he chose men outstanding for courage to follow him into battle; the rest, borne on smooth waters, lazily floated down the stream to bring Ascanius news of what had happened to his father. Horses were given the Trojans, who set out for the Etruscan fields; for Aeneas they led forth a special charger, entirely covered by a lion's tawny skin, gleaming with gilded claws.

EVANDER BIDS FAREWELL TO PALLAS

The story that the horsemen were soon going to the threshold of the Etruscan king quickly traveled through the little town. Mothers redoubled their prayers in their anxiety, fear moved closer to danger, and the image of Mars already loomed larger.

Then father Evander, weeping without restraint, seized the right hand of his departing son and clinging to him, uttered these words:

"Oh, if Jupiter were to bring back the years that are past and I were the man I was under the very walls of Praeneste—when I laid low the first battle line and victoriously put fire to a pile of shields and by this right hand send down to Tartarus King Erylus, to whom at birth his mother Feronia had given—a horrible story!—three souls and three sets of weapons that he could handle; three times he had to be laid low in death; from whom this right hand took away all his lives and stripped him of just as many weapons—I should not be tearing myself away from your sweet embrace anywhere, my son, nor would Mezentius, scorning me, his neighbor, have caused so many cruel funerals with his sword or deprived the city of so many citizens. But, gods above, and you, O Jupiter, great ruler of the gods, have mercy, I pray, on a king from Arcadia, and listen to a father's prayers. If your power, if the Fates bring Pallas back to me unharmed, if I shall live to see him and to meet him, I beg for life; I will suffer any trial, no matter how harsh. But if, Fortune, you are threatening any unspeakable disaster, may I be permitted to end my cruel life now, while anguish is in doubt, while hope of the future is uncertain, while I hold you in my embrace, dear boy, my late and only pleasure. May no sadder message wound my ears."

These words the father poured forth at this last parting. He collapsed and his servants bore him into the house.

And now the cavalry had gone out through the open gate, Aeneas and faithful Achates among the first, then the other nobles of Troy, and Pallas himself in the midst of the battle line, conspicuous for his cloak and his painted armor, as when, dipped in the wave of the ocean, the Morning Star, which Venus loves above all the other fiery stars, raises its sacred face to the heavens and scatters the darkness. Trembling mothers stood upon the walls and followed with their eyes the cloud of dust and the troops gleaming in bronze. The armed band proceeded through the thickets by the shortest route to its goal: a din arose and when the line was drawn up, the hoofs struck the dusty plain with galloping sound.

There is a great grove near the cool stream of Caere, held sacred far and wide because of ancestral devotion; on all sides the hollow hills enclose and surround this forest of dark fir. The story goes that the ancient Pelasgians, who at one time held the Latin borders, consecrated this grove and a day of festivity to Silvanus, the god of field and herd. Not far from here Tarchon and the Etruscans had camped in a safe location. Already all the legion, whose tents were pitched in the broad field, could be seen from the lofty mountain. To that point father Aeneas and the youths chosen for the war repaired and wearily looked to themselves and their horses.

VENUS BRINGS AENEAS HIS ARMOR

Now the gleaming goddess Venus suddenly appeared among the clouds of heaven, bearing gifts. When she saw her son, far away by the cool stream in a secluded valley, she addressed him with these words and even appeared to him:

"Lo, here are the promised gifts, made by the art of my husband. Hereafter do not hesitate to challenge either the proud Laurentians or fierce Turnus in battle."

Venus spoke and sought the embrace of her son. The radiant armor she placed under an oak in front of him. Happy over the gifts from the goddess and an honor so great, he could not satisfy himself with gazing at each object. Marveling, he turned over in his hands the helmet with its terrifying crests pouring forth flames, the deadly sword, and the corselet. This was stiff with bronze, huge and blood-colored as when a cloud in heaven gleams with the rays of the sun and shines afar off. Then he examined the polished greaves of electrum and refined gold, the spear, and the indescribable plating on the shield.

SCENES DEPICTED ON THE SHIELD

Vulcan, not at all ignorant of the predictions of the prophets nor uninformed about the ages to come, had engraved thereon Italian history and Roman triumphs; thereon, too, the entire race of the future offspring of Ascanius, and in their order, the wars to be fought. He had also represented a she-wolf that lay in a green cave of Mars, after having had a litter of young. Around its udders twin boys, clinging playfully, suckled the mother without fear, while she, her smooth neck drawn back, stroked them in turn and caressed their bodies with her tongue.

Not far from this he had added Rome; in the assembly of a theater the Sabine women, lawlessly seized during the progress of the great Circensian games; and a new war against aged Tatius and stern Cures suddenly rising for the descendants of Romulus. Afterward the same armed kings, the struggle between them settled, were standing before the altar of Jupiter with libation cups in their hands, agreeing to a treaty after sacrificing a sow.

Not far from there swift chariots were pulling Mettus in opposite directions—but you should have kept your word, citizen of Alba!—and Tullus was dragging the body of the deceitful man through the forest, and here and there briars dripped with blood.

And, too, Porsenna was ordering the city to receive the exiled Tarquin and was vigorously pressing its siege; the sons of Aeneas were rushing to arms in defense of their liberty. One could see Porsenna angry and threatening because Cocles was daring to tear up the bridge and Cloelia was swimming the river after breaking her bonds.

On the top of the Tarpeian citadel, Manlius, the guard, stood in front of the temple and held the lofty Capitol, and the palace of Romulus was rough with a renewed thatched roof.

And here the silver goose, flying in the gilded porticoes, cackled that the Gauls were at the gate. The Gauls were advancing through the brush and were on the point of taking the citadel, protected by the darkness, thanks to a pitch-black night. They had golden hair and golden garments; they glistened in their striped cloaks; their milk-white necks were encircled with gold; in the hands of each, two Alpine javelins gleamed, and their bodies were protected by long shields.

Here Vulcan had beat out the leaping Salii and the naked Luperci, the wool-tufted peaks of their caps, and the shields that had fallen from heaven; chaste mothers in cushioned chariots were bearing the sacred objects through the city. Far from this he added even the seat of Tartarus, the deep entrance to Pluto's realm, and the punishment for crimes, and you, Catiline, hanging from a threatening cliff, dreading the face of the Furies; and the devout, living apart, and Cato, dispensing justice among them.

Among these scenes the golden picture of the swelling main stretched far and wide, but the waters foamed with white waves. Bright silver dolphins round about, breasting the tide, swept the sea in a circle with their tails. In the midst might be seen bronze ships depicting the battle of Actium; one might see all Leucate on fire with martial lines and the shining golden waves. To one side on a high deck stood Augustus Caesar, leading the Italians in battle with the senators, the people, and his great household gods; from his blessed temples issued twin flames, and upon his head his father's star appeared. In another scene, with favoring winds and gods, Agrippa, high up on the stern of a ship, led the battle line. His temples gleamed with a naval crown of beaks of ships, a proud decoration of war. In another spot with barbaric help and varied arms, Antony, coming victorious from the peoples of the East and the red seashore, brought with him Egypt and the powers of the East and remote Bactra; and—shameful sight!—his wife, Cleopatra, followed him. All rushed forward together, and the whole sea foamed when churned by the pulled oars and the three-pronged beaks. They sought the deep. One might think that the Cyclades were tossing lightly on the sea or that high mountains were clashing with mountains, of such vast size were the men who stood on the towering decks. Burning tow and flying iron weapons were hurled by hand; the surface of the sea was red with fresh slaughter. In the midst of all, the queen summoned the battle line with the traditional rattle and looked back upon two serpents behind her. Shapes of all sorts of gods and barking Anubis held drawn weapons against Neptune and Venus and Minerva. Mars, engraved in iron, raged in the midst of the battle; the mournful Furies appeared from out of the air; gloating Discord moved with her torn mantle, and Bellona followed her with a bloody whip. Seeing all this, Apollo of Acte from above bent his bow. At that terrifying sight all Egypt and the Indians, all the Arabs, and all the Sabaeans turned in flight. After calling upon the winds, the queen herself seemed to spread wide the sails and was on the point of loosening the ropes. Vulcan had represented her, surrounded by slaughter and pale at the thought of future death, as carried along by the waves and the northwest wind; and opposite her the mourning, great-bodied Nile, opening the folds of his entire garment and calling the conquered into his dark bosom and his hidden streams.

But Caesar, borne within the walls of Rome in triple triumph, was offering his immortal pledge to the Italian gods of three hundred great shrines throughout the whole city. The streets roared with happy games and applause. In all the temples there was a chorus of mothers, in all there were altars; and the earth in front of the altars was covered with slaughtered bullocks. Caesar himself, sitting upon the snowy threshold of resplendent Phoebus, recognized the gifts of the nations and fastened them to the lofty doorposts; in a long line the conquered nations entered, as different in their language as they were in their dress and arms. Here Vulcan had forged the race of the Nomads and the unbelted Africans, here the Pelasgians and Carians and the arrow-bearing Gelonians; the Euphrates, already flowing with gentler waves; the Morini, the most remote of men, and the two-horned mouth of the Rhine; the unconquered Scythians, and the Araxes River, disdaining a bridge.

Aeneas gazed at such scenes on the shield of Vulcan, the gift of his parent, and, without comprehending the events, delighted in their portrayal as he raised upon his shoulders the fame and fate of his descendants.

Book Nine

IRIS

Book Nine

TURNUS ATTACKS THE TROJAN CAMP

While these events were occurring in a far-off region, Juno the daughter of Saturn sent Iris down from heaven to brave Turnus. As it happened, he was then seated in a grove of the sacred valley of his ancestor Pilumnus. Rosy-lipped Iris addressed him with these words:

"Behold, Turnus, time, rolling on, has unexpectedly brought around what no god would dare promise to anyone who would wish it. Aeneas, leaving behind his city, his companions, and the fleet, has sought the power on the Palatine Hill and the settlement of Evander. Nor is that all: he has penetrated to the remote towns of Corythus and to an army of Lydians; he is arming husbandmen that have been collected together. Why do you hesitate? Now is the time to call for horses, now is the time to call for chariots. Away with all this delay! Surprise the disturbed camp!"

Thus speaking, she raised herself heavenward on balanced wings and in her flight cut a great arc under the clouds.

The youth recognized her and raising his two palms to the stars, followed her with these words as she fled:

"Iris, ornament of the heavens, driven from the clouds to the earth, who sent you down to me? From where did this clear weather so suddenly come? I see the heavens parting in the middle and stars wandering in the sky. Whoever you are that call me to arms, I follow these great omens."

And with these words he proceeded to the river, took up water from the surface of the stream, and, praying long to the gods, burdened the air with his vows.

And now in the open fields the whole army marched, well equipped with horses, rich in many-colored garments, and gleaming in gold, as when the deep Ganges with its seven rivers rises silently, or when the rich flood of the Nile flows back from the fields and hides itself in the bed of the stream. Messapus commanded the vanguard, the youthful sons of Tyrrhus the rear, while Turnus [brandishing his weapons and towering head high over the others] was leader in the middle of the column. Then the Trojans saw a sudden cloud of black dust massing and darkness rising over the fields.

Caicus was the first to shout from the defenses facing the enemy: "Citizens, what mass is rolling forward in that obscure darkness? To arms at once! Bring weapons! Man the walls! The enemy is here! Come on!"

With a great clamor the Trojans rushed through all the gates and lined the ramparts, for on departing, Aeneas, their best man-at-arms, had given the order that if any serious situation should arise, they should not dare to form lines or take to the field, but only stay in camp and keep the walls safe from the ramparts. Therefore, although anger and shame favored joining in battle, still they shut the gates and followed orders, waiting under arms in the hollow towers for the enemy.

Turnus, racing ahead and outstripping the slow battle line, suddenly appeared before the city accompanied by twenty chosen cavalrymen. He rode a white-spotted Thracian charger, and a red-crested helmet of gold protected him.

"Now, young men," he shouted, "who will be the first to go with me against the enemy?"

Hurling his spear, he sent it through the air, beginning the battle, and towering high, he moved over the plain. His companions replied with a shout and followed him with a wild yell. They marveled at the lack of courageous spirit in the Trojans: that the men did not enter the level plain or offer opposition but stayed in their camp. On horseback Turnus furiously passed along the walls and here and there tried to find an approach through devious routes. As a wolf, lying in ambush for a full sheepfold, howls at the fences, suffering winds and storms in the dead of night; the lambs under their mothers keep bleating, but he, fierce and furious in his anger, rages against what he cannot attack; his long pent-up madness for food exhausts him, and his jaws are dry from lack of blood: in the same way the Rutulian's anger flared up as he looked at the walls and the camp. His great strength was grievously perplexed. How could he force an entry, how drive out the Trojans, enclosed behind their defenses, and scatter them into the plain?

He attacked the fleet, which lay close to the side of the camp but was cut off by piles of earth and flowing water, and he demanded fire of his exulting companions and eagerly filled his hand with flaming pine. Then indeed they fell to the work; the presence of Turnus urged them on, and all the youths armed themselves with smoking torches. They scattered the fire, the smoking brands gave off a pitchy light, and the flames carried mingling ashes to the stars.

THE TROJAN SHIPS ARE CHANGED INTO NYMPHS

Tell, O Muses, what god turned aside such savage fires from the Trojans, who repelled such great ruin from the ships? The story was current in ancient times, but its fame is enduring. When Aeneas was first building his fleet in Phrygian Ida and preparing to set out on the deep sea, Berecynthia, the mother of the gods, addressed great Jupiter with these words:

"Son, grant a request which your dear parent asks of you, now that you have become master of Olympus. I have a pine forest which I have cherished for many a year. There was a grove on the top of the summit, dark with gloomy pine trees and maple beams, whither men used to carry the sacred objects. I gladly gave these trees to Trojan Aeneas when he needed a fleet; now anxious fear disturbs me, and I worry. Dispel my anxiety and allow a parent to effect this by her prayers, that the ships may not be overwhelmed by any rough cruise or by any windstorm. May it be their good fortune that they grew on our mountains."

Then her son, who rules the stars of the world, replied to her: "O mother, to what are you forcing the Fates? What do you mean by these prayers? Should ships made by mortal hands have a claim to immortality? Should Aeneas pursue the uncertainties of dangers with security? To what god has such great power ever been granted? But when, their usefulness past, they rest some day for the last time in Italian ports, from whatever ones that escape the waves and bring the Trojan leader to the Laurentian fields, I will take away their mortal form and order them to be goddesses of the great sea, like Doto, the daughter of Nereus, and Galatea, who breast the foaming sea."

He finished speaking and nodded that this was sealed by the rivers of his Stygian brother, Pluto, and by the banks flowing with black whirlpools of pitch, and he caused all Olympus to tremble at his nod.

Now the promised day was at hand, and the Fates had fulfilled the due time, when the attack of Turnus reminded the mother to ward off the torches from the sacred ships. Here first a new light flashed before men's eyes, and a great cloud and the choruses of Mount Ida seemed to cross the heavens from the east; then a terrifying voice descended through the air and reached the ranks of the Trojans and the Rutulians:

"Do not hasten, Trojans, to defend my ships or arm your bands. The power will be given Turnus to burn the seas before he burns the sacred ships. Go free! Go, goddesses of the sea! Your mother orders you."

Then the ships straightway severed their cables from the banks and submerging their beaks like dolphins, sought the depths of the sea. Thereafter there appeared—a marvelous omen—just like so many maiden faces, and as many floated on the waters [as before had rested as bronze prows on the shore].

The Rutulians were amazed. As his horse stampeded, Messapus himself was frightened; the resounding river slowed down, and Tiber flowed back from the sea. But self-confidence did not desert bold Turnus; he even raised the spirits of the men when he ranted at them with these words:

"These omens warn the Trojans. By these Jupiter himself has withdrawn his usual help; they await neither arms nor Rutulian fires. Now the seas are closed to the Trojans, and there is no hope of flight; half of the world has been taken away from them. The land, however, is in our hands, and the Italian races furnish many thousands of weapons. The fateful oracles of the gods in no way terrify me, if the Trojans make any such pretensions. Enough consideration has been shown the Fates and Venus in that the Trojans have landed on the fields of fertile Ausonia. On the other hand, I have my destiny: to destroy this criminal race with the sword because of the seizure of my intended wife. Such sorrow as this touches not only the sons of Atreus, nor is Mycenae the only city permitted to take up arms.

" 'But it should be enough to have perished once,' you say.

It should have been enough for them to have sinned once, since they hated deeply, as one might suppose, almost the whole race of womankind. They derive their courage from their confidence in the wall and the obstacles of the ditches, slight barriers against death. Yet did they not see the defenses of Troy built by the hand of Neptune sink in fire? But, chosen men, who is prepared to make a breach in the wall and to invade the panic-stricken camp with me? I do not need the arms of Vulcan nor a thousand ships against the Trojans. Let all the Etruscans become their allies. They need not fear the darkness and the sneaking theft of the Palladium after the killing of the guards on the top of the citadel; nor will we hide ourselves in the hollow belly of a horse. It is my intention to surround the walls with fire openly in the daylight. I will make them realize that they are not dealing with the Greeks and the Pelasgian youth whom Hector held off to the tenth year. But now, since the better part of the day has passed, for what remains, men, refresh your bodies in pleasant occupation and await the battle that is being prepared."

Meanwhile the task was given Messapus of besetting the gates with a watch of sentinels and of surrounding the walls with fires. Twice seven Rutulians were chosen to protect the wall with soldiery; but a hundred purple-crested youths, gleaming with gold, followed each one. They moved about, changed the guard, and, stretched out upon the grass, indulged in wine, emptying their bronze drinking bowls. The fires blazed; the watch passed the sleepless night in reveling.

NISUS AND EURYALUS

From the fort the Trojans, holding the high defenses with their weapons, looked down upon this scene. Trembling in fear, they examined the gates and joined drawbridges with the outer defenses, remaining armed all the while. Mnestheus and fierce Serestus took charge. Father Aeneas had authorized them, if at any time hostilities would demand it, to command the men and to assume charge of the situation. All the soldiers, risking the danger, kept guard upon the walls and took their turns at whatever had to be protected.

Guard at the gate was Nisus, most alert in arms, the son of Hyrtacus, who, swift with the javelin and light arrows, had been sent as companion to Aeneas by the huntress Ida. Nearby was his companion Euryalus, a young man whose unshaven face revealed his extreme youth. There was no one more handsome than he among the followers of Aeneas or those who bore Trojan arms. Their love was mutual, and together they rushed into war. At the moment they were even guarding the gate at the same post.

Nisus spoke: "Do the gods put this ardor in our minds, Euryalus, or does his own fierce desire become everyone's god? For some time my mind has been rousing me to battle or to attempt some great exploit, nor is it content with placid quiet. You observe what confidence the Rutulians have in their position. A few campfires are shining. Overcome with sleep and wine, they lie about; far and wide the region is quiet. Learn now what I am pondering and what a feeling now rises in my soul. All, the people and the leaders alike, are demanding that Aeneas be summoned and that men be sent to inform him of the state of affairs. If they promise to give what I ask with you in mind—for the fame of the deed is enough for me—I might be able to find a path at the foot of that hill to the walls and buildings of Pallanteum."

Euryalus was amazed, overcome by his great love of praise. At the same time he addressed his ardent friend with these words:

"Nisus, are you then trying to avoid taking me as a companion of these noble deeds? Shall I send you alone into such great dangers? Not in this fashion did my father Opheltes, inured to war, educate and rear me between the Greek terror and the destruction of Troy; nor have I conducted myself thus with you while following the final fate of the greathearted Aeneas. Here there is a spirit that despises the light and believes that that honor toward which you are striving is well purchased with life."

"Indeed I had no such fear about you," Nisus replied. "It would not be right. No! May great Jupiter or whoever looks upon these events with just eyes bring me back to you in triumph. But if any mischance or any god—you see how many perils there are in such an exploit—should sweep me into disaster, I should wish you to survive. Your age is more worthy of life. Let there be someone to commend me to the earth when I have been swept away by the battle or redeemed at a price, or, if by chance Fortune forbids that, let there be someone to perform funeral rites for his absent friend and honor him with a tomb. May I not be the cause of such great sorrow to your wretched mother, who alone, boy, of the many mothers has dared to follow you, refusing the protection of great Acestes."

But Euryalus said: "You are vainly joining together foolish reasons, nor does my altered opinion give way. Let us hasten."

At the same time he roused the guards. They rose and took their turn. Leaving the post, Euryalus accompanied Nisus, and they sought out Prince Ascanius.

Throughout the whole world all other living things found rest from their cares in sleep, and their hearts forgot their troubles. But the chief leaders of the Trojans and the chosen youths were taking counsel about most important matters of the kingdom—what they should do or who should now be the messenger to Aeneas. Leaning on their long spears and holding their shields, they stood in the middle of the wide camp. Then Nisus and with him Euryalus eagerly begged to be admitted at once, saying that their business was important and that delay would be costly. Julus first received the excited men and ordered Nisus to speak.

Then the son of Hyrtacus spoke: "Listen with deliberate mind, followers of Aeneas, and do not let this plan we propose be considered on the basis of our years. The Rutulians, relaxed by sleep and wine, have quieted down. We have seen a place for a stealthy escape lying open along the road at the gate nearest the sea. The first fires have died out, and dark smoke is rising to the stars. If you permit us to make use of our good fortune, to seek Aeneas and the walls of Pallanteum, soon you shall see us returning with spoils after effecting a great slaughter. Nor will we be deceived about the road as we go along; by constant searching we have descried a faint trace of the city in the dark valley and we have noted the stream all the way."

Hereupon Aletes, weighed down by years and judicious in temper, said: "Gods of our fathers, under whose protection Troy always lies, you are not, then, preparing to destroy the Trojans entirely when you put in young men such a spirit and such confident hearts." So speaking, he held the shoulder and the right hand of each in turn and tears flowed down his cheeks.

"What rewards should I think worthy to be paid you for this praiseworthy action? First of all, the gods and your virtue itself shall give the most beautiful reward. Then dutiful Aeneas shall promptly repay the rest, and Ascanius, fresh in age, shall never be unmindful of such great merit."

Then Ascanius broke in: "Indeed, Nisus, I swear to you both, by the great household gods, by the guardian god of Assaracus and the shrine of venerable Vesta—my only safety lies in my father's return—whatever fortune and trustworthiness I have, I place in your protection. Recall my parent, bring him back to my sight; there will be no sorrow once he returns. I will give you two silver goblets, finely wrought with embossed designs, which my father took from the conquered town of Arisba, and two tripods, two great talents of gold, and an ancient drinking bowl which Dido of Sidon gave him. If I in victory happen to take Italy and come to possess the scepter and to assign the shares of the booty—you have seen the horse on which Turnus rode by and what armor, all gold, he wore? —that horse, that shield, and those red crests I will withhold from the drawing. They are even now your prize, Nisus. Moreover, my father shall give you twelve choice women and twelve captives, each with his own arms; in addition to all this, whatever fields King Latinus has. And you, Euryalus, honored boy, whose age treads closely on the heels of mine, I receive with my whole heart and I embrace you as my companion in the face of all mishaps. In my exploits I will seek no glory without you. Whether I carry on peace or war, you shall always have my greatest trust in word and deed."

In reply to these words Euryalus said: "May the day never come that will prove me unfit for such bold enterprises; may the present good fortune not turn out adversely! But I beg this one boon above all gifts: I have a mother of Priam's ancient race, who, pitiful woman, was not restrained by the land of Troy or the walls of the city of King Acestes from leaving with me. I now leave her, ignorant of this danger, whatever it is, and without a word of farewell, because—may Night and your right hand be witness—I cannot bear the tears of my parent. But you, I pray, solace my poor mother and aid her when she is abandoned. Permit me to carry away this hope in you. I will go more bravely into every danger."

Deeply moved, the Trojans wept, most of all handsome Julus, the picture of a son's love for his parent impressed upon his mind.

"Promise yourself everything worthy of your great exploit," Ascanius said. "Indeed, your mother shall be my mother, and only the name Creusa shall be missing. No slight gratitude awaits a mother who brought forth such a son. Whatever misfortune will follow your action, I swear by this head of mine, by which my father before me was accustomed to swear, that whatever spoils are brought back by your successful exploit, these same, I promise, shall remain in the possession of your mother and your family."

Thus he spoke in tears. At the same time he took from his shoulder the golden sword which Lycaon of Gnossus had made with marvelous art and had cleverly fitted with an ivory sheath. Mnestheus gave Nisus the skin garment of a fierce lion; faithful Aletes exchanged shields with him. Thus armed, they immediately set out. The whole band of the nobles accompanied them as they departed with the prayers of young and old alike. And handsome Julus, showing a spirit and a manly care beyond his years, issued many orders to be carried to his father. But the breezes scattered the sound of his voice, and his vain words rose to the clouds.

On leaving, they leaped over the ditches and, in the shadow of the night, they sought the enemy's camp where they would perish, though destined to destroy many first. Here and there they saw men sprawled out on the grass in drunken sleep, chariots standing on the shore with men between the reins and the wheels, and weapons and skins of wine, too.

First Nisus the son of Hyrtacus spoke: "Euryalus, we must dare with our right hands; now the task itself demands it. Our course is along this route. Be on guard and watch afar off so that no hand can strike us from the rear. I will lay this section waste and lead you through a wide path."

As he spoke, he lowered his voice. At the same time, sword in hand, he approached proud Rhamnes, who by chance lay on a thick carpet, breathing heavily in his sleep—a prince himself and the favorite augur of Prince Turnus, but he could not ward off his own destruction with his auguries. Nearby, Nisus attacked three servants, lying here and there among their weapons, and the armor bearer of Remus. Finding the driver among the horses themselves, with his sword he severed their relaxed necks; then he lopped off the head of their master and left the trunk gurgling with blood. The earth was warm and their beds were moist with black gore. And he slew Lamyrus and Lamus and young Serranus of noble features, who had played much at dice that night and was lying stretched out, overcome by much drinking. Happy man, had he played that game throughout the night and continued it to the dawn! In the same way a starving lion, running wild in the full sheepfolds—for maddening hunger drives him—devours and drags away the gentle flock, mute with fear, and rages with his gory mouth.

Nor was the slaughter of Euryalus less extensive: he, too, raging in anger, slew many nameless men in his path and fell upon Fadus, Herbesus, Rhoetus, and Abaris, unknown warriors. Rhoetus was awake and saw everything, but in his fear he hid behind a huge drinking bowl. As he rose, at close quarters full in his chest Euryalus buried his entire sword and drew it back with a great gush of blood. Rhoetus poured forth his life's spirit and, dying, disgorged wine mixed with blood. Euryalus stealthily and eagerly pressed on. Now he approached the companions of Messapus and was looking at the last dying fire and the well-tethered horses cropping the grass when Nisus spoke to him briefly, as follows—for he felt they were going too far in their desire for excessive slaughter:

"Let us desist, for the hostile daylight is approaching. We have drunk to the full of vengeance; a path has been made through the enemy."

They left behind many of the men's possessions made of solid silver and weapons and bowls, too, and beautiful coverlets. Euryalus took the trappings of Rhamnes, the gold-embossed belt which the once-rich Caedicus had sent as a gift to Remulus of Tibur when joining, though far away, in hospitality with him. At his death Remulus gave it to his grandson, and after his death the Rutulians came to possess it during a battle in the course of the war. These things Euryalus seized and in vain fastened them to his brave shoulders. Then he put on Messapus' well-fitting helmet, decorated with crests. They left the camp and made for a safe place.

Meanwhile three hundred cavalrymen sent ahead from the Latin city with a reply to King Turnus were riding along armed with shields, under their leader Volcens, while the rest of the troops remained drawn up in the fields. Now they were approaching the camp and were entering within the wall when afar off on the left edge they saw the two men moving. The helmet betrayed the thoughtless Euryalus in the lifting shadows of the night and reflected the rays striking it. It was not seen in vain.

Volcens shouted from the column: "Halt, men! What is the cause of your traveling? Who are you under arms? Where are you going?"

They made no reply but fled into the forest, trusting in the night. On this side and that the cavalry blocked the known crossways and placed a guard at every exit. The forest, rough far and wide with thickets and black holm, was enclosed on all sides by dense briars. Here and there the path shone clear among the faint trails. The darkness under the branches and the heavy booty hindered Euryalus, and fear deceived him as to the location of his course.

Nisus sped away. Already, without thinking, he had fled from the enemy and the place which later was called Alban after Alba—then King Latinus had high stables there—when he stopped and in vain looked back for his absent friend.

"Ill-fated Euryalus, where did I leave you? On what path shall I follow, retracing again all my twisting course in the deceptive forest?"

At the same time he noted his footprints as he traced his way back and wandered about in the silent thickets. Then he heard horses, he heard the noise and signals of pursuers. Nor was he long in the middle of the forest when a shout reached his ears, and he saw Euryalus, whom now all the troop seized, though he tried many dodges to no purpose after being surprised by the sudden confusing tumult and misled by the place and the darkness. What could he do? By what power could he dare to snatch away the youth, by what weapons? Certain to perish, should he rush into the midst of the enemy and hasten his own glorious death by wounds? Quickly tensing the muscles of his arm, he aimed a javelin and looking up at the high moon, he raised his voice in this prayer:

"Goddess, glory of the stars and, as Diana, guardian of the groves, be present and aid my labor. If my father Hyrtacus ever offered any gifts for me upon your altars, if I myself ever added any by my hunting or suspended any from the dome of your temple or fastened any to the sacred pediment, grant that I may scatter this troop; guide my weapons through the air."

He finished his prayer and, straining with his whole body, hurled his weapon. The flying spear winged its way through the shadows of the night and struck the back of Sulmo, who stood in its path, and there it was broken, the splintered shaft piercing his heart. Cold in death he rolled, a warm stream of blood spurting from his chest, and his sides throbbed with long gasps. They looked around in different directions. More encouraged because of this, Nisus suddenly let go a second javelin on a level with the top of his ear. While they stood trembling, the whistling spear went through both of Tagus' temples and hung warm from his pierced brain. Seeing the hurler of the weapon nowhere, savage Volcens raged, not being able in spite of his fury to direct his attack anywhere.

"But meanwhile you," he said, unsheathing his sword as he made for Euryalus, "shall be my revenge for the warm blood of both."

Then really frightened, out of his mind, Nisus shouted aloud, nor was he able to conceal himself longer in the darkness or endure so great a sorrow:

"Kill me, me! I am present! I did it! Turn your weapons on me, Rutulians! The whole fault was mine. He dared nothing; nor could he have carried it out, had he tried. I swear it by the heavens and the all-beholding stars. He only loved his ill-starred friend too much."

But while he was saying such words, the sword, driven with force, penetrated between the ribs and pierced the snow-white chest. Euryalus rolled in death, and blood flowed over his beautiful limbs, and his limp neck fell back upon his shoulders: just as when a purple flower cut down by the plow, languishes in death or as when poppies with weary stems bend low their heads when the rain happens to weigh them down. But Nisus rushed into the midst of the enemy, attacking only Volcens among all of them, stopping only at Volcens, from around whom a mass of enemies lashed out on this side and that in hand-to-hand fighting. Nonetheless, he pressed on and whirled his flaming sword until he buried it full in the face of the shouting Rutulian, and dying, Volcens delivered his spirit to the foe. Then pierced through, Nisus fell upon his lifeless friend and finally rested there in the peace of death.

How fortunate both of you! If my songs avail anything, no day shall ever destroy your name in the memory of time, as long as the home of Aeneas rests on the immovable rock of the Capitol and a Roman ruler holds sway.

The Rutulian victors, taking possession of the booty and the spoils, in tears brought the dead Volcens into the camp. Nor was there less mourning there when the lifeless Rhamnes was found and Serranus and Numa and so many leaders who had been slaughtered. There was a great crowd around the dead and the dying, where the ground was warm with fresh gore and rivulets ran with foaming blood. On examining them, they recognized the spoils and the gleaming helmet of Messapus and the trappings regained by much toil.

And now early Dawn, leaving the saffron chamber of Tithonus, was scattering new light upon the earth. When the sun had begun to shed its rays, when everything was plainly seen in the light, putting on his armor, Turnus roused his men to arms, and each officer led his bronzed line into the battle, inciting their anger with varied reports. They even displayed the heads of Euryalus and Nisus on raised spears—a horrible sight—and they followed along with a great shout. The hardy followers of Aeneas faced the battle on the left side of the wall—for on the right the place was bounded by the river—and they held the great ditches and sadly stood on the high towers. At the same time the Rutulians kept moving the impaled heads of the men running with black gore, heads only too well known to the hapless Trojans.

THE GRIEF OF EURYALUS' MOTHER

Meanwhile Rumor, the winged messenger, rushed through the frightened city and reached the ears of the mother of Euryalus. Then suddenly warmth left the body of the wretched woman, the shuttle fell from her hands, and the web was undone. In her sorrow she darted out and tearing her hair, with womanly wailing she madly sought the walls and the front lines as she ran, mindless of the men, mindless of the danger from the weapons. Then she filled the heavens with her laments:

"Is this you that I behold, Euryalus? Are you the one that was the late solace of my age? Could you leave me alone, cruel son, without giving a chance to your miserable mother to speak a last word to you when you were sent into such great dangers? Alas, you lie in an unknown spot, the prey of the dogs and birds of Latium, and I, your mother, did not lead you and your funeral to your grave, nor did I close your eyes nor wash your wounds nor cover you with the garment which through nights and days I was hurriedly making for you, solacing an old woman's worries with my weaving. Where shall I go? What land now holds your limbs, your torn body, your mutilated corpse? Is this what you bring me back of yourself, son? Is it for this that I have followed you over land and sea? Kill me, Rutulians, if you have any feeling! Hurl all your javelins against me. Destroy me first with your weapons or, great father of the gods, have pity and strike down to hell with your weapon this hated head, since otherwise I cannot break off this cruel life."

Her weeping depressed the Trojans, and a sad lament passed through the crowd; their disheartened powers were numbed for battle. At the advice of Ilioneus and the much-grieving Julus, Idaeus and Actor lifted her in their arms and placed her indoors, since she was exciting grief.

THE RUTULIANS ATTACK THE CAMP

But afar off the trumpet sounded its terrible call from the tuneful bronze; a shout followed and the heavens reverberated. The Volscians hurried forward in even lines, their shields joined over their backs, and they prepared to fill up the ditches and tear down the ramparts. Some tried to find a place to enter and mount the walls with ladders where the line of defenders was thin and the top of the rampart was not crowded with men. The Trojans, accustomed to defending their walls through the long war, hurled all kinds of weapons against them and pushed them down with rough poles. They also threw down stones of great weight to see if they could break through the armored battle line. All the while, however, the Rutulians, under the dense, shield-protected line, with fine spirit withstood all these falling objects. But this was of no avail. For where the great crowd threatened, the Trojans rolled up and threw down a mass that laid low the Rutulians far and wide and broke up the armored defense. Nor did the bold Rutulians care to contend further in such blind attacks, but they tried to repel the Trojans from the rampart with missiles. At another spot, Mezentius—a terrifying sight—brandished a torch of Etruscan pine and hurled its smoking fire, while Messapus, the trainer of horses, the offspring of Neptune, tore away the rampart and called for a ladder to be placed against the walls.

INVOCATION TO THE MUSES

O Calliope, I beseech all you muses, inspire me to tell what slaughter was done there by the sword, what deaths Turnus caused, and what hero each one sent down to Orcus. Unfold with me the great outlines of the war, [for you remember, goddesses, and you can call them to mind.]

TURNUS DESTROYS A TOWER; MANY TROJANS PERISH

There was a tower, adapted to the terrain, of great height and high communicating bridges, which all the Italians in a supreme effort tried to take by storm and to overthrow with the complete resources at their command. On the other hand the Trojans defended themselves with rocks and, gathering in great numbers, hurled weapons through hollow openings. First, Turnus threw a burning brand and caused the flame to cling to the side of the tower. This fire, fanned by the breeze, spread and attacked the doorposts. Greatly disturbed, those within trembled and in vain wished to escape disaster. While they were massing and retreating to the section which was free from fire, of a sudden the tower fell forward heavily, and all the heavens resounded with the crash. As the huge mass fell, the wounded Trojans came down to earth, pierced with their own weapons, their chests run through by rough splinters of wood. Only Helenor and Lycus escaped. The older of these was Helenor, whom a Licymnian slave had secretly born to the Lydian king and sent to Troy, bearing forbidden weapons, light-armed with his naked sword, and inglorious with his white shield. When he saw himself among thousands of Turnus' followers, facing the Latin battle line on this side and that—as a wild animal, cut off by a thick circle of hunters, rushes against weapons and, consciously hurling itself, is impaled upon spears as it leaps forward—the youth, destined to die, rushed against the enemy and made for the place where he saw the weapons were thickest.

But Lycus, a far better runner, fleeing among the weapons of the enemy, made for the walls and strove to reach their high shelter and to grasp the right hands of his companions.

Pursuing on foot and with weapons, Turnus victoriously taunted him with these words: "Did you hope in your madness to be able to escape from my hands?" At the same time he seized Lycus as he hung and pulled him back with a great part of the wall—as when the eagle, the armor bearer of Jove, flying heavenward, has carried off either a rabbit or a swan of glistening white body, as when a wolf sacred to Mars has snatched from the stables a lamb sought by its mother with much bleating. On all sides a shout arose. They attacked, and the battle line filled the ditches; still others hurled burning torches to the top of the battlements.

Ilioneus with a huge stone fragment of a mountain laid Lucetius low as he approached the gate with fire, and Liger killed Emathion, and Asilas slew Corynaeus—Liger, an expert with the javelin, Asilas with the arrow that deceives from afar off. Caeneus killed Ortygius, and Turnus slew the victorious Caeneus as well as Itys and Clonius, Dioxippus and Promolus, Sagaris and Idas, who was standing to the front of the highest tower. Capys killed Privernus. First the light javelin of Themillas merely grazed him, and he insanely threw away his shield and reached his hand to the wound. Thereupon an arrow, flying on wings, pinned Privernus' hand to his left side and, buried deep within, punctured his lung with a deadly wound. The son of Arcens, sent by his father, a youth handsome in appearance and dazzling in his embroidered cloak of Spanish purple, stood in magnificent armor. He was born in the grove of his mother near the river Symaethus, where the rich-laden and propitious altar of Palicus is. Putting aside his spears, Mezentius, driving the whistling sling, whirled the thong three times around his head and pierced the middle of his opponent's temples with the molten bullet and laid him low on a wide waste of sand.

ASCANIUS SLAYS REMULUS

The story goes that Ascanius, previously accustomed to frighten fleeing wild animals, then, for the first time in war, shot the swift arrow and with his own hand slew brave Numanus, whose surname was Remulus and who recently had been united in marriage with the younger sister of Turnus. In the front of the battle line, shouting words fit and unfit to repeat, his spirit swelling with pride because of his new position of royalty, Remulus was strutting about and boasting in a loud voice:

"Are you not ashamed, you twice-captured Trojans, to be besieged again behind a rampart and to ward off death with walls? Well, here are those who demand marriage with us in war! What god, what madness drove you to Italy? Here there are no sons of Atreus, here there is no Ulysses, inventer of falsehoods. A hardy race from the start, we first carry our children to the rivers and toughen them with cruel, icy waves. Our boys rise early to stalk game and they continually roam the forest. Their sport is to tame horses and to shoot arrows with the bow. Our youths, inured to work and accustomed to little, either conquer the earth with hoes or crush towns in war. All our life is passed with the sword, and with the blunt end of the spear we weary the backs of bullocks, nor does slowing old age weaken our strength of spirit or change our vigor, and we press down our gray hairs beneath a helmet. It always pleases us to carry off fresh booty and to live by rapine. You have garments worked with saffron and gleaming purple. Your delight is in sloth and in taking part in dances; your tunics have sleeves, and your caps have ribbons. Phrygian men, go wander over lofty Mount Dindymus where the double flute plays a duet for those accustomed to it! Tambourines and the Berecynthian flute of the mother of Mount Ida summon you. Leave arms for men and give up the sword."

Ascanius could not stand such boasting speech and dire prophecy. Facing the enemy, he stretched his weapon with bowstring of horsehair and, spreading his two arms apart, he stood, a suppliant before Jove, promising votive offerings as he prayed:

"All-powerful Jupiter, favor my bold beginning. I myself will bring sacred gifts to your temples and I will place before the altars a sleek bullock with gilded horns, bearing its head as high as its mother's, a bullock that already attacks with its horns and scatters sand with its feet."

The father heard and, from a serene region of the heaven, thundered on the left. The deadly bow sounded at the same time. The arrow, drawn back, sped forth with a fearful whistling, and went through the head of Remulus, piercing his hollow temples with its iron. "There now, make sport of courage with boastful words! The twice-besieged Phrygians send back this reply to the Rutulians." This great deed Ascanius performed. The Trojans shouted, crying out with gladness, and their spirits rose to the stars.

Then, by chance, long-haired Apollo, resting on a cloud, looked down from the region of the heavens upon the Ausonian battle lines and the city, and addressed victorious Julus with these words: "Honor to you for your new courage, boy. By such actions you rise to the stars, you who are born of the gods and who will bring forth gods. It is just that all wars which fate has destined to come shall end under the race of Assaracus, nor does Troy contain you."

As soon as he had spoken these words, he let himself down from high heaven, brushing aside the stirring air, and sought Ascanius. He then changed the features of his face to those of aged Butes, who previously had been the arm bearer of Trojan Anchises and the faithful guard at the gates; then father Aeneas had made him a tutor to Ascanius. Apollo walked along, like an aged man in every way, in voice and coloring, with white hair and savagely clanking weapons, and addressed the angry Julus with these words:

"Let it be enough, son of Aeneas, that you, unharmed, battled Numanus with your weapons. Great Apollo has given you this first glory and does not envy your skill, equaling his own. But for the future, avoid war."

After speaking thus, Apollo left mortal sight while giving his advice and vanished far from view into thin mist.

The Trojan chieftains recognized the god and his divine weapons and his quiver sounding in flight. They therefore, because of the words and command of Phoebus, forbade Ascanius to battle, in spite of his eagerness. They returned to the fight again and risked their lives in open danger. A shout passed through the defenses along the entire wall. They stretched their springing bows and hurled their javelins. All the earth was covered with weapons; then shields and hollow helmets gave off a sound when struck. A fierce battle arose: as great as a storm which comes from the west with the rainy constellation of the Kids and beats the ground, or as the clouds of rain with much hail which rush to the sea, when Jupiter, fearful with south winds, hurls a storm of water and pierces the hollow clouds of heaven.

THE GIANT BROTHERS PANDARUS AND BITIAS

Pandarus and Bitias, born of Alcanor of Mount Ida, whom the woodland nymph Iaera brought forth in the grove of Jupiter, youths as tall as the firs of their native mountains, threw open the gate, which by the command of the leader was closed, and relying on their weapons, freely invited the enemy within the fortifications. Inside, on the right and left, in front of the towers they stood, armed with swords, their high heads gleaming with crests, like tall twin oaks that grow together along flowing rivers, either on the banks of the Po or near the pleasing Adige, and raise their leafy heads to heaven and nod their lofty tops. The Rutulians rushed in when they saw the doors open. Straightway Quercens and Aquiculus, handsome in arms, and impetuous Tmarus and warlike Haemon, together with the entire battle line, either turned and fled or gave up their lives on the very threshold of the gate. Then the anger of the Trojans increased as their spirit became more aggressive; already massed, they united at the same place, fighting hand to hand and daring to sally farther.

To the leader Turnus, raging and rousing his men in another section, the news was brought that the enemy was emerging in a new slaughter and leaving the gates open. He deserted the labor he had begun and, fired with savage anger, rushed to the Trojan gate and the proud brothers. Hurling a javelin, he first laid low Antiphates—for he was the first to appear—the illegitimate son of renowned Sarpedon by a Theban mother; the Italian shaft of cornel wood flew through the unresisting air and, burying itself in his throat, sank deep into his chest; the opening made by the dark wound poured forth foaming blood, and the lodged iron grew warm in his lungs. Then Turnus struck down Meropes and Erymas, then Aphidnus; then he killed Bitias, with bloodshot eyes and raging spirit, not by means of a javelin—for he would not have lost his life from a javelin—but a huge, loud-whizzing spear came flying, driven like lightning and ordinarily hurled by catapults. This neither two bulls' hides nor a trusty suit of mail with double scales of gold withstood. His huge limbs fell in a heap. The earth gave forth a groan, and the great shield thundered over him. So at times upon the Euboean shore of Baiae a pier of stones falls which, previously constructed of great masses, is toppled into the sea; thus it spreads ruin far and wide and comes to rest, completely dashed down, in the shallows. The seas mingle with one another, and the black sands are stirred up; now at the sound lofty Procida quakes as does Inarime, a bed of rock for Typhoeus laid upon him by the command of Jupiter.

Here Mars, powerful in arms, added spirit and strength to the Latins and turned sharp goads into their breasts and let loose Flight and dark Fear upon the Trojans. The Latins assembled from all sides, now that the opportunity to fight was given them, and the warrior god entered their minds.

When Pandarus saw that his brother's blood was shed, when he realized where fortune lay and what ill luck was directing events, with great strength he pushed the gate on the turning hinge, leaning upon it with his broad shoulders, and he left many of his comrades shut outside the walls in the hard fighting. But he enclosed others and received some dashing in—mad man, who did not see the Rutulian king rushing in midmost in the battle line. He had freely admitted Turnus into the city—a savage tiger among helpless flocks. Immediately a new light shone from his eyes, and his arms sounded savagely. His bloody crests upon his head trembled, and gleaming lightning issued from his shield. Suddenly the frantic followers of Aeneas recognized his hated face and fearful frame.

Then great Pandarus leaped forth and boiling over in anger at his brother's death, shouted: "This is not the dowry castle of Amata; nor does the center of Ardea protect Turnus behind his ancestral walls. You see a hostile camp; you have no power to leave here."

Calmly smiling upon him, Turnus said: "Begin, if there is any courage in your soul. Join battle! You shall announce to Priam that here also an Achilles was found." He finished speaking.

Straining with all his might, Pandarus hurled a spear, rough with knots and green bark. The air received it; Juno the daughter of Saturn warded off the coming wound, and the spear was embedded in the gate.

"But you shall not escape this weapon which my right hand hurls with force; for the author of this weapon and this wound is not such a man."

Thus Turnus spoke and straightening himself up, raised his uplifted sword on high and with a great blow from the blade split the middle of Pandarus' forehead between his temples and unbearded cheeks. A crash followed; the earth trembled beneath the mighty weight. Dying he stretched out upon the ground his limp body and his armor bloody with brains; on this side and that, in equal parts his head hung from both shoulders. Turning in craven fear, the Trojans scattered. Had the thought entered the mind of the victor to break the bars with his hands and admit his companions within the gates, that day would have been the last of the war and the race. But madness and the insane desire for slaughter drove the furious man against his adversaries.

TURNUS SLAUGHTERS MANY TROJANS

First he overtook Phaleris, then Gyges, after wounding the back of his knee; then with their captured spears he pierced their backs as they fled. Juno gave him the energy and the spirit. He added their companion Halys, and Phegeus, whose shield was pierced. Then he slew those on the wall, who were ignorant of the battle inside and who were cheering on the fight—Alcander, Halius, Noemon and Prytanis. Lynceus, summoning his companions, was moving toward Turnus. From the mount to the right he anticipated him by wielding his flashing sword. The head of Lynceus, severed by one blow at close quarters, lay afar off with his helmet; then, Amycus, a big-game hunter—no hand more skilled than his at poisoning missiles and swords—and Clytius, the son of Aeolus, and Cretheus, friend of the Muses, Cretheus, the companion of the Muses, who always loved poetry and the lyre and tuneful chords on its strings. He always sang of horses, men's weapons, and their battles.

Finally the Trojan leaders, Mnestheus and fierce Serestus, hearing of the slaughter of their men, came together and beheld their pale comrades and the enemy within the gate.

"Where, where, then, are you fleeing?" Mnestheus shouted. "What other walls, what further defenses do you now have? Citizens, shall one man, surrounded on all sides by your ramparts, spread with impunity such great slaughter through the city? Shall he send so many leaders of the youth to Orcus? Do you, sluggards, have no pity for your unhappy fatherland, its ancient gods, and great Aeneas? Have you no sense of shame?"

TURNUS ESCAPES BY LEAPING INTO THE TIBER

After being roused by such words, they were steadied, and they formed in a dense line. Little by little Turnus began to retreat from the battle, seeking the river and the section surrounded by water. Because of this, the Trojans all the more fiercely attacked with a great shout and massed together. As a hunting party pursues a lion with hostile weapons, while the beast, terrified, fierce, and glaring wildly, retreats—neither anger nor courage permits him to turn his back, nor is he able, though he eagerly desires it, to advance through weapons and men—in the same way perplexed Turnus retraced his unhurried steps while his mind boiled over with anger. Nay, he even invaded the midst of the enemies twice; twice he turned back the fleeing, confused battle lines on top of the walls, but from the camp all the band hurriedly massed into one place. Juno the daughter of Saturn did not dare to lend him strength, since Jupiter sent aery Iris down from the heavens, carrying commands, by no means gentle, for his sister unless Turnus retreated from the lofty walls of the Trojans. Thereafter, the young man could not resist so much either with his shield or with his right arm; so they rushed upon him with drawn weapons. His helmet about his hollow temples resounded with constant striking, its solid bronze was cracked by stones, and its plumes were struck down from his head; nor was the shield equal to the blows. The Trojans and fiery Mnestheus redoubled their attack with spears. Then sweat poured from Turnus' whole body in a pitchlike river, nor had he power to catch his breath; hard panting overcame his weary limbs. Then finally with all his weapons he leaped headlong into the river. Tiber's yellow flood received him as he dove down, and it carried him along on its gentle waves; when the signs of slaughter had been washed away, the river brought him, a rejoicing man, back to his comrades.

Book Ten

VENUS

Book Ten

THE COUNCIL OF THE GODS

Meanwhile, the palace of all-powerful Olympus was thrown open, and the father of the gods and king of men convoked a council at his starry residence, from which eminence he looked down upon all the earth, the camp of the Trojans, and the Latin peoples. The gods sat down in the halls with doors at both ends, and he began:

"Great heaven dwellers, why have you reversed your decision and why do you quarrel so much in hostile spirit? I had forbidden Italy to attack the Trojans in war. What discord is this, contrary to my prohibition? What fear has induced either side to take up arms and to unsheathe the sword? There shall come a proper time for battle—do not hasten the day—when fierce Carthage shall let loose great destruction against the Roman citadels and the route over the Alps shall lie open. Then you shall be permitted to contend in hatred, then you shall be permitted to pillage. Desist immediately and joyfully arrange the truce I have ordered."

Jupiter uttered these few words, but golden Venus replied with many words:

"O father, eternal power over men and things!—for what other power is there that we can implore?—do you not see how the Rutulians are attacking, how glorious Turnus drives his horses through the midst of the enemy and with swelling pride rushes with Mars on his side? Now the encircling walls do not protect the Trojans: nay, within the gates, even upon the top of the walls they mingle in battle, and the ditches overflow with their blood. Unwitting, Aeneas is absent. Will you never let them be freed from the siege? Again an enemy, a second army is threatening the walls of the Troy that is being born; again Diomede rises from Aetolian Arpi.

"Indeed, I believe that wounds are still in store for me, and I, your daughter, await the weapons of mortals! If without your protection the Trojans sought Italy against your will, let them pay for their sins. Do not bring them aid! But if they followed the many oracles that the gods and departed spirits revealed, why does everybody now wish to alter your commands and establish new fates?

"Why should I recall that their ships were burned on the shore of Eryx? Why recall the king of storms, the raging winds roused from Aeolia, or Iris, set down from the clouds? Now Juno excites even the spirits of the dead—this section of the universe had remained untouched—and Alecto has suddenly been let loose against those dwelling upon the earth and she rages in Bacchic frenzy through the midst of the cities of the Italians. I am not disturbed about my rule; we expected such changes while fortune was ours. Let those win whom you wish to win.

"If there is no region that your harsh spouse will give to the Trojans, I beseech you, father, by the smoking ruins of overturned Troy, permit Ascanius to escape unharmed from armed conflict, permit my grandson to survive. Let Aeneas, if you will, be tossed on unknown waves and follow whatever path fortune offers, but let me protect Ascanius and spirit him away from the awful battle. I have Amathus, lofty Paphos, Cythera, and my shrine at Idalia. Let him lay down his arms and pass his life without glory. Let Carthage press Ausonia under its mighty rule. Thereafter, nothing will stand in the way of the Tyrian cities. What did it avail Aeneas to escape the curse of war, to flee through the midst of the Greek fires, to experience to the full so many dangers of the sea and the vast earth while the Trojans sought Latium and a Pergamus destined to fall again? Would it not have been better to settle down on the last ashes of the fatherland and the soil where Troy was? Return, I beg you, the Xanthus and the Simois rivers to the miserable

Trojans and, father, permit them to relive the disaster of Ilium."

Then royal Juno, driven by deep fury, began: "Why do you compel me to break profound silence and to speak my hidden grief in public? Has any god or man compelled Aeneas to declare war or to become hostile to King Latinus? He has sought out Italy under the direction of the Fates—let us grant that—impelled by the madness of Cassandra. We did not urge him, did we, to leave the camp or commit his life to the winds, to entrust the conduct of the war or his walls to a boy, to disturb Etruscan loyalty or peaceful nations? What god, what harsh power among us drove him to destruction? Where is Juno in this, or Iris, sent down from the clouds? It is unjust, you say, that the Italians surround the new Troy with flames and that Turnus, whose grandfather was Pilumnus and whose mother-goddess was Venilia, take a stand on his ancestral soil. What about the fact that the Trojans are attacking the Latins with smoking torches, that they are overrunning the fields of other men and are driving off the booty? What about laying claim to a father-in-law and leading an espoused maiden away from the arms of her lover, begging peace with their hands while mounting weapons on their ships? You can spirit Aeneas away from the hands of the Greeks and stretch out in front of the hero a cloud and empty winds, and you can convert the fleet into an equal number of nymphs. Is there anything wicked in our having helped the Rutulians in opposition?

" 'Unwitting, Aeneas is absent.' Well, let him be absent unwitting. You have Paphus and Idalium and lofty Cythera. Then why do you harass a city of fierce passions, teeming with wars? Are we trying to overturn the waning powers of Phrygia to your harm? Are we—or is it not rather the one who pitted the miserable Trojans against the Greeks? What reason was there for an armed uprising in Europe and Asia and for breaking the treaty by treachery? Was it under my leadership that the Trojan adulterer took Sparta by storm? Did I furnish the weapons or promote wars by lust? That was the time to enter-tain fears for your Trojans; now tardily you rise up with unfair complaints and you hurl vain reproofs."

With such words Juno made her plea, and all the dwellers of heaven applauded with varying degrees of approval, as the first blasts of wind wail when slowed down by the forests, and the muffled murmurs roll along, warning sailors of winds to come. Then the all-powerful father, whose control of the universe is supreme, began. As he spoke, the lofty palace of the gods grew quiet, and the earth trembled to its very foundations; high heaven was silent; the winds abated, and the seas calmly leveled off their waves:

"Listen to these words of mine and fix them deep in your minds. Since it is hardly permissible that the Ausonians be joined by treaty with the Trojans and since your discord is not coming to an end, whatever fortune everyone enjoys today, whatever hope each one, either Trojan or Rutulian, entertains, I will regard with no distinction, whether it is by the destiny of the Italians that the camp is besieged, or by some unfortunate error of Troy or some unsound advice. Nor do I exempt the Rutulians. Each one's beginnings will bring labor and fortune. Jupiter is the same king for all men. Fate will find a way."

By the rivers of his Stygian brother, by the banks flowing with pitch amid a dark abyss, he shook his head and caused all Olympus to tremble with his nod. This marked the end of his speaking. Then Jupiter arose from his golden throne, and the heaven dwellers led him in their midst to his threshold.

THE TROJANS CONTINUE THEIR RESISTANCE

Meanwhile, around all the gates the Rutulians continued to slaughter men and to surround the defenses with flames. But the besieged host of the followers of Aeneas was held within its ramparts, nor was there any hope of flight. With a feeling of futility, the miserable men stood upon their high towers and defended the walls with a scant garrison; Asius the son of Imbrasus, Thymoetes the son of Hicetaon, the two Assaracuses, and the elder Thymbris with Castor—these formed the first line; in their company were the two brothers of Sarpedon, both Clarus and Thaemon, from lofty Lycia. Straining with his whole body, Lyrnesian Acmon wielded a great stone, no small piece of a mountain, nor was he inferior to his parent Clytius or his brother Mnestheus. Some strove to defend themselves with javelins, others with stones, some by hurling fire, and others by fitting arrows to their bowstrings.

Behold, the Trojan boy Ascanius, the most natural concern of Venus, stood out, his fair head uncovered in the midst of the men, like a gem that sets off yellow gold, or an ornament about the neck or head, or like ivory that shines when framed with boxwood or Orician ebony. His milk-white neck received his flowing hair, bound up with a circle of soft gold. A great-hearted nation saw you, too, Ismarus, inflicting wounds and arming arrows with poison, a high-born scion of the house of Maeonia, where men cultivated rich fields and the Pactolus ran with gold. Mnestheus was there, too, raised to fresh glory for having repelled Turnus from the top of the walls, and Capys, from whom the name of the Campanian city was taken.

THE ETRUSCANS JOIN AENEAS

In this way both sides had fought the battles of the fierce war. Aeneas was sailing along at midnight. After leaving Evander, he entered the Etruscan camp, approached King Tarchon, told him his name and his race, what help he sought, and what he himself could offer. He revealed what allies Mezentius was winning to his side and the violence of the heart of Turnus, and warned the Etruscan king what little confidence could be placed in human affairs, interspersing his entreaties all the while. There was scarcely any delay. Tarchon joined forces and agreed to a treaty. Then, freed from fate, the Lydian race, committed to a foreign leader, boarded the fleet. The ship of Aeneas was in the lead, with Phrygian lions low on its prow; from above, Ida threatened, a most pleasing sight to the exiled

Trojans. Here great Aeneas sat and went over in his mind the various events of the war. Pallas, clinging to the left side, now asked about the stars and their course through the dark night and again what the hero had suffered by land and sea.

Open now the gates of Helicon, goddess, and inspire my song, telling what band was then accompanying Aeneas from the Etruscan shores, arming the fleet that was borne over the sea.

First, Massicus cut through the waters with his bronze Tigris; under him was a band of a thousand youths who left the town of Clusium and the city of Cosae. Their weapons were arrows, in light quivers upon their shoulders, and the deadly bow. Fierce Abas went along, whose whole battle line bore resplendent armor and whose stern gleamed with a golden Apollo. Their mother city, Populonia, had given him six hundred youths expert in war, while Elba, an island of the Chalybes, generous with its plenteous supply of metals, gave three hundred. The third, that famous interpreter between men and the gods, Asilas, to whom the entrails of cattle, the stars of the heavens, the tongues of birds, and the fire of prophetic lightning lie open, marshaled a dense battle line of a thousand men with bristling spears. Pisa, a city Alphaean in origin but Etruscan in location, ordered them to obey. Handsome Astyr followed, Astyr trusting in his horse and his armor of varied hues. Those whose home was Caere and those who lived in the fields along the Minio, men from ancient Pyrgi and unhealthful Graviscae added three hundred, all with the single purpose of following Aeneas.

Nor should I pass over you, Cupavo, brave leader of the Ligurians in war, accompanied by Cinar and a few men, from whose crest the feathers of swans rose, the indication of his father's transformation—shame, Cupid, on you and your mother! For they say that Cycnus, in sorrow for his beloved Phaëthon, while he sang amid the poplar trees and the shadows of his sisters and consoled his sad love with his singing, passed a hoary old age covered with soft plumage, rising from the earth and following the stars with his voice. The son, accompanying a crowd of his age in the fleet, rowed forward the huge Centaur, whose image hung over the water and from high above threatened to hurl a huge rock at the waves as the ship plowed the deep seas with a long keel.

Moreover, that famous Ocnus, the son of the prophetess Manto and Tiber, recruited a force from his ancestral shores, Ocnus who gave the walls and the name of his mother to you, Mantua, rich in ancestors, though all are not of the same race. She has three races, each with four towns. She herself is the chief, but her strength is from Etruscan blood. From there, too, five hundred men took up arms against Mezentius, men whom Benacus' offspring, Mincius, crowned with dark reeds, led down to the sea in a hostile ship. The slow vessel of Aulestes moved along and, rising, struck the water with a hundred oars; the waves foamed as the sea was churned. His prow was fierce Triton, who frightened the sea with his dark-blue horn. In the water his shaggy front was pictured down to the sides as a man but the belly tapered off as a sea monster; the foaming water murmured under his half-savage breast.

These many chosen chieftains in three times ten ships went to the aid of Troy and plowed the surface of the sea with bronze beaks.

THE NYMPHS BRING AENEAS WORD OF THE ATTACK

Now day had departed from the heavens, and the gentle Moon in her night-wandering chariot was riding in the midst of the heavens. Aeneas himself—for his concern gave him no rest—sat handling the tiller and managing the sails. And lo, in the midst of his course, a throng of his companions met him: nymphs, to whom dear Cybele had granted the protection of the sea and who had changed from ships, were swimming side by side and breasting the waves, as many as the bronze prows that had been anchored before at the shore.

They recognized their king afar off and encircled him in a dance. Cymodoce, the cleverest of the nymphs in speaking, following in its wake, seized the stern with her right hand and raising her back from the water, swam along with her left hand under the silent waves. Then she addressed the unsuspecting hero with these words:

"Are you awake, Aeneas, offspring of the gods? Awake and loosen the ropes from the sails. We are your fleet, pines from the sacred mount of Ida, but now nymphs of the sea. As the treacherous Rutulian with fire and sword pressed us to the point of disaster, we unwillingly broke your cables and have sought you over the waters. Our mother in pity made over our appearance and gave us the right to be goddesses and to pass our lives under the waves. But the boy Ascanius, enclosed by a wall and ditches, is in the midst of weapons and Latins fierce in war. Already the Arcadian cavalry, mingling with brave Etruscans, holds the positions you have ordered them to take. Turnus has the fixed intention of putting his troops between them so that they may not join camp. Rise then and with the coming of the dawn, first order your allies to be summoned to arms, and take up the unconquered shield which Vulcan himself, binding its borders with gold, gave you. Tomorrow's light shall see great piles of Rutulian slaughter, if only you will trust my words."

She finished speaking. Departing, she pushed with her right hand the high ship, well aware how it was done. It sped through the waves more quickly than a javelin or an arrow as fast as the wind. Then the other ships hastened their course. The Trojan son of Anchises was stupefied in his bewilderment; nevertheless, his spirits rose with the omen. Then gazing for a short time at the vaulted heavens above, he prayed:

"Dear Cybele, mother of the gods, close to whose heart is the shrine of Dindyma and the tower-crowned cities and the lions yoked with bits, you are now my leader in the battle. Grant that the augury may duly come to pass, and help the Trojans, goddess, in favorable combat."

THE LANDING OF THE SHIPS OPPOSED BY TURNUS

This much he spoke. Meanwhile, the full light of returning day was already rushing on and had put to flight the night. First he ordered his companions to follow the signals, to dispose their minds for combat, and to prepare themselves for battle. Standing upon the lofty stern, he soon sighted the Trojans and his own camp, and then he raised his gleaming shield with his left hand. From the walls the Trojans shouted to the stars; new hope roused their anger, and with their hands they hurled weapons, just as when Strymonian cranes signal their approach under the dark clouds and fly through the heavens with a whirring sound and flee the south winds with joyful cries.

This seemed strange to the Rutulian king and the Ausonian leaders until they noticed that the sterns were turned toward the shore and the whole sea was rolling in with the fleet. The helmet on Aeneas' head was all afire, flame poured out from the crests on top, and the golden boss of his shield vomited forth vast fires, just as at times in the liquid night bloody comets glow ominously or the flame of Sirius, bringing thirst and disease to sick mortals, rises and casts gloom over the heavens with its baneful light. However, bold Turnus did not lack confidence that he would be able to occupy the shore and repel the Trojans from the banks when they landed. [Moreover, he raised the spirits of his men with these words and freely urged them:]

"What you have wished in your prayers to crush with your might is here; Mars himself is in your strong hands. Now let everyone be mindful of his wife and his home. Now imitate great deeds, the glory of your fathers. Let us straightway rush to the water while they are fearful; let the first steps of those who disembark falter. Fortune helps the daring."

So he spoke and turned over in his mind the names of those whom he could lead in the attack or trust with the siege of the walls.

Meanwhile, Aeneas launched his allies from the high ships by means of gangways. Many watched for the ebbing of the languid sea and, leaping, trusted themselves to the shoals; others landed by means of their oars. Tarchon, observing the shores where, he hoped, there were no shallows and where no choppy waves resounded but the smooth sea spread out with the increasing tide, suddenly turned his prow and besought his companions:

"Now, chosen band, bend to your powerful oars! Rise up, drive your ships forward! Split this hostile shore with your beaks, and let the keel itself dig its own furrow. Nor do I shrink from breaking up a ship at such an anchorage, once the land has been reached."

After Tarchon had spoken such words, his companions rose to their oars and rammed their foaming ships upon the Latin fields until their beaks rested on dry land and all their keels settled unharmed. But not your ship, Tarchon, for being dashed against the shoals while it hung on an uneven ridge, long balanced in uncertainty and wearied by the billows, it broke up and threw the men into the midst of the waves. Fragments of oars and floating benches blocked their way, and at the same time the receding waters caused them to lose their footing.

Nor did slothful delay hold Turnus back; instead he quickly hurried all the battle line against the Trojans and stood opposing them on the shore. The trumpets sounded. Aeneas, first of all, attacked the rustic throng, an omen of the battle, and laid low the Latins, after killing Theron, a man of great size who deliberately singled out the hero Aeneas. Cutting through a bronze coat of mail, through a corselet rough with gold, he wounded Theron's bare side. Then he struck Lichas, taken from his mother when she was already dead, a man sacred to you, Phoebus, because, at birth, he was permitted to escape death by the knife. A little later, he slew tough Cisseus and huge Gyas, who were laying low the battle line with clubs. The arms of Hercules were of no avail to them, nor their powerful hands, nor their father Melampus, the companion of Alcides while the earth still presented serious labors. As Pharon was hurling vain words, Aeneas, aiming a javelin, struck him in his mouth as he was shouting. You, too, unlucky Cydon, pursuing your new love, Clytius, whose cheeks were blond with the first down, would have been a pitiful sight, lying stretched out by a Trojan right hand, unconscious of the affection that youths always showed you. However, your legion of brothers, seven in number, the offspring of Phorcus, crowded in the way and hurled seven weapons. Some harmlessly bounded back from the helmet and shield of Aeneas; others, grazing his body, dear Venus turned aside.

Aeneas spoke to faithful Achates: "Hand me weapons: my right hand shall not hurl a single one against the Rutulians in vain, weapons which stuck in the bodies of the Greeks on the Trojan plains."

Then he seized and threw a huge spear. Flying, it pierced the bronze of the shield of Maeon and at the same time it broke through his breastplate into his chest. His brother Alcanor came to him and with his right hand sustained his falling brother; straightway a hurled spear, after piercing Alcanor's shoulder, came out and, covered with blood, kept its course, and his right arm hung lifeless from the shoulder by its sinews. Then Numitor, after seizing the spear from the body of his brother, attacked Aeneas. However, it was not permitted to wound him, but it grazed the thigh of the Great Achates.

Then Clausus, who came from Cures, advanced, trusting in his youthful strength, and from the distance struck Dryops under the chin with a rigid spear, which, buried deep, took away the voice and the soul of the speaker together by piercing his throat. He struck the earth with his forehead and poured forth thick blood from his mouth. Clausus also laid low by different deaths three Thracians from the exalted race of Boreas and three whom their father Idas and the country of Mount Ismarus had sent. Halaesus and bands from Aurunca rushed to the attack; the offspring of Neptune, Messapus, noted for his horses, joined the fray. Now this group, now that, strove to repel them; the battle raged on the very threshold of Ausonia. As discordant winds battle in the great vault of heaven with equal spirit and force, they do not yield among themselves, nor do the clouds nor the sea; the battle is long in doubt and the struggle is general: in just the same way the Trojan and Latin lines battled; foot stayed close to foot and man to man.

THE EXPLOITS OF PALLAS

But in another region where the torrent had scattered rolling stones far and wide and where trees were uprooted from the banks, Pallas saw that the Arcadians, unaccustomed to infantry formations, were fleeing from the pursuing Latins, since the roughness of the place had convinced them that they should send away their horses. Now by entreaties, now by bitter words, he roused their courage—the only thing that remains in adversity:

"Whither are you fleeing, comrades? By your own brave deeds, by the name of your leader, Evander, by the wars you have won, by my hopes which are now rising to my father's merit, do not place your trust in flight. A path must be cut through the enemy with the sword. Where that crowd of men attacks in greatest numbers, there your noble fatherland summons you and your Pallas. No gods are pressing upon us; mortals ourselves, we are attacked by a mortal enemy. We have just as much spirit, just as many hands. Look, the sea shuts us off by its great watery barrier. Now no land remains for flight. Shall we make for the sea or the new Troy?"

So saying, he plunged into the midst of the battle where the enemy was thickest.

The first to meet him was Lagus, guided by an unlucky fate. While he was pulling loose a stone of great weight, Pallas, hurling his spear, struck him where the middle of the spine separated the ribs, and recovered his spear, clinging to the bones. Hisbo did not surprise Pallas, although he hoped to do so; for Pallas met Hisbo as he rushed head on, raging and incautious because of the cruel death of his companion, and buried his sword in his expanded lungs. Then Pallas attacked Sthenius and Anchemolus, of the ancient race of Rhoetus, who had dared to defile the marriage of his stepmother.

You twins, Larides and Thymber, identical offspring of Daucus, indistinguishable even to your own people and a most pleasing source of confusion to your parents, fell in the Rutulian fields. But now Pallas made a harsh distinction between you: for the sword of the son of Evander cut off your head, Thymber; and your severed right hand, Larides, sought you, where it belonged, and the half alive fingers trembled and grasped at the sword.

Mingled sorrow and shame armed the Arcadians, roused by the scolding and the sight of the noble deeds of their hero. Then Pallas pierced Rhoeteus, who was racing along in his chariot. Just so much distance, just so much reprieve was given Ilus; for from afar Pallas had directed against Ilus his strong spear, which the oncoming Rhoeteus intercepted when he was fleeing you, noble Teuthras, and your brother Tyres. Rolling from the chariot, dying Rhoeteus struck the Rutulian fields with his heels. And as with the rising of the winds in the summer the shepherd intentionally lights various fires in the forest; suddenly spreading to everything in the intervening space, a horrifying line of fire is extended through the wide plains while the seated victor looks down upon the triumphant flame; in just the same way all the courage of your companions united together and aided you, Pallas. But Halaesus, fierce in war, made for his adversaries and protected himself with his weapons.

Halaesus slew Ladon and Pheres and Demodocus. With his gleaming sword he cut off Strymonius' right hand, raised to wound his throat; with a stone he struck the mouth of Thoas and scattered his bones mixed with bloody brains. Prophesying evil fates, the father of Halaesus had concealed him in the forest. As the graying old man closed his eyes in death, the Fates laid hold of Halaesus and promised him as a sacrifice to the weapons of Evander. Pallas attacked him, after first uttering this prayer:

"Give now, O father Tiber, good luck and a way through the breast of hardy Halaesus for this shaft which I send flying.

These weapons and the armor of the hero shall hang from your oak."

The god heard these words. While covering Imaon, Halaesus, unfortunate man, offered his unprotected breast to the Arcadian weapon.

But Lausus, a mighty force in the war, did not allow the battle lines to be frightened by such great havoc wrought by the hero. First he slew Abas, the center and bulwark of the battle, who opposed him. The offspring of Arcadia was laid low, the Etruscans were laid low, and you, O Trojans, who had escaped destruction at the hands of the Greeks. The armies rushed together, equally matched in leaders and men. The soldiers in the rear pushed the front lines together, and the throng did not permit the movement of weapons and hands. On the one side, Pallas pressed the attack; on the side opposite, Lausus—both of outstanding physique, nor were they very far apart in age; but Fortune had refused to let them return to their fatherlands. However, the ruler of great Olympus did not suffer them to clash with each other. Soon their individual fates awaited them from a greater enemy.

TURNUS SLAYS PALLAS

Meanwhile, Turnus was advised by his dear sister to take the place of Lausus, who was cutting through the midst of the battle line in his swift chariot. As he saw his comrades, he shouted:

"It is time to desist from battle. I am attacking Pallas unaided. Pallas is due me alone. Would that his father were here as a spectator!"

He spoke these words, and his companions left the field at his command. But at the departure of the Rutulians, the youth, marveling at these arrogant commands, was amazed at Turnus and let his eyes wander over his huge body. From afar he surveyed the scene with savage gaze and opposed the words of Prince Turnus with these words:

"I shall soon be praised for having taken choice spoils or for meeting a glorious death; my father is prepared for either fate. Away with your threats." So saying he proceeded to the middle of the plain. The blood ran cold in the heart of the Arcadians.

Turnus leaped down from his chariot; as a foot soldier he prepared to go into hand-to-hand combat. As a lion flies to the encounter when from a high vantage point he sees a bull standing afar off in the fields meditating battle, such was the picture of the advancing Turnus. When Pallas believed that Turnus was close enough for a shot with his spear, he advanced first, in the hope that fortune might aid a man who had shown daring against uneven powers. Thus he spoke, directing his words to high heaven:

"By the hospitable tables of my father, at which as a stranger you were present, I beseech you, Hercules, aid my great beginning. May Turnus see me snatch his bloody arms from him when he is half dead, and may his dying eyes be forced to behold me as his victor."

Pressing down in his heart a great sigh, Hercules heard the youth and poured forth vain tears. Then Jupiter addressed his son Hercules with friendly words:

"Everyone has his day; brief and irreparable is the space of the life of all; but to lengthen one's fame by deeds, that is the work of virtue. So many sons of the gods fell under the high walls of Troy; nay, Sarpedon, an offspring of mine, fell. Even Turnus is summoned by his fate, and he has reached the goal of his allotted time." Thus he spoke and turned his eyes away from the fields of the Rutulians.

But Pallas hurled his spear with great force and from his hollow scabbard pulled out his gleaming sword. Flying, the spear struck where the top protection for the shoulder rose, and forcing its way through the border of the shield, finally glanced from the huge body of Turnus.

Then he, balancing for a long time an oak shaft tipped with sharp iron, hurled it against Pallas and spoke as follows: "See now whether my weapon can penetrate deeper."

He finished speaking. With a vibrating blow, the point pierced the middle of the shield, so many layers of iron, so many of bronze, which the surrounding bullhide so often encircled, and perforated the resistance of the corselet and his great chest. In vain he snatched the warm weapon from the wound: by one and the same route, his blood and his life left him. He collapsed upon his wound; his arms clashed about him, and dying he fell, striking the hostile earth with his bloody face.

Standing over him, Turnus said: "Arcadians, remember to carry back these words of mine to Evander: I am returning Pallas as he deserved to be returned. I freely give whatever honor there is in the tomb, whatever solace in burial. He shall pay no little price for his cordial reception of Aeneas."

As he spoke, he stamped on the lifeless youth with his left foot and seized the huge, heavy belt with a sacrilegious deed impressed thereon: a band of youths foully slain on one nuptial night and bloody marriage chambers which Clonus the son of Eurytus had carved with much gold. Then Turnus gloated over this trophy and rejoiced on obtaining it. How ignorant of fate and future destiny is the mind of man! How witless in not practicing restraint when elated by prosperity! There shall come a time for Turnus when he shall wish that Pallas, redeemed at a great price, had never been touched; when he shall hate these spoils and this day.

But Pallas' comrades, amid groans and tears, crowding around in great numbers, brought him upon his shield. O sorrow and great honor, soon to return to your father! This day first gave you to war and this same day bore you away; at the same time, however, you leave great piles of Rutulians!

AENEAS KILLS MANY WARRIORS

The rumor of such a great disaster had not yet reached Aeneas, but a trustworthy messenger arrived saying that his followers were on the brink of destruction and that it was time to aid the defeated Trojans. The hero struck down everything near him with his sword and, raging through the broad battle, cut a path with his blade, seeking you, Turnus, arrogant over your recent slaughter. Pallas, Evander, the banquet in which first as a stranger he had taken part, and the pledges that were given—all these things rose before his eyes. He took alive four young men, the sons of Sulmo, and just as many whom Ufens had reared, to offer them as victims to the departed shades and to pour the blood of captives over the flames of the pyre.

From afar he had hurled a hostile spear at Magus, who cleverly dodged, as the quivering weapon flew over his head, and embracing Aeneas about the knees as a suppliant, he pleaded: "By your father's spirit and the hopes of growing Julus, I beg of you, save my life for my son and father. I have a lofty house where deep-buried talents of chased silver lie; I have a quantity of gold, wrought and unwrought. The victory of the Trojans does not turn on me, nor will one life make such a great difference."

He finished speaking, and in reply Aeneas uttered these words: "Save for your children the many talents of silver and gold of which you speak. Turnus was the first to rule out such exchange in war at the moment when he slew Pallas. This is what the spirit of my father Anchises feels, this is what Julus feels."

So speaking, he seized the helmet of Magus with his left hand and bending back the neck of the pleading man, he buried his sword up to the hilt. Not far away was the son of Haemon, the priest of Apollo and Diana, resplendent in his garments and outstanding armor, whose fillet bound his temples with a sacred band. Encountering him, Aeneas drove him over the field and, standing over the fallen man, slew him, covering him with the great shadow of death. Serestus bore away upon his shoulders these choice weapons as a trophy to you, mighty Mars.

Caeculus, born of the race of Vulcan, and Umbro, coming from the mountains where the Marsi live, rallied the battle lines. Aeneas raged against them. With his iron sword he had just struck down Anxur's left hand and the whole circle of his shield. He had spoken boastfully, believing that there would be power in speech. His hopes raised to heaven, he had, no doubt, promised himself a white-haired old age. Exulting Tarquitus, whom the nymph Dryope had borne to the forest-dwelling Faunus, threw himself in the path of the raging Aeneas. Drawing back his spear, Aeneas nailed together the corselet and the heavy shield. Then he dashed to earth the head of the vainly pleading man, who was preparing to say many things, and rolling his warm body forward, Aeneas uttered these words with hostile heart:

"Lie there now, fearful warrior. Your blessed mother shall not bury you in the earth, nor shall she cover your corpse in your father's tomb. You shall be left to the fierce birds, or the wave shall bear you along under its flood, and the hungry fish graze against your wounds."

Straightway he pursued Antaeus and Lucas, the first battle lines of Turnus, and brave Numa and blond Camers, born of the greathearted Volcens, the richest landholder among the Ausonians, the ruler over quiet Amyclae. As Aegaeon, who, they say, had a hundred arms and a hundred hands, poured forth fire from fifty mouths and chests while crashing just as many corresponding shields against the thunderbolts of Jupiter and wielding as many swords, so Aeneas raged victoriously over the whole plain, once his sword grew warm. Now behold! he made for the opposing chests of the four-yoked horses of Niphaeus. And they, on seeing him advancing afar and uttering dire threats, turning in fear and rushing away, tossed out their driver and ran with the chariot to the shore.

Meanwhile Lucagus and his brother Liger drove into the middle of the battle in their chariot drawn by two white horses; Liger reined in the horses, while fierce Lucagus brandished his drawn sword. Aeneas could not bear their raging with so much fury; he rushed up, looming large with his threatening spear.

Liger said to him: "You do not see the horses of Diomede, the chariot of Achilles, or the plains of Phrygia. Now an end of this warring age shall be given this land." These words spoken by the insane Liger flew far and wide.

But the Trojan hero did not frame words in reply; instead

he hurled his javelin against his enemy. As Lucagus, bending forward and leaning over the reins, urged on the horses with his spear while with his left foot forward he made ready for the fight, a spear entered the lowest edge of his gleaming shield and then pierced his left groin. Tossed from his chariot, he rolled in death upon the fields.

Aeneas addressed him with bitter words: "Lucagus, it was not the cowardly flight of your horses that betrayed your chariot, nor did empty phantoms turn them from the enemy. You yourself, leaping from the wheels, deserted your chariot."

Speaking these words, he seized the team of horses. The unfortunate brother, Liger, stretched out his unarmed hands and descended from the same chariot: "By yourself, by the parents who produced a man like you, O Trojan hero, spare this soul and have mercy on one crying for your pity."

As he pleaded with many words, Aeneas answered him: "Just a moment ago you were not uttering such talk. Die, and as a brother, do not desert your brother." Then with his spear he laid bare his breast, the hidden seat of the soul.

The Trojan leader produced such destruction throughout the fields, raging like a torrent of water or a black tornado. Finally the boy Ascanius and the young men, besieged in vain, burst forth in a sally from their camp.

JUNO DELAYS THE DEFEAT OF TURNUS

Meanwhile, Jupiter voluntarily addressed Juno: "O my sister and pleasing wife, too, just as you thought, Venus—nor does her plan deceive you—is sustaining the Trojan arms; it is not the mighty warring strength of the men, their proud spirit, or their endurance in danger."

"Why, my handsome husband," Juno answered meekly, "do you rouse one who is distressed and fearful of your grim words? If I offered you the attraction in love that I once did—and how fittingly so!—you would certainly not deny me this favor, all-powerful one, that I might rescue Turnus from the battle and preserve him unharmed for his father Daunus. Now let him perish and let his sacred blood suffer punishment from the Trojans. He, however, is descended from our lineage, for Pilumnus was his ancestor four generations back; often with a generous hand he has laden your altars with many gifts."

The king of ethereal Olympus briefly spoke to her as follows: "If you ask for a delay of present death and an extension of time for the perishing youth and you understand this proposal of mine, then take Turnus away by flight and snatch him from impending fate: thus far it is my pleasure to have indulged you. But if any deeper favor lies hidden beneath these prayers and you imagine that the entire war can be influenced or changed, you are feeding a vain hope."

Juno tearfully replied: "What if your mind would concede what your voice refuses and life would be granted to Turnus? Now grave disaster awaits a guiltless man or I am greatly in error. Rather may it be that I am deceived by a false fear, and that you, who are able, will change your orders for something better!"

TURNUS PURSUES A PHANTOM AENEAS

After uttering these words, straightway she descended from high heaven, surrounded by a cloud and driving a storm through the air, and she sought the Trojan battle line and the Laurentian camp. Then the goddess fitted out an unsubstantial, powerless shade of hollow cloud with Trojan weapons and the features of Aeneas—a sight marvelous to behold—and she copied the shield and the crests of his divine head, gave it empty speech, a sound without mind, and it imitated the steps of a man walking. It was like such figures as flit about, they say, after death or such dreams as deceive the senses in sleep. But the happy image exulted in front of the first battle lines and irritated the hero by brandishing weapons and hurling taunts. Turnus attacked it and from afar hurled a spear; turning its back, it changed its direction.

Then indeed, as Turnus believed that his opponent Aeneas was giving ground, his mind drank in empty hope in his confusion: "Where are you fleeing, Aeneas? Do not desert the promised marriage! This right hand will give you the land you have sought over the waves."

Shouting such words, he pursued him as he brandished his drawn weapon; nor did he realize that the winds bore away the joy of victory. By chance a ship, moored to the edge of a high rock, stood with ladders in position and its bridge ready; on this King Osinius had arrived from the shores of Clusium. The frightened image of Aeneas, fleeing thither, hurled itself into the hold of the ship; nor did Turnus attack with less vigor, overcoming obstacles and overleaping the high bridges. He had hardly touched the prow when Juno cut the rope and hurried the loosened ship over the rolling sea.

But Aeneas challenged the absent Turnus to battle and sent many men in his path to their death. Then the light phantom did not stay in the hold but, flying high up, mingled itself with a black cloud, while in the meantime a whirlwind tossed Turnus in the middle of the sea.

Ignorant of what had taken place and not at all grateful for his escape, he raised his two hands to the stars and prayed: "All-powerful father, have you thought me worthy of being treated as so great a criminal, and did you wish me to suffer such punishments? Whither am I borne? Whence did I come? What flight is this that rescues me? What kind of man am I that flight rescues? Shall I ever again see the walls of the camp of Laurentum? What will that band of men do who followed me and my arms, all of whom I left to an unspeakable death—an impious thing—and whom I now behold retreating and hear groaning as they die? What am I to do? What land can now yawn deep enough for me? Rather have mercy, winds. Dash my ship into the cliffs, into the rocks—I, Turnus, honestly beg of you—and guide me into the treacherous shallows of sandbanks where neither Rutulians nor rumor that knows my disgrace may follow me."

Going over these matters in his mind, he veered now this

way, now that. Should he madly slay himself with his sword because of so great a disgrace and drive its bare blade between his ribs, or throw himself into the midst of the waves and by swimming reach the curved shores and again do battle with the Trojans? Three times he tried both ways; three times great Juno restrained him and, being compassionate in spirit, she held him back. Cutting through the deep, he glided with favoring flood and tide and was borne to the ancient city of his father, Daunus.

THE EXPLOITS OF MEZENTIUS

But meanwhile Mezentius, fired by the inspiration of Jupiter, entered the battle and attacked the rejoicing Trojans. The Etruscan battle lines converged and they attacked this one man with all their hatred and numerous weapons. As a rock jutting out into the vast ocean, meeting the fury of the winds and exposed to the billows, withstands all the threatening force of the sky and the sea, yet still remains unmoved itself, so he dashed Hebrus, the offspring of Dolichaon, upon the ground and with him Latagus and the fleeing Palmus, striking Latagus full in the face with a great piece of stone from the mountain while allowing Palmus to roll about helpless with a deep cut in his knee. To Lausus he gave the victim's armor to be worn on his shoulder and crests to fasten on his helmet. Phrygian Evanthes he also slew, and Mimas, the companion of Paris and his equal in age, whom one night Theano brought into the light for his father Amycus, the very night Queen Hecuba, pregnant with a torch, brought forth Paris. He now sleeps in the city of his father; the Laurentian coast holds Mimas, a stranger. As a boar that the pine-bearing Vesulus and the Laurentian swamp have protected for many years, feeding him on its reedy growth, is driven by the bites of dogs from the high mountains into the nets, then stops, fiercely rages, and bristles its shoulders, and none has the spirit to show his courage by approaching closer, but from afar they attack with spears and safe shouts; so it was with those who justly hated Mezentius. None had the courage to meet him with drawn sword but from afar they assailed him with missiles and a great uproar. He, however, fearlessly held his ground from every direction, grinding his teeth and shaking off spears from his back. Acron, a Greek, who had fled from his unconsummated marriage, had come from the ancient region of Corythus. In the distance Mezentius saw this man mingling in the midst of the battle lines. He was decked with red feathers and a purple cloak from his espoused wife. As a starving lion, driven by mad hunger, often roaming around high-fenced enclosures, if by chance he has caught sight of a fleeing roe or a stag with lofty horns, rejoices savagely as he opens his mouth, bristles his mane, and leaps upon his prey, clinging to its body as foul blood bathes his savage face, so Mezentius swiftly rushed into the thick of the enemy. Ill-starred Acron was laid low, and he beat the dark earth with his heels and stained the broken weapon with his blood.

Mezentius did not stoop to slay Orodes in flight nor to wound him from the rear by throwing a spear. He met him face to face and attacked him man to man, superior not by treachery but by armed courage. Then with his foot placed on his prostrate opponent, leaning on the spear, he said:

"Men, tall Orodes, a power hardly to be scorned in the war, lies low."

In unison the comrades of Mezentius shouted the happy song of victory.

"Victor, whoever you are," Orodes said as he died, "you shall not long rejoice over me without my being avenged. A like fate also awaits you; soon you shall be in the same place."

Scoffing in anger at these words, Mezentius said: "Now die. Let the father of the gods and the king of men see to me."

Saying this, he drew the weapon from his victim; heavy silence and an ironlike sleep pressed down upon Orodes' eyes, as they closed for an eternal night.

Caedidus slaughtered Alcathous, Sacrator killed Hydaspes, Rapo both Parthenius and Orses, a man of sturdy strength. Messapus slew Clonius and Erichaetes the son of Lycaon, the former lying on the earth because of a fall from his unbridled horse, the latter advancing as a foot soldier. Agis of Lycia, a foot soldier, had come forward, but Valerus, not lacking in the courage of his fathers, laid him low. Moreover, Salius slew Thronius and Nealces slew Salius, the one from ambush with a javelin, the other with a treacherous arrow from afar.

Now hard fighting made the struggle and the slaughter equal on both sides; the victors and the vanquished killed and attacked by turns, nor was one or the other known to flee. In the palace of Jupiter the gods deplored the futile anger of both and such great sufferings among mortals. From one side, Venus looked on; from the opposite, Juno the daughter of Saturn. Pale Tisiphone raged in the midst of thousands. Now furious Mezentius, brandishing his huge spear, entered the field. As when great Orion, cutting his way on foot through the deep waters of mid-sea, towered over the waves, his shoulders out of the water, or when bringing back an aged ash from the top of the mountains, he walked on the earth while his head was hid among the clouds, so Mezentius presented himself with his huge weapons.

AENEAS SLAYS LAUSUS AND HIS FATHER MEZENTIUS

Sighting him in the long battle line, Aeneas prepared to move to the attack against him. Mezentius remained unperturbed, awaiting his noble enemy, and, standing in his massive power, measured with his eyes the distance he could throw a spear, and said:

"Now may my right hand and this missile that I balance come to my aid! I vow that you yourself, Lausus, as a memento of Aeneas, shall be clothed with the spoil taken from the body of this robber."

He spoke and hurled from the distance a strident spear; but in its flight it was knocked down from Aeneas' shield and far away pierced noble Antenor between his side and his belly, Antenor, the companion of Hercules, who, on being sent from

Argos, had sided with Evander and had settled in the Italian city. The unlucky man was laid low by a wound intended for another. He gazed on the heavens and, as he died, remembered his sweet Argos.

Then dutiful Aeneas hurled his spear. It pierced Mezentius' round, hollow shield of triple bronze, the flaxen folds, and the work interwoven with three hides of bulls, and it settled low in his groin, but its power was spent. Aeneas, happy at the sight of the blood of the Tyrrhenian, quickly seized the sword at his thigh and furiously attacked the panic-stricken man.

At the sight, Lausus, with tears streaming down his face, wept bitterly because of his love for his dear parent. Here indeed I will not pass over in silence the tragedy of your hard death and your noble conduct, nor you yourself, illustrious youth, if any age to come will believe your great feat.

Mezentius, stepping back, powerless and impeded, gave ground and dragged along the enemy's spear attached to his shield. The youth rushed forward and mingled in the battle, and then with his right hand met the sword of Aeneas, who rose up and struck a blow; but Lausus withstood him by delaying tactics. His companions followed with a great shout until the parent, protected by the shield of his son, escaped, and they hurled weapons and from the distance disturbed the enemy with missiles. Aeneas lunged forward, yet kept himself protected. As when at times a storm breaks with a shower of hail, the traveler lies sheltered in some safe retreat either on the banks of a river or in a recess of some high rock and while it rains on the land, all the plowmen and farmers flee from the fields, so that they may carry on their day's work when the sun returns, so, harassed on all sides by weapons, Aeneas withstood the storm of war until all the din died down. Then he railed against Lausus and threatened him:

"Where are you rushing, youth, destined to die? Are you daring what is beyond your power? Your sense of duty lures you into a disregard for caution."

But Lausus, nonetheless, exulted in his madness. Wild anger mounted higher now in the Trojan leader, and the Fates spun the last threads for Lausus; for Aeneas thrust his powerful sword into the bowels of the youth, completely burying it. The point pierced his little shield—light armor for one threatening so—and the tunic which his mother had woven from pliant threads of gold. Blood completely covered his chest. Then his sad soul departed through the air to the spirits below and left his body.

But when the son of Anchises saw the look on the face of the dying man, a face surprisingly pale, he groaned deeply in his sorrow and stretched forth his hand, and the picture of his love for his own father flashed through his mind.

"Miserable boy, what will dutiful Aeneas give you now in consideration of such praiseworthy action, what that is worthy of such great spirit? Keep those arms of yours in which you rejoiced. I return you to the shades and ashes of your forefathers, if that causes you any anxiety. But in your unhappiness you shall relieve the misery of your death with this thought: you have fallen by the right hand of the great Aeneas."

He even chided the reluctant comrades of Lausus and raised their leader from the earth where he lay, his neatly combed locks soiled with blood.

Meanwhile, the father at the edge of the Tiber River had bathed his wounds with water and, reclining against the trunk of a tree, was resting his body. At some distance his bronze helmet hung from the branches, and his heavy armor lay upon the meadow. Picked youths stood about; he himself, wounded and panting, inclined his neck forward while his long beard flowed upon his bosom. He asked many questions about Lausus and sent back many men to recall him and bear the commands of the sorrowing father. But the weeping comrades of Lausus bore him lifeless upon his shield, a great man, felled by a great blow.

His mind, foreboding ill, afar off recognized the wailing. He poured handfuls of dust upon his white hair, stretched his two hands to heaven, and clung to the corpse.

"Did such a great delight in living possess me, son, that I suffered you to succumb to a hostile hand in defense of me? Am I, your father, saved by these wounds of yours? Am I living because of your death? Ah, now, finally in my misery I know the unhappiness of exile, now the wound has been driven deep! I myself, son, have stained your name with crime, having been driven in hatred from the soil and realm of my fathers. I owed this penalty of death to my fatherland and to the hatred of my people. Would I had yielded up my guilty soul to every kind of death! Now I live and as yet I am not leaving men and the light of day. But I will leave them."

Saying this, he raised himself on his injured leg and although his strength was failing because of his deep wound, not at all disheartened, he ordered his horse to be led forth. This was his pride, this his solace; on this he returned victoriously from many wars.

He spoke to the grieving animal with these words: "Rhaebus, long have we lived, if any time is long for mortals. Either you shall today victoriously bring back those bloody spoils and the head of Aeneas and with me be the avenger of the pains of Lausus, or, if no force can open a way, you shall perish at the same time. I do not believe, brave animal, that you will deign to heed foreign commands and Trojan lords."

He finished speaking and, mounting his horse, seated himself as he usually did and filled both his hands with sharp spears, while the bronze of his helmet gleamed and his crest of horsehair waved. Thus he rapidly charged into the midst of the enemy. At the same time there welled up in his heart great shame and fury with mingled sorrow, [rage-driven love and conscious courage]. Thereupon he hailed Aeneas thrice in a loud voice.

Aeneas recognized him and joyfully prayed: "May the great father of the gods, may noble Apollo will it so! Begin the fight."

Saying no more, Aeneas went up to meet him with a deadly spear. But Mezentius said: "In what way can you frighten me, you savage, now that my son has been snatched away? That was the only way in which you could destroy me. I have no horror of death, nor do I curry the favor of any one of the gods. Cease: for I come to die, but before I do, I bring you these gifts."

He spoke and hurled his weapon against his enemy; then another and still another he hurled, racing in a great circle: But the golden shield resisted them. Hurling weapons, three times he rode around Aeneas, standing on the left; three times the Trojan hero bore around with him the immense forest of spears that stuck in his bronze protection. Then when Aeneas grew weary of the long drawn-out delay and of tearing away so many shafts, he pressed close, though matched in an unequal struggle. After turning over many plans in his mind, at length he attacked, hurling a spear between the hollow temples of the war-horse. The beast reared up on its hind legs and pawed the air with its hoofs. Coming down, it became entangled with the thrown rider and fell head first, dislocating its shoulder. Both Trojans and Latins filled the heavens with their shouting.

Aeneas darted forth and, drawing his sword from its sheath, uttered these words as he stood over his foe: "Where now is the fierce Mezentius and that savage fury of his mind?"

In reply the Etruscan said, looking up to heaven and breathing deeply on regaining consciousness:

"Bitter enemy, why do you taunt me and threaten death? There is nothing sacrilegious in killing me, nor did I come with this spirit to battle, nor did my Lausus arrange such a pact with you in my behalf. This one thing I beg by whatever favor there is for conquered enemies: allow my body to be covered with earth. I know that the bitter hatred of my own people surrounds me; ward off this fury, I beg you, and permit me to be a companion of my son in the tomb."

He uttered these words and, still quite conscious, received the sword in his throat and poured forth his soul with the blood that streamed over his armor.

Book Eleven

DIANA

Book Eleven

TROPHY FROM ARMS OF MEZENTIUS

Meanwhile the rising dawn came up from the ocean. At the first ray of light, victorious Aeneas paid his vows to the gods, although his mind was troubled by the funeral rites and his grief urged him to take time to bury his comrades. After stripping the branches from a huge oak, he set it up upon a mound and from this he suspended gleaming armor, the spoils of the leader Mezentius, as a trophy to you, great Mars. He attached the blood-dripping crests and the shattered weapons of the man and his breastplate, dented and pierced in a dozen places, and he tied up the shield of bronze on the left and hung the ivory-hilted sword from the neck of the oak. Then he encouraged his cheering comrades with these words, for all the crowd of leaders was pressing close about him:

"Men, the greatest part of our work is accomplished. Away with all fear for what remains! These are the spoils and the first offering from a proud king; here is Mezentius in my hands. Now our course is to the king and the Latin walls. Bravely prepare your weapons. Hopefully anticipate the war. Let no delay hinder the unprepared nor any decision hold back those who are reluctant because of fear, when the gods give the order to raise the standards and to lead the youth from the camp. Meanwhile, let us commit the unburied bodies of our comrades to the earth, since burial is the only source of honor in the depths of Acheron. Go decorate with the last gifts the noble spirits that brought forth this fatherland for us in their blood, and let brave Pallas, whom a dark day has taken away and overwhelmed with bitter death, be the first to be sent to the sad city of Evander."

LAMENT FOR PALLAS

Thus he spoke in tears and turned his steps toward the threshold where the body of lifeless Pallas lay guarded by the aged Acoetes, who had previously been the armor bearer of Arcadian Evander, but who, when given as companion to his dear charge, went forth under auspices not equally happy. Round about were all the band of servants, the Trojan crowd, and the Ilian women with their hair loosened, as was the custom, in token of sadness. As Aeneas entered the lofty portal, they beat their breasts, a great wail went up to the stars, and the palace rang with mournful weeping. When he saw the raised head and face of snow-white Pallas and the wound of an Italian spear gaping in his smooth breast, bursting into tears, he addressed him in this way:

"Pitiful boy," he said, "did Fortune, when she came along in happy mood, begrudge me that you might not see our kingdom or ride victoriously to your father's home? On leaving, I did not make such promises as these to your father Evander when he sent me to a great command with an embrace, warning me of his fear that these men were fierce and that the battle would be with a hardened race. Now, greatly deceived by an empty hope, he is keeping his vows and is heaping gifts on altars, while we in sorrow accompany with empty honors a lifeless youth who now owes nothing to any gods. Unfortunate man, you will see the cruel burial of your son! Is this our return, is this our expected triumph? Has his great reliance on me come to this? But, Evander, you shall not see your son vanquished by shameful wounds; nor shall you as a father prefer sad death because your son is unharmed. Ah me, what a great safeguard Ausonia and you, Julus, are losing!"

After he had uttered these words in tears, he ordered the pitiable body to be raised, and he sent a thousand picked men from the whole battle line to accompany these final rites, to share the father's tears, a slight solace for a great grief but one due a miserable father. Others industriously wove a soft bier of wicker work from arbutus twigs and oak sprouts and shaded the raised couch with a canopy of foliage. Then upon the rude litter they placed the noble youth, like the blossom of the soft violet or the drooping hyacinth, plucked by a maiden's hand, whose brightness and beauty are not yet faded, though mother earth no longer nourishes or strengthens it.

Then Aeneas brought forth twin garments stiff with gold and purple which Dido of Sidon, happy in the work, had once made for him with her own hands, setting off the web with threads of gold. Sadly he put one of these as a final honor upon the youth, and with a cloth covered his hair that was soon to burn. Moreover, he piled up many prizes of the Laurentian battle and ordered the booty to be conveyed in a long line. He added the horses and weapons of which he had despoiled the enemy. He had bound behind their backs the hands of those youths whom he was sending as sacrifices to the gods below, intending to sprinkle the fire with the blood of these victims, and he ordered that the leaders themselves carry the trunks of trees with the weapons and the names of the enemies attached. Unlucky Acoetes, worn out by age, was led along, now marring his breast with his fists, now his face with his nails. He collapsed and lay stretched out on the ground. They led chariots, too, smeared with Rutulian blood. Then Aethon, the warrior horse, freed of his trappings, went weeping, his face wet from many a tear. Others bore the spear and helmet, for victorious Turnus had the rest of the equipment. Then the gloomy Trojan phalanx followed, together with all the Etruscans and the Arcadians, the points of their spears reversed.

After all the procession of his comrades had passed into the distance, Aeneas stood still and in deep sorrow added these words:

"The same horrible fates of war call me from here to other mourning. Hail forever, great Pallas, and forever farewell."

Without saying another word, he moved toward the high walls and entered the camp.

THE LATINS SEND ENVOYS

And now envoys arrived from the Latin city, bearing olive branches and begging favor: would Aeneas return the bodies that lay scattered by the sword over the fields and permit them to be buried beneath a mound of earth, for there could be no struggle with the conquered and those bereft of breath; would he spare those once called his hosts and his parents-in-law? Good Aeneas treated them graciously as they begged for favors that were not to be spurned. Moreover, he spoke these words:

"Latins, what unlucky stroke of fortune has involved you in such a great war that you flee our friendship? Are you asking a truce from me for those who are dead, slain in the hazards of war? Indeed I should like to grant it to them if they were still alive. Nor would I have come had not fate granted me this place and this settlement. I am not carrying on war with your people; your king deserted our pledge of alliance and preferred to trust the weapons of Turnus. It would have been fairer if Turnus had met this death. If he is preparing to end the war with his own hand and to repel the Trojans, it would be fitting for him to attack me with weapons like these. Then the one would have survived to whom god or his own might had given life. Now go—set the fire under your unfortunate fellow citizens."

Aeneas finished speaking. They stood dumbfounded in silence, turning their eyes and their faces toward one another.

Then the aged Drances, who was hostile to young Turnus because of his hateful crime, answered these words:

"O Trojan, great in fame and greater still in arms, with what praise should I raise you to the heavens? Should I first marvel at your justice or at your labors in war? Indeed we shall gratefully bear these words to our native city, and if fortune shows any way at all, we will accept you as king of the Latins. Let Turnus seek alliances for himself. In fact, it will be a pleasure to build the destined mass of walls and to carry upon our shoulders the stones for Troy."

Thus he spoke, and all shouted the same words with one accord. They agreed on twelve days, and by a peaceful arrangement the Trojans and the Latins, intermingling together, wandered on the ridges through the forests. The lofty ash struck with the two-edged ax resounded; they overturned pines that reached the stars; nor did they cease to split with wedges oaks and fragrant cedar or to haul away mountain ash in groaning wagons.

EVANDER'S LAMENT FOR PALLAS

Then swift Rumor, the messenger of a great grief, reached Evander and the walls of his palace, Rumor which shortly before was reporting Pallas as victor in Latium. The Arcadians rushed to the gates. The road was alight with a long line of torches and illumined the fields far and wide. The crowd of Trojans coming from the opposite direction joined the ranks of mourners. After the mothers saw them enter among the dwellings, they kindled the sad city with their wailing. No force was able to restrain Evander as he came into the midst of the mourners. Once the bier was set down, he fell forward upon Pallas and, weeping and groaning, clung to him. Finally, he controlled his voice with difficulty, so great was his sorrow:

"O Pallas, you did not make such promises to your father, that you would entrust yourself so rashly to savage Mars. I was not ignorant of how very sweet freshly won glory in arms and honor in a first encounter could be. Ah, what a pitiful beginning for a youth, what a harsh lesson in a war close at hand! And my vows and prayers heard by none of the gods! And you, my sinless wife, happy in your death, not surviving for this sorrow! But I by living have overcome my fate, to linger on, a parent surviving my children. Would that the Rutulians had attacked me with weapons as I followed the allied arms of the Trojans! Would I had yielded up my life, and this procession were bringing me, not Pallas, home! I would not accuse you, Trojans, nor the treaty nor the pledges that we gave on joining in the alliance; this lot was due my old age. But if an early death was to be the fate of my son, it will be pleasing to know that he fell leading the Trojans into Latium after thousands of the Volscians had been slain. Nay, Pallas, I do not deem you worthy of a different funeral from that which dutiful Aeneas, the great Trojans, the Etruscan leaders, and the whole army of the Etruscans would receive. They bear great trophies, taken from those whom your right hand gave over to death. You, too, would now be a hideous, hacked body in armor, Turnus, if his age had been equal to yours and the strength of his years the same. But why do I, unfortunate man, keep the Trojans from warring? Depart and be mindful to take back these commands to your prince: the reason why I linger on in this hated life since Pallas is slain is my hope in your right hand, which, you see, owes the death of Turnus to a father and son. Only this achievement remains for your merit and fortune. I do not seek the joys of life—that would not be right—but I do wish to bear my son that joyful message in the underworld."

THE TROJAN FUNERAL PYRES

Meanwhile the dawn had shed its kindly light on miserable mortals, bringing back work and labor. Already father Aeneas and Tarchon had erected pyres on the curved shore. To this point each one brought the bodies of his own kinsmen, according to the custom of their fathers, and when smoking fires were set, high heaven was hid in darkness by the smoke. Girt with gleaming arms, three times they marched around the enkindled pyres; three times they rode on horseback about the gloomy fire of the funeral and uttered laments. The earth was wet, their armor was wet with tears. The clamor of men and the clanging of trumpets rose to heaven. At this point, some hurled into the fire spoils taken from slain Latins: helmets, decorated swords, bits, and glowing chariot wheels; others hurled the personal offerings of the dead, their shields, and their unlucky weapons. Round about, many oxen were offered to Death, and they slaughtered over the flames bristle-bearing swine and cattle driven from all the fields. Then along the entire shore they watched their burning comrades and kept guard over the half-burned funeral pyres, nor could they be dragged away until the dank night changed the heavens, studded with gleaming stars.

In no less unhappy state of mind the Latins in a different section erected innumerable pyres. Some committed the bodies of many of their men to the earth while others raised their dead and carried them to neighboring fields or conveyed them back to the city. The rest, a great heap of confused slaughter, men without position or honor, they cremated; then vast fields on all sides fiercely glowed with numerous fires. The third dawn had removed the chill shades from the heavens when sadly they collected the deep ashes and the disordered bones upon the pyres and buried them under a warm mound of earth.

Now indeed in the homes of the city of wealthy Latinus, there was the principal outburst, the greatest part of the far-reaching lamentation. Here mothers and miserable daughters-in-law, here the dear hearts of weeping sisters and boys bereft of their parents cursed the cruel war and the marriage of Turnus. They ordered him to decide the issue with arms, with the sword, since he demanded the kingdom of Italy and the chief honors for himself. Drances savagely emphasized these points and testified that Aeneas invited only Turnus, demanded only him in combat. At the same time, many a contradictory view was spoken in various statements defending Turnus. The powerful name of the queen exerted its influence, and the great reputation of Turnus, based on his many trophies, supported the hero.

FAILURE OF THE LATIN MISSION TO DIOMEDE

During this trouble, in the midst of this furious tumult, behold, to add to their difficulties, sorrowful ambassadors brought a reply from the great city of Diomede: nothing had been accomplished by all the expense involved in their great effort; of no avail were the gifts, the gold, or their earnest prayers; the Latins must seek other weapons or ask the Trojan king for peace. King Latinus himself in his great sorrow lost courage. The anger of the gods and the fresh graves before his eyes admonished him that Aeneas, a man of destiny, had been brought there by the manifest power of the gods. Therefore, he assembled a great council and his own chief followers, summoned by his command, within the arched threshold. They came together and streamed along the crowded roads to the royal palace. His countenance not at all happy, Latinus, the most advanced in years and also the first in power, was seated in their midst. Then he ordered the legates who had returned from the Aetolian city to state what news they brought and to give their replies in their proper order.

Then all tongues were silent, and Venulus, obedient to the command, began to speak in this way: "Citizens, we have seen Diomede and the Argive city, and traversing the route, we overcame all mishaps. We touched the hand by which the land of Ilium was completely destroyed. He, victorious over the Iapygian fields of Garganus, was founding the city of Argyripa, named after the town of his fathers. After we had entered and were given the opportunity of speaking to him face to face, we proffered our gifts and told the name of our fatherland, who had declared war against us, and what cause had drawn us to Arpi.

"To what he had heard he replied in a calm voice with these words: 'O fortunate races where Saturn once ruled, ancient Ausonians, what fortune rouses you when you are at peace and persuades you to stir up unknown wars? Those of us who violated the fields of Ilium with the sword, a band to be pitied even by Priam, have all suffered throughout the world unspeakable hardships and punishments for our crimes—I pass over the sufferings we endured in battling under the high walls and the men over whom the famed Simois flows. The fatal star of Minerva knows and so does vengeful Caphereus, the craggy promontory of Euboea. Driven from that war to a distant shore, Menelaus the son of Atreus wanders, an exile at the pillars of Proteus, and Ulysses has seen the Cyclopes of Aetna. Shall I tell of the kingdom of Pyrrhus, of the ruined home of Idomeneus, or of the Locrians living on the coast of Libya? Even the Mycenaean leader of the famed Greeks, scarcely over his own threshold, was struck down by the hand of his perfidious wife; an adulterer lay in wait for the conqueror of Asia. To think that the gods envied my returning to the altars of my fathers and seeing my loving wife and beautiful Calydon! Yet portents of horrible aspect still followed, and my lost companions took to the air with wings and, as birds, hovered over the rivers—ah, what dire punishments for my men!—and they filled the cliffs with their mournful cries. Such happenings I was led to expect even from that very time when in my madness I attacked the heavenly gods with my sword and impiously wounded the hand of Venus. Nay, nay do not drive me to such battles. Since the destruction of Troy I have had no war with the Trojans, nor do I remember with joy those former woes. Take to Aeneas the gifts which you bring me from your ancestral shores. We have stood, our fierce lances aimed at each other, and we have fought in single combat: believe the experienced when they tell how high he towers with his shield, with what a whirlwind he hurls his spear. Moreover, if the land of Mount Ida had produced two such heroes, the Trojans would even have come to the Grecian cities, and Greece would be mourning over the reversal of its fate. Whenever we were stopped at the walls of resisting Troy, it was the might of Hector and Aeneas that delayed the Greek victory and held it back to the tenth year. Both were outstanding in courage and superior in armor, but Aeneas was the more devout. Let your right hands join in a treaty, whatever the conditions may be, but beware of headlong armed conflict.'

"Most noble king, you have heard at the same time what the reply of the king is and what is his opinion with respect to this great war."

The legates had hardly uttered these words when a rippling murmur ran through the disturbed speech of the Ausonians, as when rocks delay rapid rivers and noise rises from the enclosed swirling and the nearby banks resound with the splashing of the waves.

PEACE PROPOSALS OF LATINUS

As soon as their spirits were calmed and their fearful tongues grew quiet, the king, after calling upon the gods, began speaking from his high throne:

"Indeed I could wish, O Latins—it would have been better—that we had previously settled the question of the supreme safety of the state instead of meeting in council when the enemy is besieging the walls. We are carrying on a hazardous war, citizens, with a godlike race and unconquered heroes whom no battles weary. Even when conquered, they cannot give up the sword. If you entertained any hope in the confederate arms of the Aetolians, lay it aside. Everyone clings to hope, but you see how slender ours is. In what ruin the rest of our affairs lies, you behold before your eyes and you touch with your hands. Nor do I accuse anyone. The greatest courage that could be displayed has been displayed; the fight has been waged with all the kingdom's strength. Now, indeed, I shall make clear the judgment of my perplexed mind and in a few words—give heed—I shall explain.

"For long I have had some land near the Tuscan river, far

to the west, up to and beyond the Sicanian borders. The Auruncans and the Rutulians farm there, plowing the rough hills, and they feed their flocks in the most barren of them. Let all this region and the pine-wooded tract of the lofty mountain be handed over to the friendship of the Trojans, and let us stipulate just conditions for the treaty and invite them into the kingdom as allies. Let them settle down, if their love is that great, and let them build walls. But if they have a mind to hasten to other borders and to another race, they can depart from our soil. Let us build twice ten ships of Italian oak, or they themselves can fit out a greater fleet—all the material lies at the water's edge—and let them order the number and type of the ships; let us give them the bronze, the workmen, and the naval equipment. Moreover, it is our pleasure that a hundred Latin envoys of the nobility go carry our words and confirm the treaty and extend in their hands the branches of peace, bearing gifts, talents of gold and ivory, and the chair and the toga, symbols of our power. Take counsel for the common good and aid our distressed condition."

SPEECH OF DRANCES

Then ever-hostile Drances, whom the glory of Turnus was stirring up with cruel goads of secret envy, arose. He was a man of great wealth and still greater eloquence, though his right hand was cold to war, and he was regarded as wise in counsel and powerful in promoting sedition. His mother's nobility gave him a proud lineage, but his descent from his father was base. Heaping high the load of their anger, he spoke these words:

"O good king, you counsel what is obscure to nobody and what does not need our approval. All confess that they know the direction that the fortune of the people is taking, but they are afraid to speak. Let Turnus grant freedom to speak and control his boasting. Because of his unlucky leadership and sinister character—indeed I will speak, though he threaten me with arms and death—we see so many illustrious leaders fallen and the whole city buried in grief, while he, trusting in flight, attacks the Trojan camp and terrifies the heavens with his weapons.

"Add one more to these many gifts for Aeneas which you are ordering to be sent and one word to be said, most noble of kings: let not the violence of anyone deter you, a father, from giving your daughter to an illustrious son-in-law in a worthy marriage and from joining in this peace by an eternal treaty.

"But if such great panic possesses our minds and hearts, let us call Turnus to witness and beg this favor of him: let him yield and hand over to king and fatherland their just rights. Why do you so often hurl miserable citizens into open dangers, O source and cause of these evils to Latium? There is no safety in war; we all demand peace of you, Turnus, and at the same time the only inviolable assurance of peace. I, whom you imagine hostile to you—and I am not reluctant to be that—behold, I come as a suppliant. Have pity on your people, put aside your anger, and being vanquished, leave! Already routed, we have seen enough funerals and we have laid waste vast fields. Or, if fame goads you on, if you conceive such great courage in your heart, and if still a royal dower is close to your heart, be brave, and confidently turn your breast toward the opposing enemy. Of course, so that Turnus may have his royal spouse, we, vile spirits, an unburied and unwept throng, should lie upon the field of battle. In just the same way, if you have any vigor, if you have anything of the warring spirit of your fathers, squarely face that man who challenges you."

THE REPLY OF TURNUS

At such words the violence of Turnus flared up. He uttered a cry and from the depths of his heart broke forth with these words:

"Of course, Drances, you always have a great supply of talk

at a time when war demands action. When the senators are summoned, you are the first to be present. But the assembly must not re-echo with those big speeches you utter in safety while the defense of the walls still holds back the enemy and the ditches are not yet running with blood. So then, thunder on in your eloquence, as has been your custom. Accuse me of fear, Drances, since your right hand has slaughtered so many piles of Trojans and since you have decorated fields here and there with trophies. Suppose you prove what vigorous courage can accomplish. To that end we need not seek afar for enemies; they surround the walls on all sides. Are we going to meet them? Why do you hold back? Will war always be on your windy tongue, in those fleeing feet of yours? You say I was repulsed? Vile man, shall anybody justly accuse me of being repulsed when he sees the Tiber swollen with Trojan blood, the entire race of Evander destroyed at its very root, and the Arcadians stripped of their weapons? Bitias and huge Pandarus and the thousand whom I, enclosed within the walls and shut off by a hostile rampart, sent down to hell in one day hardly found me such a man.

" 'There is no security in war.' Madman, sing that song to the Trojan leader and to your party. Thenceforth, continue to stir up everything with your great fear, to laud the power of a race twice conquered, and to press on against the weapons of Latinus. Now the chieftains of the Myrmidons fear Phrygian weapons as do Diomede and Achilles of Larissa, and the river Aufidus flees from the Adriatic waves. Again, when this criminal schemer feigns to be fearful of my quarreling, he makes the charge more cruel by reason of his pretended terror! You shall never lose your life, such as it is, by my right hand. Do not be alarmed! May it dwell with you in that breast of yours.

"Now, father, I return to you and to your great counsel. If you no longer place any hope in our weapons, if we are so abandoned, if we have fallen utterly because our battle line has been routed once and our Fortune cannot right itself, let us beg for peace, let us stretch forth our powerless hands. And yet, if only something of our usual courage were present! In my opinion, he is above all others fortunate in his labors and noble in spirit who, in order not to see such a thing as this, fell in death and once and for all buried his face in the dust. But if we still have supplies and fresh youth and cities and peoples of Italy, and if glory comes to the Trojans at the cost of much blood—they have their funerals and the storm is the same for all—why do we disgracefully falter on the very threshold? Why do our limbs tremble even before the sound of the trumpet? Passing time and the different troubles of various ages have changed things for the better; Fortune in alternate visits has made sport of many and again placed them on dry land. We shall not have the help of the Aetolian and his town Arpi, but we shall have Messapus and lucky Tolumnius and those leaders whom so many peoples sent; nor shall the glory be slight for those chosen from Latium and the Laurentian fields. Then there is Camilla, from the noble race of the Volscians, leading a battle line of cavalry and squadrons gleaming with bronze.

"But if the Trojans are demanding that I fight in single combat and this is your pleasure, if I am obstructing the common good so much, Victory has not fled from my hands with so much hatred that I should refuse to try anything to realize such a great hope. I will go against him with courage, even though he show himself as great as Achilles, even though he wear armor equal to that made by the hands of Vulcan. I, Turnus, hardly second in courage to any of the ancients, have vowed this soul to you and to Latinus, my father-in-law. 'Aeneas invites me alone.' And I pray that he may invite me rather than that Drances suffer death in my place, if this is the anger of the gods, or that he win the prize, if it carries with it heroism and glory."

PREPARATIONS FOR RENEWING THE WAR

They debated among themselves about these doubtful issues while Aeneas was moving his camp and his battle line. Suddenly a messenger rushed with great speed through the royal palace and filled the city with great terror, saying that the Trojans, drawn up in battle array, and the Etruscan band were descending from the Tiber River over all the fields. Of a sudden their spirits were disturbed, their hearts panic-stricken, and their anger aroused by no gentle prods. With trembling hands they called for arms; youths cried for arms. The elders sadly wept and spoke in whispers. Here on all sides, a great clamor with varying dissent rose heavenward, much as when, by chance, flocks of birds have settled in a high grove, or raucous swans in the fish-filled river Padusa make a sound throughout the noisy swamps.

"Well, now, citizens," said Turnus, seizing the opportunity, "assemble a council, and sitting down praise peace: the enemy in arms is rushing into the kingdom." And saying no more, he stalked out, quickly leaving the lofty palace.

"You, Volusus," he said, "order the troops of the Volscians to be armed, and lead the Rutulians. Messapus, once you are armed, and Coras, with your brother, deploy the cavalry over the wide plain. Let some guard the approaches to the city and man the towers; let the rest of the troops attack with me where I command."

Straightway there was a scurrying throughout the whole city to the walls. Father Latinus himself left the council and deferred its great proposals, disturbed by this deplorable crisis. He greatly berated himself because he had not freely received Trojan Aeneas and recognized him as his son-in-law to rule over the city. Some dug trenches in front of the gates or carried stones or stakes. The blaring horn gave the bloody signal for battle. Then matrons and boys, a varied throng, defended the walls; the final crisis invited all. Moreover, the queen rode along in company with a great crowd of mothers to the temple of Pallas Athene on the lofty heights, carrying gifts; beside her was her companion, the maiden Lavinia, the cause of so great a disaster, her modest eyes cast down. The mothers followed, filling the temple with incense, and they poured forth their mournful voices from the lofty threshold: "Minerva, powerful in arms, arbiter of war, break with your hand the weapon of the

Phrygian robber and cast him prone upon the ground and lay him low under the lofty gates."

Furious Turnus eagerly girded himself for battle. And now armed with a gleaming breastplate, he looked dreadful with bronze scales. He had encased his legs with gold; his temples were as yet unprotected, and he had fastened a sword to his side. As he ran down from the high fort, he gleamed in gold and gloated in his mind, already looking forward with hope to the conflict with the enemy, just as when a horse, breaking his halter and finally free, escapes from the stalls, and reaching the open plain, either makes for the pastures or the herds of mares, or, accustomed to swim in the familiar river, darts forth and neighs as he proudly rears his head high in the air, while his mane plays over his neck and shoulders.

THE PROWESS OF CAMILLA

Queen Camilla, in company with a battle line of Volscians, met him, and at the very gates leaped down from her horse, and the entire cohort, imitating her, dismounted from their horses. Then she spoke as follows:

"Turnus, if a brave person may have any self-confidence based on merit, I dare and I promise to meet the host of the followers of Aeneas and to attack alone the Etruscan cavalry. Permit me to risk the dangers of war in the first wave: you remain on foot near the walls and guard the defenses."

At these words, Turnus, fixing his eyes on the warlike maiden, said:

"O maiden, the pride of Italy, what gratitude can I begin to show, what thanks to return? But now, since that spirit of yours rises above all difficulties, share the labor with me. As the rumor runs—and the scouts sent out have brought back the certain report—Aeneas has wickedly sent ahead light-armed horsemen to ravage the plains. He himself, gaining the ridge, is advancing toward the city by the deserted steeps of the mountain. I am preparing an ambush of war along a sloping trail in the forest so that I may attack the defile from both ends with armed soldiers. After the battle is joined, cut off the Etruscan canalry; valiant Messapus shall be with you, and the Latin hosts, and the band under Tiburtus; you, too, take over the duties of a leader."

Thus Turnus spoke and with like words he urged Messapus and his fellow leaders to battle; then he set out against the enemy. In a valley suited to the stratagem of an armed ambush, there is a winding ravine, both sides of which are dark with dense foliage. There a narrow footpath leads through a close gorge with scant approaches. Upon the heights and on the very top of the mountain above this valley, there lies a little-known stretch of level land and a safe retreat, whether one wishes to attack either on the right or on the left, or to take a position on the ridge and roll down huge stones. To this point the youth made his way along the familiar route of the path and, occupying the place, settled in the treacherous forests.

Meanwhile, in the heavenly realms, Diana spoke to swift Opis, one of the sacred train of her companion maidens, and uttered these sorrowful words:

"Maiden, Camilla is going forth to a cruel war, and though she is dear to me above all others, in vain is she girt with our weapons. This love on the part of your Diana has not come into being recently and moved her mind with sudden sweetness. Metabus was expelled from his kingdom because of hatred due to his haughty display of power, and he left the ancient city of Privernum. Though fleeing in the midst of the conflicts of war, he sustained the infant as his companion in exile and called her by the name of her mother Casmilla, slightly changed to Camilla. Carrying her close to his chest, he sought the long ridges of the lonely groves. Savage weapons were flying about on all sides, and the Volscians were circling about with their scattered troops. Suddenly, in the middle of his flight, the swollen Amasenus was foaming over the top of its banks, so great was the storm that had broken from the clouds. Preparing to swim, he was held back by his love for the infant and his fears for his dear burden. Suddenly he made this decision after turning everything over in his mind. Rolling the child in the bark of a wild cork tree, he fastened her gently around the middle of a spear, a huge weapon of solid knots and seasoned oak which, by chance, the warrior carried in his mighty hand. As he let it go from his powerful right hand, he directed this prayer heavenward:

"'O dear virgin Diana, protectress of the groves, I, her father, vow this servant to you. Holding your weapons for the first time, she, your suppliant, flees the enemy. Goddess, receive, I pray, your child, now committed to the uncertain breezes.'

"He spoke, and drawing back his arm, hurled the spear. The waves roared; over the rapid river, unfortunate Camilla sailed upon the whistling javelin. But Metabus, when a great troop was already bearing down upon him, threw himself into the river and victoriously snatched up from the grassy turf the child with the spear, his gift to Diana.

"No cities received him within their homes or walls, nor would he have submitted, being of a fierce nature. He passed his life among the lonely mountains of the shepherds. Here in the thickets and among the rough dens of wild animals he nurtured his daughter with milk from an untamed mare, directing the flow from the teats into her tender lips. When the infant had begun to set her foot down with a firm tread, he armed her hands with the swift javelin and hung a bow from the little girl's shoulder. In place of a golden clasp for her hair, in place of the cover of a long mantle, the skin of a tiger fell from her head over her back. Even then she held in her tender hand the weapons of boys and whirled about her head a sling with a polished thong, striking down the Strymonian crane or the white swan.

"In vain did many mothers throughout Etruscan towns wish her for a daughter-in-law; content with Diana alone, she purely cultivated the eternal love of weapons and virginity. I wish she had not been caught up in such a military expedition, attempting to battle the Trojans: she would now be one of my dearest companions. Since she is now pressed by a premature fate, go, slip down from heaven, nymph, and visit the Latin borders where a sad battle is being fought under unfavorable omens. Take these weapons and draw forth an avenging arrow from the quiver. With this arrow let whoever wounds her holy body, no matter whether Trojan or Italian, pay for his crime with his blood. Later under the veil of a cloud I will carry the hapless maiden's body and her weapons intact to her tomb and I will bury her in her native land."

She finished speaking and the nymph with resounding weapons descended through the gentle breezes of heaven, her body surrounded by a dark, swirling cloud.

But, meanwhile, the Trojan host moved toward the walls, together with the Etruscan leaders and all the army of the cavalry, their numbers arranged in squadrons. Over the entire plain the leaping chargers neighed, and wheeling this way and that, they fought the tightly drawn reins. Then far and wide the iron acres bristled with spears, and the fields gleamed with upraised weapons. Opposite them upon the plain appeared Messapus and the swift Latins, Coras, with his brother, and the battalion under the maid Camilla. With their right arms drawn back, they held their spears far out in front of themselves and flourished their javelins. The approaching men and the neighing horses became more furious. Now both sides had taken up their stand after advancing within javelin range. Suddenly both broke forth with a shout and urged on their fiery horses. At the same time they released their swift weapons, thick as falling snow, and the heavens were clouded by the shadow.

Straightway Tyrrhenus and fierce Aconteus, their lances poised, rushed to the attack, straining every nerve. Colliding with a great crash, they were the first to fall, and their chargers clashed, dashing against each other's chests. Aconteus was thrown afar, as if by lightning or by an engine throwing a great weight, and he scattered his life to the breeze. Suddenly the battle lines gave way, and the fleeing Latins put their shields to their backs and turned their horses toward the walls. The Trojans drove on, Prince Asilas leading the squadrons. Already they were approaching the gates, when the Latins again raised a shout and turned around the yielding necks of their horses;

the attackers fled and rode afar off with relaxed reins: as when the sea with alternate swell now rushes toward the land and falls upon the cliffs with its flood, all foam, and soaks the farthest sand with its waves, then rapidly flees back, sucking the rolling stones with the tide and leaving the shore as the shallows ebb. Twice the Etruscans drove the Rutulians in retreat to the walls; twice repulsed, the Etruscans looked behind them, covering their backs with their shields. But after clashing in the third encounter, the battle lines became completely intermingled, and each man chose a man. Then indeed were heard the cries of the dying. Weapons, bodies in deep blood, and half-dead horses, mixed in with slaughtered men, rolled about. A fierce battle started. Shuddering at the approach of Remulus, Orsilochus hurled his spear into the horse and left the weapon under the animal's ear. The fierce charger went wild at this blow and, raising his breast high, furious from the wound, reared into the air. Remulus, unseated, rolled upon the ground. Catillus struck down Iollas and Herminius, great in mind, great in body and weapons, whose head of blond hair was unprotected and whose shoulders were bare; nor did wounds terrify Herminius. So huge he appeared in the face of arms! The spear, driven through his broad shoulders, trembled and, piercing the man, doubled him up in pain. Everywhere dark blood was pouring out; as they fought, they slew with the sword and sought an illustrious death through their wounds.

Like an Amazon, quiver-bearing Camilla, her one side uncovered for battle, exulted in the midst of slaughter. Now her hand scattered, as if in a shower, tough spears, now she tirelessly wielded with her right hand a powerful two-edged ax; a golden bow and the arms of Diana sounded on her shoulder. If, repulsed at times, she retreated to the rear, in flight she directed the shafts from her bow turned back toward the enemy. Round about her were chosen companions, the maiden Larina and Tulla and Tarpeia brandishing a bronze ax, Italian girls whom the divine Camilla chose as an ornament for herself, good servants either in peace or in war. Such as these are the Thracian Amazons who tread the ice of the river Thermodon and battle with their painted weapons, either when they escort Hippolyte or when warlike Penthesilea returns in her chariot; as the great crowd cries aloud, the ranks of the women with their crescent-shaped shields exult in triumph.

Who was the first, who the last, fierce maiden, that you killed with your javelin? How many bodies did you strew in death upon the ground? First, Eunaeus the son of Clytius, whose unprotected chest faced her, she pierced with a long fir lance. Pouring forth rivers of blood, he fell and bit the blood-stained earth, and, as he died, he twisted and turned in his pain. Then she laid Liris low and Pagasus upon him. Headlong they fell together: one, as he was picking up the reins when rolling over upon his wounded horse; the other, as he rose and stretched forth his unarmed right hand to his fallen comrade. To these she added Amastrus the son of Hippotas, and leaning forward, she pursued in the distance with her spear Tereus, Harpalycus, Demophoön, and Chromis. For as many javelins as the maiden let fly from her hand, the same number of Trojans fell. Afar off, Ornytus, a hunter with unusual weapons, rode upon an Apulian horse, a warrior whose broad shoulders were protected by the hide of a bullock, whose great head was covered by the yawning mouth and jaws of a wolf with white teeth, and whose hands held a rustic hunting spear as a weapon. He whirled about in the midst of the squadrons, towering above them by a head. On overtaking him—it was no great task when the battle line was turned back—she ran him through and then said these words with hostile feeling:

"Did you think that you were driving wild animals from the forest? The day has come that shall refute with the weapons of a woman the boasting of you and your people. You shall carry this distinction, no slight one, to the ghosts of your fathers, that you fell by Camilla's weapon."

Thereupon she slew Orsilochus and Butes, two of the most powerful of the Trojans. She struck Butes sideways with a spear between his cuirass and helmet where the rider's neck appeared and his shield hung low from his left arm. Fleeing Orsilochus and, driven in a great circle, she escaped to the center and followed the one who was following her; then rising higher, with a powerful ax she rained blows upon the weapons and body of the man, who cried for pity and uttered many a prayer. His wound sprinkled his face with warm blood from his brain. The warlike son of Aunus, who dwelt in the Apennines, not the least treacherous of the Ligurians as long as the Fates permitted him to deceive, met her, and terrified at the sight, was frozen to the spot. And when he saw that he could not by any course escape from the battle nor turn aside the approaching queen, he attempted to deceive her by a crafty plan and began in this way:

"What is there so marvelous in this, if, though you are a woman, you put your trust in a brave horse? Stop your flight and trust yourself in equal hand-to-hand combat with me; gird yourself for battle on the ground. You shall soon know to whom vain glory brings ruin."

He finished speaking. She, raging and fired with fierce resentment, gave her horse over to a companion and as a foot soldier, unaffrighted, resisted with equally matched weapons, a bare sword and unmarked shield. But the youth fled, thinking he had won by his deception, and with scarcely any delay, wheeling around, rode away and wearied his swift charger with his iron spurs.

"Foolish Ligurian, elated in your proud mind to no purpose, in vain have you cunningly tried the deceit of your race, nor shall your deception deliver you unharmed to treacherous Aunus."

Thus the maid spoke, and with the speed of light her swift feet crossed the horse in its course, and, seizing the reins, she met him face to face and wreaked punishment upon the enemy's blood, as easily as the sacred bird, the hawk, from a lofty rock pursues in flight a dove high up in a cloud and holds it fast, disemboweling it with its hooked claws while blood and plucked feathers fall from the sky.

But the father of gods and men sitting high on the summit of Olympus cast an observant eye on all these happenings. He roused the Etruscan Tarchon to savage battle and stirred up his anger with prods that were not at all gentle. Thereupon Tarchon rode on his horse amid slaughter and retreating battle lines, and encouraged the cavalry on the wings with varied shouts, calling each man by name and reorganizing for battle those who had been repulsed.

"What fear, what great cowardice has come over your spirit, Etruscans, you who are never willing to suffer pain, you who are always sluggards? To think that a woman is driving you in retreat and is turning these lines! Where are your swords? Why do you carry these unused weapons in your right hands? But you do not hang back in the nightly battles of Venus, nor when the curved flute has signaled the Bacchic dances. Wait for the banquet and the wine cups on a full table—this is your love, your interest. Wait until the approving soothsayer announces the sacred rites and the fat offering calls you to the deep groves."

Saying these words, he spurred his horse into the midst of the enemy, ready to die himself. Like a whirlwind he bore down upon Venulus and seizing his enemy, he lifted him from his horse with his right hand. Holding him in front of himself, with great might Tarchon swiftly carried him away. A shout rose to the heavens, and all the Latins turned their gaze. Tarchon sped like lightning over the plain, bearing the man and his weapons. Then he broke off the point from the very top of Venulus' spear and sought for an open spot where he might inflict a deadly wound; but Venulus, fighting back, kept Tarchon's right hand from his throat and repelled force with force. As when a dark eagle, flying high, carries a serpent that it has seized, and entwines it in its feet, and though wounded, holds on with its claws while the serpent turns its winding coils and rising high up, bristles with its scales erect and hisses with its mouth; nonetheless the eagle, as it beats the air with its wings, plucks at the struggling serpent with its hooked beak: in like manner triumphant Tarchon bore his booty out of the battle line of the Tiburtians. The Etruscans, following the example and the fortune of their leader, rushed to the attack.

Then Arruns, destined by fate to die, circled about swift

Camilla with his javelin, very craftily anticipating her movements and searching out his easiest chance. Wherever the furious maid moved in the midst of the battle line, there Arruns tracked her and silently followed her course; where she returned victorious and retreated from the enemy, there the youth stealthily turned aside his swift reins. He tried this approach and again that and the entire circuit on all sides, and wickedly leveled his deadly lance.

By chance, Chloreus, consecrated to Mount Cybelus and once a priest, brightly shining afar off in Trojan armor, spurred his foaming horse, covered with bronze scales arranged like feathers and fastened below with gold. He himself, outstanding in dark-tinted foreign purple, was shooting his Cretan arrows from his Lycian bow; from his shoulders hung the golden bow, and his helmet was golden, since he was a priest. His saffron mantle and its rustling linen folds were caught up into a knot by yellow gold; his tunic and foreign hose were decorated with needle work. Like a hunter, the maiden, either to hang up his Trojan arms in the temple or to array herself in captured gold, blindly kept following him alone, without regard to the whole struggle of the battle, and was carelessly raging along the whole line with a woman's desire for booty and spoils, when finally, Arruns, taking advantage of the moment, flourished his javelin from ambush and prayed to the powers above in this way:

"Greatest of the gods, Apollo, guardian of holy Mount Soracte, whom we were the first to honor, Apollo for whom the pine fire is heaped up and for whom we worshipers, full of piety, tread upon a bed of hot coals through the midst of fire, grant, O supreme father, that our weapons be cleansed of this disgrace. I do not seek her arms, a trophy for defeating the maiden, or any spoils. The rest of my deeds will bring me praise. If only this dire scourge be repelled and fall by a wound from me, I will return inglorious to my ancestral city."

Phoebus heard, let a part of the vow enter his mind, and scattered the rest into the swift air. He conceded that the man who uttered the prayer should strike down and slay Camilla in sudden death, but he did not grant that Arruns should return to see his mountainous home. The storm blew his voice into the winds. Thereupon, when the spear released from his hand sounded through the air, all the attention of the fierce Volscians was arrested, and they turned their gaze toward the queen. She was not at all conscious of the breeze or the sound of the weapon coming from the sky until the hurled spear stuck under her naked breast, and driven deep, drank the maiden's blood. Her fearful companions rushed together and sustained their falling mistress. Frightened Arruns fled before all, with mingled feelings of joy and fear, nor did he any longer trust in his javelin or dare to face the maiden's weapons. As a wolf, after killing a shepherd or a great bullock, conscious of its bold deed, hides itself afar off in the high mountains before hostile weapons can follow it, and, lowering its trembling tail and drawing it up under its belly, makes for the forests; in much the same way the startled Arruns disappeared from sight and, content to flee, vanished in the midst of the weapons. Dying, Camilla pulled out the weapon with her hand, but the iron point stayed in a deep wound between the bones of the ribs. Lifeless she slid down; her eyes closed, cold in death, and her once bright color left her cheeks.

While she was thus breathing her last, she addressed one of her companions, Acca, who, faithful above all the others, had shared Camilla's troubles, and she spoke to her in this way: "Thus far, sister Acca, I have been able to fight; now a painful wound is ending my life, and everything around is turning black in the darkness. Flee and carry these, my very last orders, to Turnus: let him come into the battle and ward off the Trojans from the city. And now, farewell!"

With these words she dropped the reins, sliding helpless to the earth. Then little by little, in the chill of death, she freed her soul from her body and, letting her weapons fall, laid down her relaxed neck and conquered head in death. With a groan her spirit fled all too soon into the shadows. Then, indeed, a great shout struck the golden stars. With the death of

Camilla the battle grew fierce; at the same time all the force of the Trojans and the Etruscan leaders and the Arcadian cavalry of Evander attacked in dense array.

But Opis, the sentinel of Diana, had for some time been seated high on top of the mountains, observing the battle in safety. When afar off, in the midst of the turmoil of angry youths, she saw Camilla punished in sad death, she groaned and uttered these words from the depths of her heart:

"Ah, too, too cruel a punishment have you paid for trying to harm the Trojan in war! Nor did it help you to have worshiped Diana in lonely thickets or to have borne our quivers upon your shoulder. However, your queen has not left you unhonored now in the very moment of death; nor shall this death be nameless among the nations, nor shall you suffer the fame of being unavenged, for whoever has marred your body with a wound shall atone for his crime in a death well deserved."

At the foot of the lofty mountain was the grave of Dercennus, the ancient Laurentian king, piled high with earth and covered with shady oak. In a quick flight the beautiful goddess took up her position before Arruns and watched for him from the top of the tomb. When she saw him rejoicing in spirit and swelling in his vanity, she said:

"Why are you going away? Direct your steps here, come here, you who are destined to perish, and receive suitable rewards for slaying Camilla. Shall you, too, not die by the weapons of Diana?"

Thus spoke the Thracian nymph and, taking a speedy arrow from her golden quiver, she savagely stretched the bow and drew it far back until each of the curved heads came together and her hands, moving apart an equal distance, were touching, the left, the point of the iron, the right, her breast with the bowstring. Suddenly Arruns heard the whizzing weapon and the whistling breezes just as the weapon stuck in his body. His forgetful companions left him expiring and uttering his last lament in the ignominious dust of the fields. Opis was borne on her wings to lofty Olympus.

After losing its mistress, the light cavalry of Camilla was the first to flee; the panic-stricken Rutulians and fierce Atinas fled; the dispersed leaders and their deserted troops sought a safe place and, wheeling about on their horses, made for the walls. Nor was anyone able to withstand the attack of the death-dealing Trojans or make a fighting stand; instead, they slung their bows over their weary shoulders, and the hoofs of the galloping horses struck the dusty plain as they ran.

Dust whirling in a dark cloud rolled toward the walls. Mothers on the lookout towers, beating their breasts, raised their womanly wailing to the stars. A hostile throng fell upon those who first in a confused formation ran through the open gates. They did not escape a miserable death, but on the very threshold of their fathers' walls and in sight of the safety of their homes, pierced through, they breathed out their life. Some closed the gates: nor did they dare to open the way for their comrades or admit them, in spite of their pleas, within the walls. There arose a most deplorable slaughter of those defending the approaches with their arms and of those rushing against the arms of their comrades. Some, locked out before the eyes and the faces of their weeping parents, turned into the deep ditches as disaster approached; others in blind anger, letting their reins fall, charged against the gates and the solidly bolted jambs. The mothers themselves with supreme fighting spirit—they showed true love for their country, following Camilla's example—though fearful, hurled javelins with their hands and hastily imitated iron weapons with posts and fire-hardened stakes of tough oak, and they were eager to be the first to die in defense of the walls.

Meanwhile, the disastrous news reached Turnus in the forests, and Acca pictured for the youth the great tumult: that the lines of the Volscians had been destroyed, that Camilla had fallen, that the fierce enemy was furiously advancing, that everything had collapsed with the help of Mars, and that panic had already reached the walls. Raging Turnus—the dreadful divinity of Jupiter demanded that it be so—deserted the hills he had occupied, and left the rough groves. Hardly had he gone out of sight and reached the plain when father Aeneas, entering the undefended woodland pastures, mounted the ridge and left the dark forest. Thus it was that both, with their entire battle lines, moved rapidly to the walls; nor were they very far apart from each other.

As soon as Aeneas sighted in the distance the plains billowing with dust and saw the Laurentian battle lines, as soon as Turnus recognized fierce Aeneas in arms and heard the tramping of feet and the snorting of horses, straightway they would have begun the fight and attacked in battle, but rosy Phoebus was already bathing his weary horses in the Iberian sea, and, as the day slipped away, was bringing back the night. The Trojans settled down in their camp in front of the city and threw up defenses.

Book Twelve

JUPITER

Book Twelve

TURNUS DETERMINES TO FIGHT AENEAS

When Turnus saw that the crushed Latins were discouraged because of the opposition of Mars, that the promises he had made were now demanded of him, and that the eyes of all were on him, his unappeasable rage was uncontrolled, and his arrogance mounted and mounted. Just as a lion, injured in the chest by a serious wound from hunters in the fields of the Carthaginians, finally prepares to do battle and, raising the mane-covered muscles of his neck, fearlessly breaks the imbedded lance of the enemy and roars from his bloody mouth: in much the same way violence glowed in the angered Turnus. Then he addressed the king and furiously began in this way:

"There is no delay on the part of Turnus, and there is no reason why the cowardly followers of Aeneas should retract what they said or go back on what they agreed. I am going to battle. Bring forth the sacred objects, my lord, and seal the pact. Either I will send the Trojan, Asia's deserter, to hell by this right hand—let the Latins sit down and watch—and alone refute with my sword the crime he imputes to us all, or Lavinia may have the conquered Trojans and yield as spouse to Aeneas."

Latinus answered him in a calm tone: "O youth, outstanding in spirit, the more you excel in gallant courage, so much the more fitting it is that I take earnest counsel and in my fear weigh all the dangers. You have the realm of your father Daunus, many towns captured by your hands. Moreover, Latinus has gold and is liberal with it; there are other maidens in Latium and the Laurentian fields, nor are they of ignoble race. Permit me, speaking frankly, to reveal things that are not easy to say; at the same time, let this sink deep in your mind. As all the gods and men have prophesied, it is not right that I give my daughter in marriage to any one of her former suitors. Won over by love of you, by the ties of kinship, and by the tears of my sad wife, I violated all my obligations: I snatched the promised maiden from my destined son-in-law; I declared unholy war. Wherefore you see, Turnus, what disaster, what wars overtake me, and what trials you, most of all, are suffering. Conquered in two great battles, we uphold with difficulty the hopes of Italy in this city. The flowing Tiber is still warm with our blood, and the wide fields are white with our bones.

"Why do I so often come back to this subject? What insanity changes my purpose? If, supposing that Turnus is slain, I am prepared to take on allies, why do I not rather end the fighting while he is unharmed? What will my kinsmen, the Rutulians, what will the rest of Italy say, if I hand you over to death—may Fortune prove it false—when you are seeking our daughter in marriage? Consider the varying fortunes of war; pity your sad, aged father, who now is far away in your ancestral Ardea."

The violence of Turnus was not at all affected by these words; he became even more enraged and, in spite of the soothing plea, his anger mounted. When able to speak, he began in this way:

"Whatever concern you bear for me, my good king, I beg that you set it aside and permit me to risk death for glory. With my right hand I scatter weapons of iron that are by no means ineffective; the blood flows from *my* wound. His mother goddess, who, as he flees, hides him in the womanish cloak of a cloud, will be far away from him, concealing herself in deceptive shadows."

But the queen wept, frightened by his new risk of battle, and, on the brink of death, clung to her ardent son-in-law:

"Turnus, by these tears, if the good name of Amata is of any concern to you at all—you are now our one hope, the solace of our miserable old age; the honor and rule of Latinus is in your hands, and all our tottering house rests upon you—

I beg this one thing: desist from battling with the Trojans. Whatever disasters await you, Turnus, in this proposed combat await me, too; at the same moment I will leave this hated light of day, nor will I as a captive behold Aeneas as my son-in-law."

Lavinia heard her mother's voice, her flushed cheeks wet with tears, while a deep blush kindled a fire that ran over her fevered face. As when someone has shaded ivory with blood-colored purple or as white lilies seem red when mingled with many roses, so such colors appeared on the face of the maiden. Love disturbed Turnus, and he fixed his gaze on the maiden. He was so much the more eager to fight and he addressed Amata:

"Please, mother, do not harass me with your tears or with such an ill omen as I go into a combat of rough fighting, for Turnus has no power to delay death. Messenger Idmon, take these unpleasant words to the Trojan tyrant: when tomorrow's Dawn, borne on purple wheels, reddens the sky, let him not drive the Trojans against the Rutulians; let the weapons of the Trojans rest, and let the Rutulians rest, too. Let us end the war with the shedding of our blood; let the prize upon that field be Lavinia."

When he had uttered these words and rapidly returned to the palace, he demanded horses and rejoiced as he looked upon them whinnying before his face. These, surpassing the snow in whiteness and the winds in speed, Orithyia herself had given as an honor to Pilumnus. The enthusiastic drivers stood about and slapped with their cupped hands the horses' resounding chests and combed their flowing manes. Thereupon, he put about his shoulders a coat of mail, embossed with gold and white brass; at the same time he made ready his shield, the horns of his red crests, and the sword which the fire-god himself had made for his father Daunus and had dipped, while still glowing, in the Stygian wave. Then, with might he seized the powerful spear which stood leaning against a great column in the midst of the palace, spoil taken from Actor of Aurunca. He brandished the dreadful weapon and shouted:

"Spear that has never failed to heed my call, now is the time! Great Actor wielded you; now the right hand of Turnus wields you. Grant that I may with my strong arm lay low the body and rend the pierced armor of the half-living Trojan and spoil his hair, curled with a hot iron and dripping with myrrh."

By such madness was he driven. Sparks flew from the entire face of the furious man; fire gleamed from his fierce eyes, just as when a bull raises his dreadful bellowing before a fight and charging into the trunk of a tree, tries to put all his anger into his horns and wounds the winds with his thrusts or prepares for battle by pawing the sand.

Meanwhile, Aeneas, no less savage in the armor given him by his mother, whetted his martial spirit and roused himself in anger, happy that the combat was to be settled by the proposed pact. Then he consoled his companions and the fears of gloomy Julus by explaining the fates, and he ordered the men to carry a definite reply to King Latinus and to lay down the rules of the peace.

On the morrow, the rising day had hardly showered the tops of the mountains with light when the horses of the sun rose from the deep ocean and poured forth fire from their upraised nostrils. The Rutulians and the Trojans measured off the field for combat under the walls of the great city and prepared fires and grassy altars in the center to their common gods. Others, wearing the sacrificial apron, with their temples bound with sacred wreaths, carried water and live coals. The army of the Italians moved forward, and the javelin-armed lines poured from the crowded gates. From another direction all the Trojan and the Etruscan army rushed forth with different kinds of weapons, hardly less armed for war than if Mars were calling them to battle. In the midst of thousands the leaders themselves, proudly arrayed in gold and purple, swept by—Mnestheus, offspring of Assaracus, brave Asilas, and Messapus, the trainer of horses and offspring of Neptune. As each one at a given signal retired to his place, he stuck his spear in the ground and laid aside his shield. Then the mothers in eager throngs and the unarmed masses and the weak old men settled down on the towers and the roofs of the houses, while others stood near the lofty gates.

JUNO ROUSES JUTURNA TO BREAK THE TRUCE

But Juno, looking down from the top of the mount which is now called Alban—then it had neither name nor honor nor glory—viewed the field and both the battle lines of the Laurentians and of the Trojans, and the city of Latinus. Suddenly the goddess thus addressed Turnus' sister, a goddess who presided over pools and rivers—an honor which Jupiter, king on high of the heavens, made sacred to her for ravishing her virginity:

"O nymph, ornament of streams, most pleasing to my spirit, you know how I preferred you alone above all other Latin women who ascended the ungrateful couch of great-spirited Jupiter, and how I gladly placed you in the region of heaven. Learn your sorrow, Juturna—do not blame me. Insofar as Fortune seemed to allow it and the Fates permitted that victory be on the side of Latium, I protected Turnus and your walls. Now I see the youth battling against an unequal lot. The day of the Fates and a hostile power approach. I cannot let my eyes rest on this battle nor on this treaty. If in defense of your brother you dare anything more effective, take courage; it is fitting. Perhaps better things are in store for the miserable men."

Hardly had she uttered these words when tears poured forth from the eyes of Juturna, and three times, four times with her hand she beat her beautiful breast.

"This is not a time for tears," said Juno the daughter of Saturn. "Make haste and snatch your brother from death, if there is any way, or stir up war and violate the treaty that has been planned. I am the author of this daring."

With this exhortation, she left her wavering and disturbed by the dire wound in her mind.

Meanwhile, the chieftains came forth—Latinus in a chariot drawn by four horses, a man of massive frame, whose gleaming temples were bound around with twice six golden rays, symbol of his forefather, the Sun, and Turnus in a car pulled by white horses, carrying two spears of broad iron in his hand. Thereupon, father Aeneas, the seed of the Roman race, gleaming with his star-studded shield and his heavenly arms, and Ascanius at his side, the second hope of great Rome, proceeded from the camp. The priest in unstained garments brought forth the offspring of a bristle-bearing swine and an unsheared sheep and led the animals to the flaming altars.

Turning their eyes to the rising sun, they spread out salted cakes with their hands, marked the top hair of the animals' temples with a sword, and poured out libations upon the altars.

Father Aeneas, drawing his sword, uttered this prayer:

"Now may the Sun be my witness as I pray and this Earth for which I was able to endure such great trials, and all-powerful father and you, his spouse, O daughter of Saturn—I pray you are now better disposed, goddess—and you, glorious Mars, who control all wars with your power. I invoke the Fountains and the Streams, whatever divinity there is in the sky above and whatever powers there are in the dark-blue sea. If by chance the victory goes to Italian Turnus, it is agreed that the conquered shall leave for the city of Evander; Julus shall depart from these fields, nor shall the warring followers of Aeneas ever renew the attack or harm this kingdom with the sword. But if Victory concedes the battle to us—as I rather suppose, and may the gods approve that by their power—I will not order the Italians to obey the Trojans, nor do I seek a kingdom for myself. Let both races, unconquered, submit by just laws to an eternal treaty. I will introduce my rites and my gods; my father-in-law Latinus shall have his power and shall exercise his solemn offices of government. The Trojans shall erect walls for me, and Lavinia shall give her name to the city."

Thus spoke Aeneas first. Then Latinus followed with these words, as he looked up at the heavens and raised his right hand toward the stars:

"I swear by these same powers, Aeneas, by Earth and Sea and Stars, by the dual nature of Latona, by double-faced Janus, by the power of the gods below and the sacred realm of harsh Pluto; may the father of all, who enforces treaties with his thunderbolt, heed these words. I touch these altars and I call these fires between us and the power of the gods to witness. The day shall never come when the Italians shall break this treaty of peace, no matter what may happen; nor shall any force turn me aside from my strong purpose, no, not even if that force were to pour the earth into the sea, mingling them in a deluge, not if it were to set loose the heavens against hell; just as this scepter"—he happened to hold a scepter in his right hand—"shall never put forth shoots with tender leaves or shade, since it has been severed completely from its roots in the forest and has lost its parent trunk, and, though once a tree, its foliage and branches have been lopped off by an ax. Now the hand of the artist has enclosed it in decorative bronze and given it to the Latin chieftains to carry."

With such an exchange of words they ratified the treaty in open view of the elders. Then over the fire they sacrificed the duly consecrated animals, tearing the quivering entrails from them, and piled high the altars with the laden platters.

But for some time it had seemed to the Rutulians that the fight was not an even match, and their hearts were disturbed by various misgivings, especially when they noted on closer view the unequal strength of the two. Venerating the altar as a suppliant with downcast eyes, Turnus deepened this feeling as he came forward with silent tread. His cheeks were wan and his youthful body was pale. As soon as Juturna noted that this word was spreading and the confidence of the crowd waning, assuming the appearance of Camers—who had an illustrious origin from his ancestors and a name famous because of his father's courage, though he himself was most valiant in the use of arms—she threw herself into the midst of the battle line, not at all ignorant of the state of affairs, and sowed various rumors, speaking as follows:

"Is it not a shame, Rutulians, that one life should expose itself in defense of such a host as we are? Is it in numbers or in strength that we are not their match? Look! This is all of them, Trojans and Arcadians together and these doomed men of Etruria, hostile to Turnus. We would hardly have an enemy if every other one of us were to attack them. The fame of Turnus shall rise to the gods, to whose altars he is dedicating himself, and he shall live on the lips of men. We, who are now quietly settled in these fields, shall be compelled to obey proud masters when we have lost our fatherland."

The feelings of the youths were more and more enkindled by such words, and a murmur stole along the lines; even the Laurentians and the Latins were changed. Those who a moment before were hoping for rest from battle and safety for their possessions now wished for arms and begged that the treaty be broken, and they pitied the unfair lot of Turnus. To these Juturna added a still greater deception, by giving from high heaven a sign most effective in disturbing the minds of the Italians and deceiving them with its portent. For the golden bird of Jove, flying in the red sky, was chasing shore birds and a noisy flock of the winged throng when suddenly the fierce eagle, gliding down to the water, seized a beautiful swan in its hooked claws. The attention of the Italians was arrested as all the birds with a cry reversed their course—a wonderful sight—and darkened the air with their wings and in the shape of a cloud pursued the enemy through the air until the eagle, overcome by the power and weight of the swan, weakened and dropped its booty from its claws into the river and fled far away into the clouds.

Then, indeed, the Rutulians hailed the omen with a shout and prepared themselves for the fight. Tolumnius the augur spoke first:

"This, this was what I have often sought in my prayers. I receive it and I recognize that the gods are here. With me, with me as your leader, seize the sword, unfortunate men, whom a wicked stranger terrifies with war, as if you were weak birds, and whose shores he lays waste with his might. He shall seek flight and sail far over the sea. With one accord form your lines and in battle defend your king, before he is snatched from you."

He spoke and, running forward, hurled his javelin against the enemies opposite him. The whizzing cornel spear sounded and cut through the air in a straight line. As soon as this happened, a great shout arose, and all the assembled men were disturbed, their hearts fired by the tumult. Nine handsome brothers, sons that a faithful Etruscan wife had borne to Gylippus the Arcadian, happened to be standing together on the opposite side. The flying spear struck one of them, a youth of magnificent figure with gleaming weapons, near the middle of his body where the stitched belt rubbed against the waist and the buckle joined the clasps on the ends. The weapon pierced his ribs, and he died on the yellow sand. Now the brothers, a courageous band, were furious in their grief. Some seized their swords in their hands, others snatched up weapons to hurl, and blindly attacked. Against them the lines of the Laurentians dashed forward; thereupon, waves of Trojans and men from Agylla and Arcadians with painted weapons poured forth. Thus, the same desire possessed everyone—to settle the matter with the sword.

THE WOUNDING OF AENEAS

They tore down the altars; a whirling storm of weapons flew through the whole heavens, and a rain of iron descended. They bore away the bowls and the fire. Latinus himself fled, carrying back his rejected gods, the rites of the truce unfinished. Others harnessed their chariots or with a leap sprang upon their horses and were ready with drawn swords. Messapus, eager to break the truce by charging with his horse, frightened away King Aulestes the Etruscan, bearing the royal insignia. He fell as he retreated and, unfortunate man, was thrown backward upon his head and shoulders across the altars in his path. Now furious Messapus raced up with his spear, and looking down from his horse, with a beamlike weapon gravely wounded the man as he uttered many a prayer.

"This is the end of him," Messapus said. "This better victim has been offered up to the great gods." The Italians rushed to the spot and despoiled his still warm body.

As Ebysus came carrying a whip, Corynaeus in his path seized a blazing torch from the altar and pushed the flame into his face. His long beard took fire and gave off a burning odor. Moreover, moving in close, Corynaeus seized the hair of his confused enemy with his left hand and bearing down with a heavy knee, he pinned Ebysus to the ground and pierced his side with a rigid sword. Podalirius, pursuing with a naked sword, pressed upon Alsus the shepherd, who was rushing through the weapons in the first line of battle. Raising high his ax, Alsus split the middle of his opponent's forehead and his chin, and stained his armor with blood that spattered far and wide. Grim silence and an ironlike sleep overpowered the eyes of Podalirius; his eyelids closed in an eternal night.

Then devout Aeneas, his head bare, stretched forth his unarmed hand and called to his men with a shout: "Where are you rushing? What sudden discord is this that is starting? Ah, restrain your anger! The truce is already made, and all the rules are settled. I alone have the right to battle! Let me fight! Lay aside your fear! I will see to it that the conditions of the treaty are carried out with a firm hand. By these sacred rites Turnus is already due me."

During this appeal, in the midst of these words, suddenly a whizzing arrow came flying and struck the hero, though it was uncertain what hand shot it, what whirlwind drove it to its mark, or what chance or god brought such great fame to the Rutulians. The glory of this noteworthy deed was kept secret, nor did anyone boast of inflicting this wound on Aeneas.

TURNUS SLAYS MANY

Turnus, seeing Aeneas leave the battle line and noting the anxiety of the leaders, feverishly glowed with sudden hope. He demanded horses and arms at the same time. With one leap he bounded into his chariot and seized the reins in his hands.

Hurrying along, he sent many a brave man to his death and rolled many over half dead, either crushing the battle line with his chariot or hurling the spears he had seized at those who were fleeing. As when swift, bloody Mars along the cool Hebrus River rattles his shield and, fomenting war, lets loose his furious horses; they fly over the open plain, outstripping the south and the west winds; the distant borders of Thrace groan under the pounding of feet, and round about hover grim-visaged Fear, Wrath, and Deceit, in company with the god: so spirited Turnus in the midst of the battle lashed his steaming horses over his enemies who had been miserably slain. The rapid hoofs splattered drops of blood, and the tramping mixed gore with sand. Then he sent Sthenelus to his death and also Thamyrus and Pholus, the last two in close fighting, the first from a distance. From afar, he slew Glaucus and Lades, sons whom Imbrasus himself had reared in Lycia and equipped with like armor so that they could fight in hand-to-hand combat or outstrip the winds on horseback.

In another section of the field, Eumedes rode into the midst of the battle. He was the offspring, illustrious in war, of ancient Dolon, recalling his grandfather in his name and his father in mind and action, who once, on approaching the camp of the Greeks as a spy, had dared to demand for himself the chariot of Achilles; for such daring, Diomede rewarded him with a different prize, and thereafter he did not aspire to the horses of Achilles. As Turnus sighted Eumedes afar off on the open plain, after pursuing him with a light javelin for a long space, he reined in his team of horses and, leaping down from his chariot, stood over the half-living, fallen man. Pushing his foot into Eumedes' neck, Turnus wrested the sword from his victim's right hand and stained the gleaming weapon with a deep thrust into his throat, while uttering these words:

"Now, Trojan, lying there, measure the fields of Italy which you sought in war. Those who have dared to match me with the sword receive this reward; in this way they build their walls."

Hurling a spear, Turnus sent Asbytes, the companion of

Eumedes, to his death and Chloreus and Sybaris and Dares and Thersilochus and Thymoetes, tossed over the neck of his plunging horse. As when the wind of Thracian Boreas resounds over the Aegean Sea and follows the waves to the shores where the winds press on and the clouds flee from the heavens: so wherever Turnus cut a path, the battle lines yielded, and the opposing lines collapsed; his impetus carried him along, and the air struck his flying crest as the chariot headed into the wind. Phegeus could not bear the sight of Turnus as he attacked with raging spirit: he threw himself in the path of the chariot and turned aside with his right hand the mouths of the swift horses foaming on the bit. While he was being dragged along, hanging to the yoke, a long spear reached him, unguarded as he was. Being thrust deep, it pierced the double-plated cuirass and slightly wounded him. But after turning toward his enemy with upraised shield, Phegeus was walking along, seeking help after pulling out the weapon, when the wheel of the swiftly advancing chariot threw him headlong and dashed him to the ground. Turnus, following with his sword, cut off Phegeus' head between the base of the helmet and the edge of the top of the cuirass, and left his trunk upon the sand.

AENEAS IS CURED BY VENUS

While Turnus victoriously spread death over the field, meantime Mnestheus and faithful Achates and Ascanius, his companion, led to the camp the bleeding Aeneas, who leaned at every other step upon a long spear. Wild with rage, he attempted to pull out the weapon with its broken reed and demanded that they use the quickest method to bring him relief; that they cut the wound with a broad sword, lay bare the deep hidden spot where the weapon was, and return him to the battle.

Iapyx the son of Iasus, beloved above all others by Phoebus, happened to be present. To him Apollo, smitten with fierce love, once would have gladly given his arts and his gifts—

prophecy, the lyre, and his swift arrows. In order that he might defer the fate of his dying parent, he preferred to know the power of herbs and their use in healing and to practice without glory the quiet arts. Leaning upon a huge spear and raging bitterly, Aeneas, unmoved by their tears, stood surrounded by a great crowd of youths and by weeping Julus. The aged Iapyx, with his garment drawn up in medical fashion, tremblingly tried to do much with his healing skill and the powerful herbs of Apollo, but in vain. In vain he attempted to draw out the point of the dart with his right hand and to catch hold of the iron with his gripping pincers. No luck attended his effort; his patron Apollo aided him in no way. The wild turmoil on the plains increased more and more, and disaster came closer. Already the air was thick with dust, the horsemen rode up, and darts fell thick in the middle of the camp; the sad clamor of youths, battling and falling in the grim struggle, rose to the heavens.

Then his mother Venus, crushed by the undeserved pain of her son, plucked on Cretan Ida some dittany, a stalk of mature leaves, blooming with purple flowers. This plant was not unknown to wild goats when swift arrows pierced their hide. Concealing her face in a dark cloud, Venus descended with this herb. With this she tinged the water poured out in magnificent vessels, mixing the drug secretly, and she sprinkled the healing juice of the ambrosia and the sweet-smelling panacea. Without realizing this, the aged Iapyx bathed the wound in this water, and suddenly all the pain left Aeneas, all the blood stayed in the bottom of the wound. Then the arrow, following the physician's hand, though no one forced it, fell out, and Aeneas' strength returned anew to its former state.

"Quickly hasten with arms to the hero! Why do you stand there?" Iapyx shouted out, the first to rouse their spirits against the enemy. "This is not the result of human effort or of a physician's skill. Aeneas, my right hand does not save you; a greater force is active here and sends you back to greater deeds."

Aeneas, eager for combat, had encased his legs round about in gold, and brandishing his spear, resented the delay. After his shield was fitted to his side and his cuirass to his back, he put his arms around Ascanius in an iron embrace and, lightly kissing his lips through the helmet, he said:

"My boy, learn courage and true labor from me, but fortune from others. Now my right arm shall defend you in war and lead you within reach of great prizes; when soon you grow to mature manhood, see that you remember, and that both your father Aeneas and your uncle Hector stir you to noble deeds, as you recall to mind the example of your kinsmen."

JUTURNA KEEPS TURNUS FROM AENEAS

When he had said these words, towering high, he left the camp through the gate, brandishing a huge javelin in his hand. At the same time in a dense line, Antheus and Mnestheus rushed forth and all the multitude poured from the abandoned camp. Then the plain was covered with blinding dust, and the shaken earth trembled with the beating of feet. Turnus saw them coming from the opposite hill; the Italians saw, and a cold tremor ran through their very marrow. Juturna was the first of all to hear the Latins, and recognizing the sound, she fled trembling. Aeneas flew ahead, hurrying the dark ranks to the open field. As a rain cloud, when a storm has broken out, moves toward the land through the midst of the sea; alas, the prophetic hearts of the unfortunate farmers afar off are terrified, for it will bring ruin to the trees and disaster to the crops and will destroy everything far and wide; the winds fly ahead and carry the sound to the shore: so the Rhoeteian leader hurled his battle line against the opposing enemy, and everyone joined in close formation with the driving battalions. Thymbraeus struck bulky Osiris with his sword, Mnestheus slew Arcetius, Achates killed Epulo, and Gyas laid Ufens low; even Tolumnius the augur fell, the first to hurl his javelin against the opposing enemy. The noise rose to the heavens, and the retreating Rutulians in turn showed their dust-covered backs as they fled through the fields. Aeneas did not even deign to lay low in death those who turned away from him or met him on an equal footing, nor did he pursue those who hurled weapons at him. Looking about in the dense clouds of dust, he hunted for Turnus only; he challenged him alone in single combat.

Warlike Juturna, whose mind was disturbed by this fear, pushed out Turnus' driver, Metiscus, as he stood with the reins about him, and left him lying far from the chariot. She mounted the chariot and seized the flowing reins in her hands, assuming everything about Metiscus, his voice, his appearance, and his weapons. As when a dark swallow flies through the great buildings of a rich lord and wings its way through the lofty halls, picking up little bits of food for the chattering nests, now crying out in the empty porticoes or again around the dank pools: likewise Juturna was carried by the horses through the midst of the enemy and, as she sped, traveled everywhere in her speedy chariot. Now here and now there she displayed her triumphant brother; yet she did not allow him to fight, but raced afar beyond reach.

Nonetheless, Aeneas followed these whirling turns to meet him, and he tracked down the man and shouted with a loud voice through the scattered battle lines. As often as he caught sight of his enemy, Aeneas by running attempted to equal the flight of the wing-footed horses, and just as often Juturna turned the chariot aside. Alas, what was he to do? Helplessly he tossed on a shifting tide of anger, and various worries beckoned his mind in different directions. Messapus happened to be carrying in his left hand two tough spears tipped with iron and, turning with a sudden spurt, he hurled one of these with deadly force. Aeneas stopped and, dropping to his knees, took a position behind his armor; the swift spear struck the peak of his helmet and knocked the top of his crest from his head. Then indeed his anger rose; when he saw the horses and the chariot turning away from him, exasperated by the deception, he called many times on Jupiter and the altar of the broken truce, and then finally attacked in the center. Now terrible with the favor of Mars, he rekindled savage slaughter indiscriminately and loosened all the reins of his wrath.

What god can now describe for me so many bitter clashes?

Who can express in poetry the diverse slaughter, the death of the leaders whom, by turns, now Turnus, now the Trojan hero drove over the whole plain? Was it your pleasure, Jupiter, that by reason of this great struggle future races should live in eternal peace? Aeneas struck Rutulian Sucro in the side. That fight was the first to hold back the onrushing Trojans. He did not offer much opposition, and Aeneas thrust his bloody sword through the ribs that protect the breast, where death comes swiftest. Meeting them on foot, Turnus struck Amycus, who had been knocked down from his horse, and his brother Diores —the one he slew with a long spear as he was approaching, the other with his sword—and he suspended the severed heads of the two from his chariot and carried them along dripping with blood.

Aeneas sent to their death Talos and Tanais and brave Cethegus, the three in one combat, and sad Onites, with a Theban name, of the race of his mother Peridia. Turnus dispatched the brothers sent from Lycia and the fields of Apollo, and the Arcadian Menoetes, the youth who vainly detested war, who had skill along the rivers of fish-stocked Lerna and a poor home; he had no access to the palaces of the powerful, and his father sowed his crops on rented land.

And as fire let loose from different directions upon a burning forest and shrubs of crackling laurel, or when in a rapid descent from high mountains foaming rivers sound and run into the plains, each laying waste what is in its path—not less sluggishly did both Aeneas and Turnus rush through the battle lines. Now, now their anger tossed within them; their breasts that knew nothing of defeat were on the point of bursting. Now with all their force they fell to inflicting wounds.

Then Murranus, who boasted of his grandparents and their grandparents of ancient name, and of all his race descended from Latin kings, Aeneas knocked headlong with the whirling mass of a great stone and dashed upon the ground. As he lay beneath the reins and the yoke, the wheels rolled over him; the swift hoofs of the horses, heedless of their master, again and again beat upon him from above. Turnus blocked the onrushing Hyllus, who was furiously fuming in his arrogance, and he hurled a javelin at the Trojan's gold-protected temples. Piercing his helmet, the spear clung fixed in his brain. Your right hand, Cretheus, bravest of the Greeks, did not save you from Turnus, nor, as Aeneas came up, was Cupencus protected by his gods. His breast met the sword; the resistance of his bronze shield was of no avail to the unlucky man.

The Laurentian fields saw you, too, Aeolus, meet death and cover the earth with your broad back. You fell, whom neither the Greek phalanx nor Achilles, the destroyer of the kingdom of Priam, was able to vanquish. Here was your goal, your death. Your lofty home was beneath Mount Ida, your lofty home at Lyrnesus, and your grave in Laurentian soil! The entire battle lines converged to that point—all the Latins and all the Trojans; Mnestheus and fierce Serestus and Messapus the horse trainer and brave Asilas; the phalanx of the Etruscans; and the Arcadian cavalry of Evander. Each and every one of the men battled for himself with all the strength at his command. There was neither delay nor rest; in a vast struggle they drove forward.

AENEAS ATTACKS THE WALLED CITY

Thereupon the beauteous mother of Aeneas put the thought in his mind to go to the walls and quickly wheel his battle line to the city and confuse the Latins with a sudden defeat. As he turned his gaze this way and that while tracking down Turnus through the scattered lines, he noticed that the city was unscathed by the great battle and free from attack. Straightway the vision of a greater battle kindled his imagination. He called Mnestheus and Sergestus and brave Serestus, the leaders, and he stood on a mound where the rest of the Trojan legion assembled in close formation without laying aside their shields or spears.

Standing in the center upon a high bank he spoke: "There must be no delay in heeding my commands. Jupiter is on this side. Let no one go along with me with greater reluctance because of this sudden decision. Today I will destroy the city, the cause of the war, the very kingdom of Latinus, unless they are willing to submit and obey as conquered people. I will level the smoking rooftops to the ground. Should I perhaps wait until it pleases Turnus to submit to a battle with me, until that conquered man wishes to meet me again? Here, citizens, is the source, here is the heart of this unholy war. Bring up torches quickly and demand back by fire what was pledged me."

He finished speaking, and all with equally energetic spirit formed a wedge and moved in a dense mass toward the walls. Unexpectedly ladders and a sudden fire appeared. Some ran aside to the gates and killed the defenders; others hurled weapons and darkened the air with javelins. Aeneas himself in the van stretched his right hand toward the walls and with a loud voice reproached Latinus and called the gods to witness that he was again forced to war, that twice before the Italians had been his enemies, and that already this second truce was broken. Disagreement arose among the panic-stricken citizens. Some ordered the city to be thrown open and the gates to be unlocked for the Trojans, and they favored dragging the king himself to the fortifications; others brought arms and proceeded to defend the walls: as when a shepherd has tracked bees enclosed in a secret, stony crevice and has filled it with stifling smoke, those within, panic-stricken at the turn of affairs, run about through the waxen camp and sharpen their anger with loud buzzing; the odorous black smoke rolls through the hive; inside, rocks resound with a muffled murmur, while smoke rises into the free air.

AMATA COMMITS SUICIDE

The weary Latins experienced a new misfortune, which shook the whole city with grief to its very foundations. When the queen saw the enemy advancing toward the houses, the walls assailed, fires flying to the roofs, and nowhere any opposing battle lines of the Rutulians, no battalions under Turnus, the unhappy woman believed that the youth had perished in the conflict of battle. Of a sudden, disturbed by her sorrow, she exclaimed that she was the guilty cause and the source of these evils. Insanely uttering many things in her pitiful madness, destined to die, she tore her purple garment with her hands and tied the knot of hideous death from a high beam. After the miserable Latin women heard of the calamity, the daughter Lavinia tore her flowerlike tresses and her rosy cheeks with her hands, and then the throng became frantic with grief; the buildings resounded far and wide with wailing. Thereupon, the news of the misfortune spread through the whole city. They gave themselves over to despair. Latinus with rent garments went about, dazed at the death of his wife and the ruin of the city, soiling his white hair by sprinkling it with foul dust. [He reproached himself for his many failings, for not receiving Trojan Aeneas before and not freely recognizing him as his son-in-law.]

TURNUS RECOGNIZES HIS DRIVER AS JUTURNA

Meanwhile, warlike Turnus, now slowing up a bit, was pursuing a few stragglers at the extreme end of the plain and was less and less happy with the speed of his horses. The breeze carried that din mingled with faint cries of terror to him, and the mournful, rumbling sound of the confused city reached his straining ears.

"More woe! Why are the fortifications disturbed by such great lamentations? What great noise comes from the distant city?" Thus he cried and, frantically pulling on the reins, stopped.

His sister answered him in these words, for having taken on the appearance of his driver Metiscus, she was managing the chariot and the reined horses:

"Turnus, let us pursue the Trojans along this route where victory first opens a path. There are others who can defend the battlements with their strength. Aeneas is attacking and mingling in battle with the Italians; let us deal out fierce death to the Trojans with all our might. You shall not kill fewer men, nor shall you be rated below him in the honor of battle."

To these words Turnus replied: "O sister, even then I recognized you when first you broke up the truce by your cunning and threw yourself into the battle, and now you vainly disguise your divinity. But whose wish was it that you, sent down from Olympus, should suffer such great hardships? Was it that you might see the cruel death of a miserable brother? For what am I to do, or what chance now offers me safety? Before my eyes I saw Murranus perish—no man dearer to me survives—as he called upon me—a huge man, laid low by a great wound. Ill-starred Ufens died lest he should see our shame; the Trojans took possession of his body and his armor. Shall I suffer our homes to be destroyed—the one thing lacking to complete our disaster—and not refute with my right arm the words of Drances? Shall I turn my back? Will this land see Turnus fleeing? Is it so very miserable to die? Gods of the underworld, be good to me, since the will of the gods above is averse! I will descend to you, an innocent soul, guiltless of this fault, not at all unworthy of my great ancestors."

He scarcely finished speaking these words when Saces, plainly bearing an arrow wound on his face, suddenly flew through the midst of the enemy, borne upon a foaming charger, and rushed up, imploring Turnus by name:

"Turnus, in you is our last hope of safety! Have pity on your followers! Aeneas thunders in arms and threatens to cast down the highest Italian citadels and hand them over to destruction. Already the torches are flying toward the roofs. To you the Latins turn their faces, to you their gaze. King Latinus doubts whom he should call son-in-law or to what arrangement he should consent. Moreover, the queen, who placed her greatest trust in you, has perished by her own hand and fled the light of day in her terror. Alone in front of the gates, Messapus and fierce Atinas hold the line; around them on both sides are compact battalions, and an iron crop bristles with drawn swords. You are turning your chariot upon the deserted meadows."

Turnus was stupefied, confused at the changed picture of events, and he stood silently gazing. At the same time there welled up in his heart great shame and fury with mingled sorrow, rage-driven love, and conscious courage. As soon as the shadows were driven away and the light of reason returned to his mind, troubled he turned his angry gaze toward the fortifications and from his chariot looked back at the great city. But lo, the whirling column of fire between the floors leaped toward the heavens and enveloped the tower which he himself had erected from closely laid beams and had mounted on wheels and fitted above with lofty bridges.

"Now indeed fate conquers, sister. Cease to delay; let us pursue where the god and bitter fortune call. I have decided to fight Aeneas, to suffer whatever bitterness there is in death. You shall not see me dishonored any longer, my sister. I beg of you, allow me to vent my fury before I die."

He finished speaking, and from his chariot he swiftly leaped to the ground and, deserting his tearful sister, rushed through the enemy, through the weapons, breaking through the middle of the battle line in his swift course. As a rock rushes precipitously down from the top of a mountain when the wind tears it away or a turbulent rainstorm washes it down or passing age loosens it over the years; the destructive mass is borne headlong with great speed and bounds upon the ground, dragging with it forests and cattle and men: so Turnus dashed through the scattered lines to the walls of the city, where the earth was wet with bloodshed, and the air was shrill with spears. He made a gesture with his hand and at the same time began in a loud voice:

"Cease now, Rutulians, and you Latins, hold back your weapons! Whatever the fortune of this war, it is mine; it is more right that I alone, in place of you, atone for the broken truce and settle the outcome with the sword."

All who were in the center moved back and left a space for the combat.

SINGLE COMBAT BETWEEN AENEAS AND TURNUS

Then father Aeneas, on hearing the name of Turnus, left the walls, left the height of the citadel, and quickly ending all delay, broke off all his toil. Exulting with joy, he made a thunderous sound with his weapons, as great as Athos, as great as Eryx, or as great as father Apennine when, raising himself to the breeze, he shrieks amid waving oaks or rejoices in his snow-crowned peak. Now, indeed, the Rutulians and the Trojans and the Italians turned their gaze to him, both those who held the lofty fortifications and those who were pounding the base of the walls with battering rams, and they put down their weapons from their shoulders. Latinus himself was amazed that these great heroes, born in widely separated parts of the world, had reached an agreement with each other and that they would settle matters with the sword. Once they appeared on the cleared level of the field, they hurled their spears from the distance and, running forward rapidly, attacked with shields and resounding bronze. The earth sent up a groan; then they redoubled their frequent sword blows; luck and courage effected the same result. As in the great forest of Sila or on the top of Taburnus, when two bulls with locked horns attack in battle to the death—the fearful herdsmen have retired and all the herd stands mute with fear, silently waiting to see which one shall rule the grove, which one the entire herd shall follow—they with all their might inflict wounds upon each other, and in their struggle, they thrust forth with their horns, and their necks and shoulders are bathed in profuse blood, and all the grove reechoes with their bellowing: in the same way Trojan Aeneas and the Daunian hero raised a din with their shields, and a great sound of crashing filled the air.

Jupiter himself held up the two scales equally balanced, and placed therein the diverse fates of the two men, to determine whom the struggle would doom, which side death would weigh down. Thereupon Turnus leaped forward and, thinking he might do so without risk, raised himself high with his upraised sword and struck. The Trojans and the fearful Latins cried out, and the battle lines of both were tense. But the faithless sword broke and failed the enraged Turnus in the midst of the blow, and he would have perished had not flight come to his aid. Faster than the wind he was flying when he saw the unknown hilt in his defenseless right hand. The story goes that when he was climbing into his chariot behind the harnessed horses for the very first battle, leaving behind his father's weapon, in his headlong haste he seized the sword of his driver, Metiscus. This served for a long time, while the straggling Trojans were in retreat, but when it encountered the arms of the god Vulcan, the man-made sword broke at one blow, as if it were brittle ice. The fragments shone upon the yellow sand. Then crazed Turnus sought the plain, fleeing now here, now there in different directions, and he dashed about in confused circles, for everywhere the dense throng of Trojans hemmed him in, while on one side a vast swamp and on the other steep fortifications blocked his course.

Nevertheless, Aeneas continued in pursuit, feverishly treading on the heels of the fearful Turnus, although at times his knees, slowed down by the wound from the arrow, held him back and hindered his running: just as at times, a hunting dog, catching up with a deer that is cornered in the river or held back by fear of ropes with purple feathers, pursues as he runs and barks, while the deer, terrified by the snare and the high bank, flees this way and that over a thousand paths; the swift Umbrian hound with open mouth stays with him and ever so often reaches him, and, as if catching him, snaps with his jaws and is deceived when he bites on nothing. Then indeed a tumult arose, and the banks of the lake round about returned the sound, and all the heavens thundered with the uproar. As he fled, Turnus railed at everyone, calling each person by name, demanding his well-known sword. On the other hand, Aeneas menaced with death and immediate destruction anyone who approached, and he terrified his trembling enemies, threatening to destroy their city, and though wounded, he pressed on. The two ran around in a circle five times and just as often retraced their steps now this way, now that; nor were the trifling prizes of the games at stake, but they were fighting for the life and blood of Turnus.

As it happened, there had stood here a wild olive tree with bitter leaves. Sacred to Faunus, its wood was once venerated by sailors. There, when saved from the waves, they were accustomed to fasten gifts to the god of Laurentum and to hang their vowed garments. But the Trojans with utter indifference had removed the sacred trunk so that they might fight in a clear field. Here the spear of Aeneas stood. To this spot his power had driven it, and it remained fixed in the tough root. Aeneas leaped to it and wished to pull up the weapon with his hand and hurl it at the man whom he could not overtake by running.

Then, indeed, Turnus, panic-stricken with fear, cried: "Faunus, I pray, have pity! And you, dear land, hold the javelin, since I have always promoted your honor, unlike the followers of Aeneas who have profaned it in war."

He spoke and not with vain prayers did he invoke the help of the god, for, though struggling long and delaying at the tough root, Aeneas was not able with all his strength to loosen the hold of the hard wood. While he pushed and struggled fiercely, Juturna, again changing her appearance to that of the driver Metiscus, ran forward and handed a sword to her brother. Venus, indignant that this was permitted the audacious nymph, approached and pulled the javelin from the deep root. The heroes, towering high, now renewed in arms and spirit, the one trusting in the sword, the other fierce and giantlike with his spear, stood opposite each other, panting from the exertion of the battle.

Meanwhile, the king of all-powerful Olympus addressed Juno, who was looking at the battle from a bright cloud:

"What is to be the end of this, wife? What is in store at last? You yourself know, and you admit you know, that Aeneas is a divine hero, that he is destined for heaven, and that he will be raised by the Fates to the stars. What are you scheming? With what hope do you stay in these cold clouds? Would it be fitting that a god be dishonored with a wound from a mortal? Was it fitting that the sword—for what could Juturna accomplish without you?—snatched away from him be returned to Turnus, and that the power of the vanquished should increase? Cease now at long last and yield to my prayer, so that such a great sorrow may not quietly consume you, and mournful complaints may not so often issue from your sweet lips. The end has been reached. You were able to harass the Trojans on land or sea, to enkindle an unspeakable war, to ruin a home, and to bring a marriage to grief: I forbid you to attempt to go farther."

Thus Jupiter spoke. The divine daughter of Saturn with downcast countenance answered with these words:

"Indeed, great Jupiter, because this, your will, was known to me, I unwillingly left Turnus and the earth; otherwise, you would not now see me seated alone in the sky, a worthy goddess, suffering undeservedly, but I would be standing surrounded by flames in the very battle line, drawing the Trojans into fatal conflict. I induced Juturna, I admit it, to aid her miserable brother, and I approved her daring still more for his life, but not that she should hurl darts or bend the bow. I swear it by the inexorable source of the Stygian river, the one oath that is reverenced by the gods. And now, indeed, I yield, and hating battles I retire. I beg of you for Latium, for the majesty of your kin, that boon which is forbidden by no law of fate: when soon they will arrange the peace with a happy marriage—let it be so—when soon they will agree on laws and treaties, do not order the native Latins to change their ancient name, nor that they become Trojans and be called Teucrians, nor that the people change their language or alter their dress. Let there be a Latium, let Alban kings exist through the ages, and let the Roman stock be strong in Italian courage. Troy has perished, and let it perish with its name."

Smiling at her, the creator of men and the world said: "You are the sister of Jupiter and the second offspring of Saturn. What great waves of anger toss in your breast! Come now, quiet the fury that has risen to no purpose. What you wish I give, and I yield, willingly conquered. The Italians shall retain their native speech and customs, and the name shall be as it is. The Trojans, mingling only their blood with the Latins, shall disappear as Trojans. I will add the usage and the rites pertaining to their sacred services, and I will make all the Latins of one tongue. From them shall rise a race mixed with Italian blood which you shall see go beyond men, beyond the gods in piety, nor shall any race celebrate your honors with equal devotion."

Juno assented to these proposals and joyfully changed her attitude. Meanwhile, she departed from the heavens and left the cloud.

After doing this, the creator himself turned over another matter in his mind and prepared to dismiss Juturna from the service of her brother. There are twin fiends, known by the name of Furies, which, together with infernal Megaera, gloomy Night brought forth in one and the same birth and bound with equal coils of serpents, adding wings with the speed of the wind. These Furies serve near the throne of Jupiter and in the region of savage King Pluto. They incite fear in miserable mortals whenever the king of the gods plans fearful death by disease or terrifies cities with the war they so richly deserve.

Jupiter sent down from highest heaven one of these swift Furies and ordered her to appear to Juturna as an omen. The fiend took wing and was borne earthward in a swift whirlwind. Just as an arrow, driven through the clouds by a bowstring and armed with the deadly poison of gall, a fatal weapon shot by a Parthian or a Cretan, speeds, twanging and unperceived, through the swift shadows, in just the same way the offspring of Night moved in her course to the earth. After she sighted the Trojan battle lines and the army of Turnus, she suddenly took on the appearance of a tiny bird which, at times, on tombs and on deserted housetops, sits late at night, ominously singing through the shadows. In this guise, the fiend, croaking, flew back and forth in front of the face of Turnus and beat his shield with her wings. A numbness that he had never experienced before now paralyzed him. He was horrified; his hair stood on end, and his voice stuck in his throat. But unhappy Juturna recognized afar off the whirring wings of the Fury.

His sister tore her loosened hair, scratched her face with her nails, and beating her breast with her fists, said: "How can your sister help you now, Turnus? What is left for me to do, hard-hearted as I am? By what stratagem can I prolong life for you? Can I oppose such a monster? Right now I am leaving the battle lines. Obscene birds, do not change my fear into terror; I recognize the beating of your wings and the fatal sound, nor do the arrogant commands of the noble-minded Jupiter deceive me. Does he issue these in payment for my virginity? For what reason did he give me unending life? Why was the common lot of death taken away? Now I would be able definitely to end such great sorrow and go as my unfortunate brother's companion through the underworld. So I am immortal? But is there anything at all that I have that will be pleasurable to me without you, brother? Ah, would that the earth could open deep enough for me, and send me, a goddess, down to the lowest shades!"

After saying this much, the goddess covered her head with a bluish hood and, weeping much, hid herself in the deep river.

Aeneas charged against Turnus and brandished a huge, tree-like spear. With savage spirit he spoke these words: "What is the cause of the delay now? Why are you still drawing back, Turnus? You must fight not by retreating but by battling with fierce weapons in hand-to-hand combat. Turn yourself into any form you will and bring together whatever you can, whether by courage or trickery; wish to follow the burning stars on wings or to hide yourself deep in the hollow earth."

But Turnus, shaking his head, said: "Your heated words do not terrify me, savage; the gods and my enemy, Jupiter, terrify me."

Saying no more, he looked around at a huge rock, an ancient, massive rock which happened to be lying on the field, placed on the ground as a marker to settle a quarrel over boundaries. It could hardly be raised up on the shoulders of twice six chosen men with such bodies as the earth produces today. The hero, straightening himself up and running swiftly, tried to hurl at his enemy the rock he had snatched up with trembling hand. But he did not recognize his former self either when he ran or walked or raised his hands or moved the mighty rock; his knees gave way, his chilled blood began to grow sluggish with cold. Then the very stone hurled by the hero through the empty air did not cover the entire distance or strike its mark. As in dreams, when languid quiet has weighed the eyelids down in darkness, and it seems we vainly will to hasten our eager course and feebly sink down in the midst of our attempt; the tongue is powerless, the known strength of the body fails, and the sound of words does not come forth: so the dire goddess denied Turnus success in every way that he sought to show his courage. Then varying feelings troubled his heart: he glanced at the Rutulians and the city, he hesitated in fear and began to tremble at the approaching javelin, nor did he see any place where he might flee, nor by what means he might attack the enemy, nor did he sight his chariot or his charioteer sister anywhere. Aeneas, risking his lot on a lucky aim, strained afar off with every sinew of his body. Never did stones hurled from wall-crashing engines of war whine so; nor such great peals burst from thunder bolts. Like a deadly whirlwind the spear flew, bearing awful destruction, laying open the border of the cuirass and the outer layers of the seven-fold shield. With a shrill sound it pierced the middle of his thigh. Great Turnus, wounded, fell to the earth as his knees buckled. With a groan the Rutulians rose, and all the mountain round about resounded and the deep groves re-echoed their cry far and wide.

Suppliantly raising his humble eyes and stretching forth his beseeching right hand, Turnus said: "Indeed I have received my reward, nor do I cry for pity. Use your good fortune. If any consideration for a miserable parent can touch your soul, I beg of you—you had such a father in Anchises—have pity on the old age of Daunus and return me, or my dead body if you so wish, to my people. You have conquered, and the Italians have seen me stretch forth my hands in defeat. Lavinia is your wife. Proceed no farther with your hate."

In his armor fierce Aeneas stood rolling his eyes, and he held back his right arm. The plea had begun to move the hesitating hero when suddenly the fatal belt shone high up on the victim's shoulder, and there was a gleam from the well-known embossed work on the belt of young Pallas. When Turnus had overcome that youth, he laid him low with a wound; thenceforth he wore upon his shoulder the distinguishing ornament of his enemy.

Aeneas, after gazing upon the reminder and the relic of a cruel grief, on fire with rage and terrible in his anger, shouted: "Are you, wearing the spoils of my ally, going to escape from me? Pallas, yes, Pallas immolates you with this wound and wreaks vengeance on the blood of a criminal."

So saying, he eagerly buried his sword in his enemy's breast. Then the limbs of Turnus relaxed in cold death, and with a groan his ill-deserving spirit fled into the darkness.

Genealogical Table

The mythical founder of the Julian gens, to which Augustus belonged, was Ascanius, also known as Julus, descended on both his father's and his mother's side from divinity, since both had a common ancestor in Tros, whose grandfather was Dardanus, the offspring of Jupiter and an ocean nymph Electra. In the following table are shown the descendants of Tros whose names occur in the *Aeneid*.

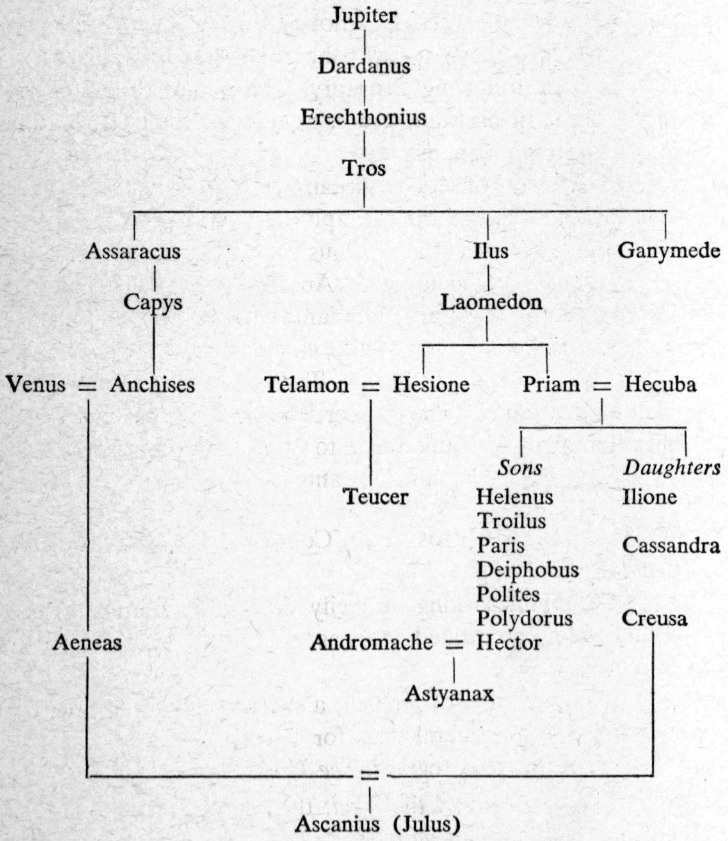

Glossary

One of the difficulties encountered in reading the *Aeneid* is the great number of unfamiliar proper names. In the main, the following items have been omitted from this glossary: names whose meaning is clear from the context; warriors about whom nothing is known or need be known for an understanding of the epic; obscure place names whose location is unknown or unnecessary for following the story. The names of places visited by Aeneas in his wanderings, as told in Book III, may be found on the map (pp. xiv–xv).

For the sake of variety or because of the demands of dactylic hexameter, Vergil often employs several different names for the same person or place. Thus the Greeks are called Argives, Danaans, Pelasgians, or Achaeans; the Trojans may be referred to as Teucrians, Dardanians, sons of Dardanus, or Phrygians. Ascanius is sometimes called Julus; Venus, Cytherea; Juno, the daughter of Saturn. Troy is meant by Ilium, Pergamus, or Dardania. The reader should bear in mind that Vergil often gives the same name to more than one person, e.g., Abas, Pallas, Pandarus, and Serranus.

ABAS. 1. A king of Argos. 2. A Companion of Aeneas. 3. An Etruscan warrior.

ACESTES. A mythical king of Sicily descended from a Trojan mother. He entertained Aeneas when the latter came to Sicily.

ACHAEANS. Inhabitants of Achaia, a district in the north of the Peloponnesus. A general term for Greeks.

ACHERON. The infernal regions. *See* Hades.

ACHILLES. Famed hero of the *Iliad;* the son of Peleus, a king of Thessaly, and Thetis, a goddess.

ACTIUM. A promontory on the west coast of Greece where Octavian defeated the forces of Antony and Cleopatra in 31 B.C.

AEACUS. Father of Peleus and Telamon.

AENEAS. Son of Anchises and Venus. By Creusa, his first wife, who did not survive the destruction of Troy, he had a son called Ascanius or Julus. After the fall of Troy, Aeneas led a band of exiles to Latium where he founded the city of Lavinium, named after Lavinia, the daughter of King Latinus, whom he married. He is regarded as the founder of the Latin race.

AEOLUS. God of the winds.

AESCULAPIUS. The god of healing.

AGAMEMNON. King of Mycenae and leader of the Greek forces in the Trojan war. He was the son of Atreus of the house of Pelops and the brother of Menelaus, whose wife Helen fled with Paris to Troy under the protection of Venus.

AGATHYRSI. Scythian tribesmen who tattooed their bodies.

AGENOR. A king of Phoenicia and ancestor of Dido.

AJAX. 1. Son of Telamon and hero in the Trojan war. 2. Greek warrior, son of Oileus. Because he dragged Cassandra from the temple of Pallas, the goddess destroyed his ships.

ALBA LONGA. Most ancient city of Latium, built by Ascanius.

ALCIDES. Hercules.

ALECTO. See Furies.

ALLIA. A small river, flowing into the Tiber, near which the Gauls defeated the Romans in 387 B.C.

ALPHEUS. A large river in the Peloponnesus which rises in Arcadia and flows through Elis. The river god Alpheus fell in love with the nymph Arethusa, who bathed in the river. Fleeing from him, she was transformed into a fountain in Sicily; but Alpheus flowed beneath the sea and mingled his waters with those of her fountain.

AMAZONS. A legendary tribe of warlike women living near the Euxine Sea. Under Penthesilea, their queen, they fought as allies of the Trojans.

AMPHRYSIAN. An epithet of Apollo, who fed the flocks of Admetus near the Amphrysus, a river in Thessaly. The sibyl of Cumae was given the same name because she was a priestess of Apollo.

ANCHISES. Father of Aeneas by Venus.

ANDROMACHE. Wife of Hector and mother of Astyanax.

ANTENOR. Trojan leader, who, after the fall of Troy, founded the city of Patavium (Padua).

ANUBIS. An Egyptian god with the face of a dog.

APOLLO. Son of Jupiter and Latona, brother of Diana; a god of many attributes.

ARCADIA. A district in the center of the Peloponnesus.

ARETHUSA. *See* Alpheus.

ARGILETUM. A section of Rome near the Forum where there were many shops. According to Vergil's etymology, the name is derived from the death of Argos, a treacherous guest of Evander.

ARIADNE. *See* Minos.

ASCANIUS. Julus, son of Aeneas.

ATLAS. 1. A king of Mauretania noted for his knowledge of the stars. He is also represented as a giant who supported the world on his shoulders. 2. A mountain range of northwestern Africa.

ATREUS. *See* Agamemnon.

ATRIDAE. Sons of Atreus.

AUGUSTUS. *See* Introduction, p. v*ff*.

AURORA. See Tithonus.

AUSONIA. Italy.

AVERNUS. A lake near Cumae on the site of an extinct volcano. Nearby was the sibyl's cave through which Aeneas descended to the lower world.

BACCHUS. The god of wine; also called Lyaeus, Liber, and, by the Greeks, Dionysus.

BACTRIA. A province of the Persian Empire.

BAIAE. A town in Campania on a small bay west of Naples; celebrated for its baths.

BELLONA. Roman goddess of war.

BENACUS. An Italian lake near Verona, the modern Lago di Garda.

BERECYNTHIA. A surname of Cybele (q.v.).

BOREAS. The north wind.

BRIAREUS. A hundred-handed giant, friendly to the gods in their struggle with the Titans.

BYRSA. Citadel of Carthage.

CACUS. A giant slain by Hercules; his name suggests the Greek word for an evil man.

CAENIS. A maiden changed by Neptune into a man. In VI, 448, Caeneus is represented as again restored to womanly form.

CAMPANIA. A region of Italy, south of Latium. Here many wealthy Roman nobles had their villas.

CASSANDRA. Daughter of Priam, who received the gift of prophecy from Apollo, whose attentions she spurned. In revenge the god saw to it that her prophecies, though true, would never be believed. After the fall of Troy, Agamemnon took her with him to Mycenae, where both were slain by Clytemnestra.

CASTOR. Twin brother of Pollux. They were regarded as patrons of athletic contests, and their aid was sought in war. As the constellation Gemini they guided travelers, according to popular belief.

CATILINE. A conspirator whose plot against the state was foiled by Cicero during the latter's consulship in 63 B.C.

CATO, MARCUS PORCIUS. 1. The Elder, also called the Censor (234–149). An uncompromising foe of Carthage and an opponent of Hellenic influence in Roman society. 2. The Younger who is 46 B.C. committed suicide in Utica.

CELAENO. One of the Harpies (q.v.).

CENTAURS. Fabled monsters, half animal, half man, who lived on Mount Pelion in Thessaly.

CERBERUS. The three-headed dog guarding the entrance to Hades. In some accounts he has fifty, even one hundred heads.

CERES. Goddess of agriculture; identified with Demeter of the Greeks.

CHARON. An unkempt old man who rowed the shades of the dead across the river Styx.

CHARYBDIS. *See* Scylla.

CHIMAERA. A monster that spat flames. She is represented as having a lion's head, a goat's body, and a dragon's tail.

CIRCE. An enchantress who dwelt on the island of Aeaea.

CLOELIA. *See* Cocles.

COCLES, PUBLIUS HORATIUS. A Roman hero, who, battling on a narrow bridge over the Tiber, held off the Etruscan army under Porsenna. The exploit is celebrated by Macaulay in his *Lays of Ancient Rome.* At the time, Cloelia escaped from Porsenna and swam the river to Rome.

COCYTUS. *See* Hades.

CORYBANTS. *See* Cybele.

CREUSA. Wife of Aeneas (q.v.).

CUMAE. A town in Campania, west of Naples. The sibyl who led Aeneas through the underworld lived here in a cave.

CURETES. Cretan attendants of Rhea, the wife of Saturn. With their noisy dancing they drowned out the infant cries of Jove, who, if discovered, would have been swallowed by his father.

CYBELE. A goddess of Asia, typifying the powers of nature, known by various names such as Dindymene; the Great Mother; Mother of the Gods; Idaean Mother, because of Mount Ida, sacred to her. The principal seat of her worship was at Pessinus. Her eunuch priests were called Galli. (Other attendants of hers were called Corybants and Dactyli.) Cybele is identified with the Greek goddess Rhea, who was attended by the Curetes.

CYCLOPS. One of the race of giants that inhabited Sicily. As the name indicates, they had one round eye.

CYLLENE. Mountain in Arcadia where Mercury was born.

CYMOTHOE. A Nereid. *See* Nymphs.

CYNTHUS. A mountain on the island of Delos where Latona brought forth Diana and Apollo, who are often called Cynthia and Cynthius.

CYTHERA. An island off the southern coast of Greece where

there was a shrine to Venus.

DAEDALUS. Mythical Greek genius, gifted in architecture and the crafts; credited with planning the Labyrinth. He was banished from Athens for the murder of his nephew, a crime that was prompted by his jealousy of the young man's inventive talent. At Crete he displeased Minos, but escaped by making wings for himself. His son Icarus was killed in this venture.

DANAË. Mother of Perseus by Jupiter, who came to her in a shower of gold while she was imprisoned in a tower by her father Acrisius, who had learned from an oracle that he would be killed by his daughter's child.

DARDANUS. Son of Zeus (Jupiter to the Romans) and Electra; ancestor of the Trojan race.

DEIPHOBUS. Son of Priam, slain by Menelaus.

DELOS. Island in the midst of the Cyclades.

DELPHI. A town in Phocis where there was an oracle to Apollo; also called Pytho.

DIANA. An Italian goddess, identified with Artemis; sister of Apollo.

DICTE. Mountain on island of Crete where Jupiter was reared.

DIOMEDE. Son of Tydeus; hence called Tydides. Leader of the soldiers from Argos at the siege of Troy. Returning from the war he found his wife had been unfaithful. Later he was driven by a storm to the coast of Italy. The Latins sent an embassy to Diomede in the hope of enlisting him in their war against the Trojans, but he declined the invitation.

DIS. PLUTO. See Hades.

DODONA. Seat of an oracle to Jupiter in central Epirus, in northwestern Greece.

DOLOPES. Thessalians who took part in the siege of Troy.

DRANCES. One of the opponents of Turnus within his own ranks.

EGERIA. A nymph with whom Numa held converse concerning the worship he introduced.

ELIS. A district on the western coast of the Peloponnesus.

ELISSA. Dido.

ELYSIUM. The place where all worthy persons were to enjoy a pleasant life after death.

ENCELADUS. One of the giants who attempted to overthrow the gods, but the former were defeated and rendered powerless. He was imprisoned under Mount Etna.

ERATO. Muse of amorous poetry and the lyre.

EREBUS. Son of Chaos. The word means "darkness."

ERIPHYLE. After betraying her husband for a necklace that she coveted, Eriphyle was slain by her son Alcmaeon.

ERYX. 1. A mountain in Sicily where there was an ancient temple to Venus. 2. A Sicilian giant, son of Venus and Butes, and therefore a half brother of Aeneas.

EUBOEA. The largest island in the Aegean Sea.

EUROTAS. The most important river in Laconia. Sparta, the capital of Lacedaemon, was situated on this river.

EVADNE. Devoted wife of Capaneus, one of the seven heroes who fought against Thebes. She threw herself on her husband's burning funeral pyre.

EVANDER. A son of Hermes, said to have emigrated from Arcadia to Italy, there founding Pallanteum on the Tiber.

FABIUS. The name of a famous Roman gens. See Maximus.

FABRICIUS, GAIUS. A type of incorruptible Roman; prominent in the war against Pyrrhus, king of Epirus.

FAUNUS. King of Latium and father of Latinus; worshiped as protecting deity of husbandmen and agriculture and identified with Pan. As Inuus he is a god of fertility.

FURIES. Three avenging goddesses called Erinyes or Eumenides by the Greeks. In the *Aeneid* they bear the names Alecto, Tisiphone, and Megaera.

GABINE. Pertaining to the ancient Latian town of Gabii whose inhabitants arranged the toga in a distinctive manner.

GAETULIA. An inland section of northern Africa.

GANYMEDE. According to one account, a son of Laomedon. Because of his beauty, he was seized by Jupiter's eagle and carried to heaven where he became Jupiter's cupbearer, replacing Hebe, the daughter of Jupiter and Juno.

GARAMANTES. A tribe living in the interior of Africa.

GORGONS. Three daughters of the sea-god Phorcus. The head of one of these, Medusa, changed anyone looking upon it into stone. Minerva later placed it in the center of her shield.

GRYNEAN. Pertaining to Grynia or Grynium in Asia Minor, where a temple to Apollo was located.

GYARUS. A small, barren island in the Aegean.

HADES. 1. Pluto, the ruler of the nether regions. 2. The realm over which Pluto ruled with Proserpine, his queen. The shades of the dead were ferried across the river Styx by Charon. Other streams in the nether world were Lethe, the river of forgetfulness; Cocytus, the river of wailing; Phlegethon, the river of fire; and Acheron, the river of woe.

HAMMON. A name of Jupiter. There was a shrine to him in an oasis of the Libyan desert.

HARPIES. Birds sent by the gods to torture Phineus, a king of Thrace, who blinded his sons and was himself so punished. In his wanderings Aeneas encountered these vile creatures at the Strophades (q.v.). Vergil mentions only one of these, Celaeno.

HECATE. A goddess of widely extended powers: in heaven she is the moon (Luna, Selene); on earth, Diana; in Hades, Proserpine. She is most frequently known as mistress of sorcery and witchcraft.

HECTOR. Son of Priam, slain by Achilles.

HECUBA. Wife of Priam.

HELENUS. A son of Priam who was taken captive to Epirus by Neoptolemus (Pyrrhus), who had received Andromache as a share of the Trojan spoils. Upon the death of Neoptolemus, Helenus married Andromache and became the ruler of Chaonia.

HELICON. A mountain in Boeotia where Apollo and the Muses dwelt.

HERCULES. Heracles among the Greeks; son of Jupiter by Alcmene. He possessed unparalleled physical strength and performed many exploits, including his famed twelve labors.

HERMIONE. Daughter of Menelaus and Helen; wife of Orestes.

HESPERIA. A poetical name for Italy.

HESPERIDES. Nymphs who guarded the golden apples that Earth gave Juno at her marriage to Jupiter.

HIPPOLYTUS. Son of Theseus and an Amazon. Theseus' second wife, Phaedra, was attracted to her stepson. When he failed to reciprocate, she accused him to his father, who called on Neptune to avenge him. Later the father learned that his son was guiltless. Phaedra killed herself.

HYRCANIAN. Pertaining to the Hyrcani, a tribe along the Caspian.

IARBAS. King of the Mauretanians and suitor for the hand of Dido.

ICARUS. Son of Daedalus, who met disaster in his aerial flight from Crete.

IDA. 1. A mountain range in Mysia, Asia Minor. 2. A mountain in central Crete.

IDALIUM. A city on the island of Cyprus, sacred to Venus.

INUUS. *See* Faunus.

IO. A maiden loved by Jupiter. Juno's vigilance caused him to change Io into a heifer. Juno ordered Argus, who possessed a hundred eyes, to watch her. When at Jupiter's command Mercury slew Argus, Juno sent a gadfly to pursue the young heifer. After much wandering she recovered her human form in Egypt.

IXION. King of the Lapiths who murdered his father-in-law. Jove purified him, but Ixion showed his ingratitude by attempting to win the favor of Juno. He was bound to a revolving wheel in Tartarus, where he was sentenced to suffer for eternity.

JANUS. The two-faced god whose temple doors were open in time of war and closed in time of peace.

JULUS. Ascanius, son of Aeneas.

JUNO. Daughter of Saturn and wife of Jupiter; goddess of women, identified with the Greek Hera.

LABYRINTH. The name given to the maze in Crete where the Minotaur was kept. *See* Minos.

LACEDAEMON. Sparta, country in the south of the Peloponnesus.

LACINIAN. A name for Juno, derived from the promontory Lacinium on the southern coast of Italy where there was a temple to Juno.

LAERTES. Father of Ulysses.

LAODAMIA. Wife of Protesilaus, who was slain by Hector. She implored the gods to be permitted to talk with him three hours. At the granting of this request, she died with her husband when he died a second time.

LAOMEDON. Father of Priam and king of Troy.

LAPITHS. Thessalians who fought with the centaurs at Hippodamia's marriage to Pirithous, king of the Lapiths.

LAR. Household god.

LATIUM. A country of central Italy, south and east of the lower Tiber.

LATONA. Mother of Apollo and Diana.

LAVINIA. Second wife of Aeneas.

LAVINIUM. City in Latium, founded by Aeneas and named after his wife Lavinia.

LEDA. Visited by Jupiter in the guise of a swan, Leda produced two eggs, from one of which came Pollux and Helen, from the other Castor and Clytemnestra.

LERNA. A swamp near Argos where Hercules slew the Hydra.

LETHE. *See* Hades.

LIBER. Bacchus.

LUPERCAL. A cave in Rome where Romulus and Remus were suckled by a wolf. It was connected with honors to Lupercus, a pastoral deity, and named after Lycaean Pan, the word "Lycaean" being derived from a mountain in Arcadia. Priests who presided over the festival of the Lupercalia were called Luperci.

LUPERCI. *See* Lupercal.

LYAEUS. Bacchus.

MACHAON. A surgeon of the Greeks during the siege of Troy.

MAEONIAN. Lydian, voluptuous. There was a tradition that the Etruscans came from Maeonia, an ancient name for Lydia in Asia Minor.

MARCELLUS. A famous name in Roman history. Toward the end of the sixth book Vergil mentions Marcus Claudius Marcellus, a great warrior against the Gauls and Hannibal. In VI, 860–886, Vergil celebrates the virtue of Marcellus, the son of Octavia, the sister of Augustus. Augustus married his daughter Julia to him, thus indicating that he was to succeed to the chief office of the state. However, Marcellus died in his youth.

MASSYLIAN. Libyan.

MAXIMUS. Quintus Fabius Maximus called "The Delayer" because of his tactics in battling Hannibal.

MEGAERA. *See* Furies.

MEMNON. Son of Tithonus and Aurora (Dawn). Though his armor was wrought by Vulcan, he was slain by Achilles. At the request of his mother, Jupiter granted him immortality.

MENELAUS. Son of Atreus and brother of Agamemnon. He was married to Helen, who eloped with Paris.

MERCURY. A parallel of the Greek Hermes; the messenger of the gods, the god of eloquence, thieves, and commerce.

MEZENTIUS. A cruel ruler of the Tyrrhenians expelled by his own people, who sided with Turnus, and was slain by Aeneas; father of Lausus.

MINERVA. Goddess of wisdom, the arts, and crafts; identified with Pallas Athena of the Greeks.

MINOS. King of Crete and husband of Pasiphaë, to whom Phaedra, Ariadne, and Androgeus were born. The latter won all the contests at the Panathenaea and was for that reason killed at the command of King Aegeus. Minos avenged the death of his son and compelled the Athenians to send an annual tribute to Crete of seven youths and seven maidens. These were devoured by the Minotaur, a monster, the offspring of Pasiphaë. Theseus, the son of King Aegeus, slew the Minotaur with the aid of Ariadne. She then eloped with Theseus, only to be deserted by him on the island of Naxos.

MINOTAUR. See Minos.

MONOECUS. A promontory in Liguria, now Monaco.

MORINI. A Belgic tribe near the English Channel.

MYCENAE. City in Argolis over which Agamemnon ruled.

MYGDON. A king of Phrygia, allied with the Trojans.

MYRMIDONS. A Thessalian tribe that fought under Achilles.

NARYCIAN. Pertaining to Naryx, a city of the Locrians.

NEOPTOLEMUS. Son of Achilles, also called Pyrrhus.

NEPTUNE. God of the sea; builder of the walls of Troy.

NEREIDS. *See* Nymphs.

NEREUS. God of the sea and father by Doris of the Nereids.

NYMPHS. Lesser goddesses dwelling in the seas (Nereids); trees (dryads and hamadryads); lakes, rivers, fountains (naiads); mountains (oreads).

NYSA. A city in India, the birthplace of Bacchus.

OCTAVIA. Sister of Augustus.

OLEAROS. An island of the Cyclades.

OLYMPUS. A mountain between Macedonia and Thessaly, regarded as the home of the gods.

ORCUS. The underworld; Pluto. See Hades.

OREADS. *See* Nymphs.

ORESTES. Son of Agamemnon.

ORION. In mythology a hunter loved by Diana. After his death he became a constellation in the heavens.

ORPHEUS. A master of the lyre who charmed even beasts with his playing. He failed in an attempt to rescue his wife Eurydice from the underworld.

ORTYGIA. An ancient name for Delos.

PAEAN. A song or shout of victory.

PAEON. God of healing.

PALAMEDES. A Greek warrior at the siege of Troy, falsely accused of treachery by Odysseus and put to death.

PALLADIUM. Image of Pallas Athena, supposed to be a pledge of Troy's security as long as it was kept within the city. It was stolen by Odysseus and Diomede.

PALLAS. 1. The goddess Pallas Athena, whom the Romans called Minerva. 2. A king of Arcadia, great-grandfather of Evander. 3. Son of Evander.

PAN. God of the woods and of shepherds.

PANDARUS. 1. A Trojan archer in the *Iliad* who violated a truce after the single combat between Menelaus and Paris

2. A Trojan, son of Alcanor, slain with his brother Bitias by Turnus.

PAPHOS. A town on the island of Cyprus, noted for its temple to Venus.

PARIS. Son of Priam and abductor of Helen. *See* Introduction, p. xvi.

PAROS. An island in the Aegean, noted for its marble.

PARTHENOPAEUS. One of the seven chieftains who fought against Thebes.

PARTHIA. A country southeast of the Caspian Sea. The inhabitants were warlike and celebrated for their cavalry.

PASIPHAË. *See* Minos.

PELASGIANS. The earliest inhabitants of Greece.

PENTHESILEA. Queen of Amazons.

PENTHEUS. King of Thebes (Boeotia); because of his sacrilegious treatment of Bacchus and his prying into the orgies celebrated by the female followers of that god, he was torn to pieces by these women, foremost among whom was his own mother.

PERGAMUS. 1. The citadel of Troy or the city itself. 2. A name given the unsuccessful settlement Aeneas made in Crete.

PHAEACIANS. Mythological inhabitants of Corcyra (Corfu) where Odysseus lingered on his journey homeward.

PHAEDRA. Daughter of Minos. *See* Hippolytus.

PHAËTHON. 1. An epithet of the sun. 2. The son of the Sun (Helios) by Clymene, who induced his father to let him drive his chariot. The youth was unable to control the horses, and after he had done great damage to the earth, Jupiter killed him with lightning.

PHILOCTETES. A noted archer at the siege of Troy who inherited the poisoned arrows of Hercules. Among others he slew Helen's abductor, Paris.

PHLEGETHON. *See* Hades.

PHOEBUS. Apollo.

PIRITHOUS. King of the Lapiths who was chained in the nether world for attempting to abduct Proserpine. *See* Lapiths.

PLUTO. See Hades.

POLLUX. *See* Castor.

PORSENNA. An Etruscan king, an ally of the Tarquins who were banished from Rome.

PRIAM. Last king of Troy, son of Laomedon and husband of Hecuba, by whom he had a numerous progeny. *See* Genealogical Table, p. 336.

PROCRIS. Wife of Cephalus, who accidentally slew her when she, suspecting his fidelity, followed him into a forest.

PROSERPINE. Daughter of Ceres. She was seized by Pluto, the king of the underworld, who made her his queen. When Ceres presented her case to Jupiter, he ruled that Proserpine might return to the upper world if she had not eaten any food during her stay in Hades. She had eaten some seeds of the pomegranate, and therefore was obliged to spend half of the year in the realm of Pluto and the other half on the earth.

PROTEUS. A mythical king of Egypt.

PYGMALION. Brother of Dido, who killed her husband, Sichaeus.

PYRRHUS. Neoptolemus, son of Achilles.

QUIRINUS. *See* Romulus.

REMUS. *See* Romulus.

RHESUS. A Thracian king, an ally of the Trojans. His horses were captured by Diomede. According to an oracle, if these animals had fed in the Trojan plain or had drunk of the river Xanthus, Troy would not have fallen.

ROMULUS. Son of Mars and the vestal Rhea Silvia; twin brother of Remus, whom he killed in a dispute. After a rule of thirty-seven years Romulus was taken up into heaven, where he was worshiped as Quirinus.

RUTULIANS. An ancient tribe of Latium. "The Rutulian" means Turnus, the leader of the race.

SABELLIAN. A general name for certain tribes living in central Italy about 500 B.C. Among them were the Volscians, Samnites, Frentani, and Vestini.

SABINE. An ancient Italic people, living in central Italy. They were known for their simplicity and virtue.

SALII. Priests of Mars, whose duty it was to guard sacred shields that fell from heaven.

SARPEDON. A Lydian prince slain by Patroclus before Troy.

SATURN. A Latin god said to rule Italy during the Golden Age.

SCYLLA. Often mentioned with Charybdis. They were feared by mariners sailing the Strait of Messina between Italy and Sicily. Scylla, a barking monster, lived on the Italian side. Charybdis was on the Sicilian coast and created whirlpools by swallowing and belching forth the water in the strait.

SCYTHIA. A barbarous country between the Carpathian Mountains and the river Don.

SERRANUS. 1. A surname of Gaius Atilius Regulus, summoned from the plow to leadership in the government. He must not be confused with Marcus Atilius Regulus, taken captive by the Carthaginians in 255 B.C. 2. A Rutulian.

SIBYL. A prophetess; the sibyl of Cumae.

SIGEAN. Of Sigeum, a town near Troy, at the mouth of the Dardanelles.

SIMOIS. A river near Troy.

STROPHADES. Two islands west of Messenia, in the southern part of the Peloponnesus.

STYGIAN. Pertaining to Styx. *See* Hades.

SYRTES. Two gulfs on the northern coast of Africa, treacherous because of shallows and sand bars.

TANAIS. The river Don; in XII, 513, a Rutulian.

TARTARUS. That section of the lower world which was set aside for the punishment of the reprobate.

TEUCER. 1. First king of Troy; hence the Trojans are called Teucrians. 2. A noted Greek archer, son of Telamon and Hesione.

THEBES. The capital of Boeotia.

THESEUS. *See* Minos.

THETIS. Mother of Achilles.

THYMBRAEAN. Pertaining to Thymbra, a town in the Troad where there was a temple to Apollo.

TISIPHONE. *See* Furies.

TITHONUS. Brother of Priam, beloved by Aurora, who petitioned the gods that he live forever, but neglected to include perpetual youth in her petition. See Tennyson's "Tithonus."

TITYUS. A giant slain by Apollo and Diana for waylaying their mother, Latona. For this crime, vultures plucked at his liver in the underworld.

TRITON. God of the sea, son of Neptune.

TRITONIAN. Applied to Pallas (Minerva) because of her birth near Lake Triton in Africa.

TRIVIA. Diana.

TROILUS. Son of Priam, slain by Achilles.

TYDEUS. One of seven warriors famed for an attack on Thebes; father of Diomede.

TYRRHENIAN. Etruscan, Tuscan, Etrurian.

UFENS. 1. A prince of the Aequi who fought against Aeneas. 2. A river in Latium.

ULYSSES. In Latin "Ulixes," in Greek "Odysseus." Son of Laertes, king of Ithaca and husband of Penelope, by whom he had a son, Telemachus. He feigned madness to avoid going to the Trojan War, but once there, distinguished himself. His years of wandering before reaching home after the Trojan War are described in the *Odyssey*.

VENUS. The goddess of love and beauty, identified with the Greek Aphrodite.

VESTA. Goddess of the hearth, worshiped in every Roman home. Her public shrine was the most important in the Capital.

VOLSCIANS. A people in Latium, subdued with difficulty by the Romans in 338 B.C.

VULCAN. The god of fire, identified with Hephaestus. He is the god of the arts of the forge.

XANTHUS. The name of three rivers: 1. near Troy; 2. in Epirus; and 3. in Lycia.

Rinehart Editions